GATESHEAD F.C.
THE FOOTBALL LEAGUE YEARS
1930-1960

*****

A Complete Record of
'The Team Nobody Noticed'

By George Thompson

Published by:
Yore Publications
12 The Furrows, Harefield,
Middx. UB9 6AT.

© George Thompson 2002
Reprinted 2017
....

British Library Cataloguing-in-Publication Data.
A catalogue record for this book
is available from the British Library.

Printed in the UK by 4edge Limited

Dedicated
again to Jenny
with many thanks
for a decade of Friendship

~ Acknowledgements ~

I am grateful to Dave Twydell and his industrious family who continue to produce an impressive range of football history books, under the name of 'Yore Publications'.

Another person to be thanked is Roy Gourley, a Gateshead fan of old who had memories of selling programmes at Redheugh Park as a boy, and being rewarded with free admission to the match. Roy was very helpful in supplying several team group pictures which I was finding rather hard to come by. Also life-long South Shields enthusiast Robert Wray for the loan of material and many kindnesses regarding my previous book.

By a stroke of good fortune, Pat Hewson, a Gateshead defender from 1953 to 1957, got in touch with Dave Twydell just as the project was nearing completion, and agreed to provide a fore-word to the book, which is a joy to read.

The staff of the Newspaper Library at Colindale have continued to wheel their barrows and supply me with volumes of the North Eastern papers.

Thanks to all of the above, and to the many authors of books on other football clubs, both large and small. Also to members of the former A.F.S. (Association of Football Statisticians), and in particular Tony Brown.

It has been a pleasure to make a small contribution to this ever increasing body of work.

Foreword
by Pat Hewson

(Gateshead F.C.: 1953-1957)

****

Words just can't describe what it was like in an area where football was so much a passion to be able to play for a team held in so much regard by its town. For me, that was to play for my home town of Gateshead.

Being born in the Teams, I used to play in the streets next to the Ground. Then in later years I followed the congregation to Redheugh Park, to watch the heroes of the day such as Tommy Conroy, Gus Livingston, Albert Watson, Andy Dudgeon and Billy Cassidy. That's probably what sparked my passion for football, and which eventually led me to turn professional at West Bromwich Albion.

I got my opportunity to return to the North-east when I nearly signed for Hartlepool. That was until the then manager of West Brom., Vic Buckingham, rang the then manager of Hartlepool, Fred Westgarth at his office, and asked to speak to me. *"Don't sign for Hartlepool."* said Vic Buckingham, *"Go and talk to Gateshead and sign for them. If you don't then you-re still my player."* It certainly was an offer I couldn't refuse, and I didn't want to.

You just can't imagine the sense of both pride and excitement I felt as I walked out in front of my home crowd. However, it didn't stop me having to take a job on the groundstaff just to make ends meet as wages for footballers then were poor. I wasn't the only player who was forced to do this, for later Jackie Callendar did the same.

The years I spent at Gateshead were the happiest of all my football career, and there were some great players and friends I made during this time. Of course both the Callendar brothers were playing then and they were a pleasure to watch. Tommy was a quiet, unassuming gentleman, while Jackie was more outgoing; the life and soul of the party. Bob Gray was a good friend and an excellent goalkeeper, whilst Johnny Ingham was a prolific goalscorer. Johnny Campbell was another local lad and a really good player. When he left Gateshead, I got him a job in the factory where I worked.

In 1955, we had a good F.A.Cup run which took us to the third round. We demolished Chester quite easily, 6-0, in the first round, and in the second, against Barnsley, we pulled back from 3-1 down with 20 minutes to go, to draw 3-3. In the replay, at Barnsley, we won 1-0, but we were stopped in our tracks by 'Spurs in the next round, by 2-0. 'Spurs were by far the better team, and it showed towards the end, for their level of fitness outshone ours by far. It was an honour to play in that game against the likes of (Sir) Alf Ramsey and Danny Blanchflower.

Shortly after, I went part-time at the club, intending to pick up my trade in preparation for the end of my career. I had the good fortune of working on the very next machine to Albert Gregory, a man whom I had known all my working life. Albert was famous for his half-time entertainment at Redheugh Park, as after a few drinks he would take over the pitch and pretend to play a game of football, all by himself. The crowd always gave an immense cheer when he 'scored'.

The following years saw the club go into decline as we had a bad run of form, and gate attendances dropped. In 1957, the decision was made to create a new Third and a Fourth Division, this meant that the two third divisions would compete for positions, with the top twelve from each forming the new Third Division, and the two bottom twelve clubs would become the Fourth Division. The 1957/58 season was hard, and every game seemed like a cup-tie. Unfortunately we finished just outside the top half, and hence joined the League Division Four. This led to Gateshead being eventually voted out of the Football League two years later. I feel this was unfair because the team didn't even finish in the bottom two positions, but the decision may well have been because of poor gate attendances.

I'm 76 years old now, and look at the game today and can see how much it has changed, and not always for the better. The pace is faster, the rules have changed, and players seem to fall over with the slightest of body contact. I'd like to see any present player head one of the footballs we used in those days; when it was wet it was like thumping a brick wall!

Over the years I've met some of the players again, and I know some have passed away. I often see Bobby Gray walking around my local village, Whickham, and we still chat about football. It's nice to remember how football was in the old days and to take a nostalgic view of the past. But it is also just as important to look to the future, and I only hope it becomes clear on reading this book that Gateshead was a workingmans team which inspired a town through some hard times.

It's nice to think that through watching their team play, other young footballers may be inspired, just as I was, to a career in football. There's no other job like it.

Pat Hewson July 2002

Introduction

When Dave Twydell published my earlier book *"South Shields F.C. - The Football League Years"* in 2000, he suggested that I should bring the story to a logical conclusion by writing a history of Gateshead F.C., who had emerged as a result of the failure of the South Shields club being able to survive in its own town.

The idea appealed as I have memories of watching Gateshead F.C. at Redheugh Park.

When I was a boy, I saw five of the club's home games in their last season, and then some of the friendly matches they played against Scottish clubs the following season.

The last time I was there was for a Cup-tie against Workington in 1961.

George Thompson
July 2002.

Contents

ECHOES OF OLD SOUTH SHIELDS

The action of South Shields FC in removing to another town and renaming themselves was a highly unusual one, although comparison could be made with the two London clubs namely Woolwich Arsenal and South Shields' old sparring partners Clapton Orient, both of whom altered their names after moves within the Metropolis. To date no other club has transferred between provincial towns. As will be seen, some supporters of the old South Shields club travelled to Redheugh Park regularly though their numbers probably dwindled as old South Shields players disappeared from the scene.

Not that any of those who performed at Redheugh Park belonged to the era when South Shields played to crowds of twenty thousand and it was necessary to arrive at Horsley Hill an hour before the kick off. This was the case in the first two post-War seasons, but interest waned rapidly after about 1922.

A few of the most popular players from that era turned up in newspaper reports as the century progressed; the coverage of the 1931-32 season notes the varying fortunes of Henry Higginbotham and Cyril Hunter.

Former Sunderland player Arthur Bridgett had captained South Shields in the last two seasons before the First World War when they won the championship of the North Eastern League with almost contemptuous ease. After the War he managed North Shields for a while but when he was well over forty he played a few games for Port Vale and scored for them at Horsley Hill on New Years Day of 1924. The next we hear of him was when Sunderland played at Stoke on a warm day in 1947. North Eastern journalists bumped into the now elderly Arthur who was hawking fish from a cart. Unfortunately he spent so long reminiscing of bygone days that all the ice on his cart melted!

Irvine Thornley, the phenomenally high-scoring centre forward of North Eastern League days, was also in trade, running a grocer's shop near the South Shields ground. Some of the old South Shields players, notably Jack Smith and Bill Charlton, were found in the sports pages of inter-War summer editions as they assisted local cricket sides. Goalkeeper Willis Walker played for Nottinghamshire throughout that era.

Popular South Shields captain George Keenlyside took time off from a game of bowls in 1959 to chat to a journalist. His favourite memory was Jack Smith's goal with which South Shields knocked Blackburn Rovers out of the FA Cup at Ewood Park in 1923. He had fond memories of playing for Partick Thistle before the First World War.

When Aston Villa beat Newcastle United 2-0 in October 1960 the old South Shields and Portsmouth manager Jack Tinn was spotted in the Villa Park directors box. He cheered up the Northern pressmen by observing that the present Newcastle side was the worst he had seen in sixty years. Similar views were often expressed in that relegation season but at least old Jack was spared from ever seeing the 1977-78 side.

Playing for Newcastle's championship winning team of 1926-27 was the favourite memory of tough old full-back Alf Maitland who had left South Shields for Middlesbrough in 1923. In an uncanny interview in the *Coalville Times* of December 1981 (intended to draw attention to the plight of lonely old people) poor bedridden Alf said he would welcome anybody who cared to visit him on Christmas Day to talk about football, but sadly he died before that date.

THE TEAM NOBODY NOTICED
League Football in Gateshead 1930-1960

Until the last quarter of the Twentieth Century people who wished to immerse themselves in facts and figures concerning the history of professional football had to be content with a number of books (mostly annuals) which told of such players as Richardson and Scarth (both North Easterners) who scored four and three goals in double-quick time (for West Bromwich Albion and Gillingham respectively) but never mentioned a man named William Watkin who scored four goals in seven minutes. This is perhaps because his rapid scoring feat was achieved whilst playing for Gateshead (against Grimsby Town on 27th February 1954). Readers knew about Ted Drake's seven goals for Arsenal at Villa Park and sometimes reference was made to the even more famous Jimmy Hill scoring five goals away from home for Fulham, plus Jimmy Greaves and Bobby Tambling both doing the same for Chelsea, but there was never any reference to Ernie Passmore scoring all Gateshead's goals in a 5-3 victory at Hartlepools United one September evening in 1949.

Lists of FA Cup "Giantkilling" feats rarely included Gateshead's 1953 victory over Liverpool. Discussion of the early adoption of floodlights by League clubs in the 1950's failed to mention that Gateshead had installed a rudimentary system of lighting as early as 1953. This innovation was prompted by a desire to avoid playing home League matches on weekday afternoons as attendances at the Redheugh Park Stadium were so small as to be embarrassing. And that was the knub of the problem. If the football world at large paid little attention to Gateshead FC then the local populace rarely seemed to be much interested either.

This most poverty-stricken of professional clubs had come into being in a unique manner. In 1930 South Shields FC had moved lock, stock and barrel to the town after experiencing a brief but eventful career in the Football League from 1919 to 1930, all but the last two years of which had been spent in the Second Division.

In their earliest seasons South Shields had often drawn crowds of twenty thousand but this high level of interest had waned and in their last season the average attendances at their Horsley Hill ground had fallen to a paltry 3,300. A large part of their problem was their failure to compete with Sunderland, especially in their last three seasons when their home fixtures coincided with those at Roker Park, less than three miles away.

The last goal to be scored at Horsley Hill,
versus Accrington Stanley.

The move to Gateshead was seen as the only hope of keeping the club alive and at first there seemed to be cause for optimism. Gateshead Council was welcoming and a new stadium was quickly completed. The attendance at the first home match against Doncaster Rovers exceeded 15,000 but within three months a League game against Rochdale was played before a smaller crowd than had ever assembled at South Shields.

When the former Newcastle player Stan Seymour crossed the Tyne to report the Gateshead v Nelson game in March 1931 he encountered large numbers of Gateshead people travelling in the opposite direction to attend a North Eastern League game between the reserve sides of Newcastle United and Middlesbrough at St. James' Park. Throughout the 1930's, Newcastle Reserves regularly drew larger crowds than Gateshead's first team, barely a mile away, even though Newcastle were relegated to the Second Division in 1934.

Despite these ominous signs Gateshead's second season was an enjoyable one and they only missed promotion by a narrow margin. There was to be an equally close encounter with promotion after the Second World War and an impressive Cup run in 1953.

Generally, however, the 30 year history of League football in Gateshead would be one of struggle against poverty, though the club usually managed to hold their own in the Third Division (North) with their overall average position being ninth. The Fourth Division was another matter.

Was the decision to leave South Shields and relocate a wise one? Compared to the South Shields club of the 1919-1930 period the Gateshead club of the 1930-1960 era maintained a relatively tame not to say colourless career apart from the rare highlight. There was another South Shields Football Club after 1936 who played in the North Eastern League and enjoyed some success against Football League clubs in the FA Cup. But their financial situation was little different from that of Gateshead and twice in the 1950's, the South Shields Supporters Club had to dip into their funds to pay the players wages. It is unlikely that lower Division football would have prospered anywhere on Tyneside.

There was one matter in which Gateshead shamed their South Shields predecessors and that was their disciplinary record. South Shields were a rough, tough side and during their eleven year career they had five players dismissed from the field in League and Cup matches. Gateshead only had three players sent off in twenty three seasons. On the first and second occasions – at Darlington in 1936 and at Wrexham twenty years later – an equally blameworthy opponent accompanied the Gateshead culprit on the long walk, whilst the third Gateshead dismissal – at Aldershot in 1959 – was merely for violence of the tongue. Incidentally Wrexham seem to have been Gateshead's least favourite opponents with rough play and injuries being reported in several matches against the Welsh club after the War. The South Shields equivalent had been Clapton Orient. In the 1920's matches against that London club rarely passed off without trouble.

But football was always a rough game which brings us back to where we were at the start of this chapter. Those old football record books devoted a short space to fatalities – *"mercifully rare"* wrote one encyclopaedist – and told of the deaths through injury of men who played for Celtic, Sunderland, Arsenal and Gillingham. Sadly the many detailed club histories which have since appeared show that list to be an appreciably longer one. Before the Second World War professional footballers who played for Blackburn Rovers, Blackpool, Leicester Fosse, Port Vale, Sheffield United and Wolverhampton Wanderers died as a result of injuries sustained in matches. Since the War the situation has improved but one name was added to this grim chronicle. He was a young Gateshead player, John Haley, who died in 1956 a few days after being injured in a reserve match. His demise was reported locally but not nationally. After all he played for a team that "Nobody Noticed".

1930-31

The directors of South Shields Football Club, despairing of attracting enough support to their Horsley Hill ground, had decided that the club's salvation lay elsewhere. Their first target was Newcastle but when this was thwarted by opposition from United they plumped for the next best thing and looked across the River Tyne to the populous, but poor, town of Gateshead. A site with the less than promising name of Johnsons Clay Hole was inspected and deemed to be a satisfactory location for a stadium. Gateshead Council welcomed the idea of League Football in their town and in March 1930 work began on converting this worked out clay pit into a football ground. After a summer of hard work a spectacular transformation had taken place. Former Newcastle United captain Colin Veitch, now working as a journalist, was impressed to find *"a playing pitch beautiful to view with a stand and terracing of commendable accommodation"*. The stand had been purchased from a greyhound stadium at Carlisle.

The team comes out for the first match, versus Doncaster.

League football got off to a promising start. A supporters club was formed, 10,000 people attended a trial match and a week later, on 30 August, the first League game against Doncaster Rovers was watched by 15,545 including the town's Member of Parliament, the Mayor and the President of the Football League. That first Gateshead team took the field in the old South Shields strip of claret and white and nine of them had played for Shields a few months earlier. Two of them, Maycock and Barkas, scored in a 2-1 victory.

The reporter from a South Shields football paper regarded with envy the enthusiasm shown by Gateshead councillors in contrast shown by the *"icy isolation"* of their South Shields counterparts. After this near carnival occasion Gateshead FC settled down to the grim reality of the Third Division (North).

After two away defeats at Halifax and Hull the crowd for the next home game was only a third of that for the first match. However, a convincing 4-0 victory over New Brighton on a Monday evening resulted in an increased gate of 7,605 the following Saturday when Lincoln City became the first visiting side to win at Redheugh. The next two away games yielded three points with the new clubs first away victory occurring just down the Durham coast at Hartlepools.

There followed two home games against comparatively local opponents. The first, against Darlington, drew more than 10,000 and that figure was dwarfed by the 14,823 when Carlisle United were the visitors; about 3,000 came from Carlisle. It had been four years since there had been a five figure attendance for a League game at South Shields so the move seemed to have been more than justified. Some South Shields supporters continued to travel to Redheugh Park regularly for a number of years.

A promising South Shields player was Thomas Charlton, an amateur who had scored a hat-trick against Carlisle United in the penultimate match at Horsley Hill. He repeated his achievement for Gateshead when Wigan Borough were beaten 4-2 on 27 September and signed professional forms soon afterwards. Reporter Stan Seymour criticised the Gateshead crowd for barracking the legendary old Aston Villa bruiser Frank Barson who was playing for Wigan.

We are fortunate to have the comments of Stan Seymour who was long regarded as something of a guru in North Eastern football matters. In later years he would be the manager of Newcastle United before serving as a director, but for Gateshead's first five years he reported most of their home and away matches for the Newcastle paper the *Sunday Sun*. He was never slow to make constructive criticisms but he must have been glad he spent all his playing career in the First Division when he saw some of his old team mates and opponents ekeing out their last seasons in more modest company.

Four League games in November yielded only one point and the home game against Rochdale was watched by a sub-South Shields crowd of 1,129 in atrocious weather. The Gateshead directors were not downhearted and announced that they had offered terms to former Newcastle United star Hughie Gallacher if he wished to return to Tyneside from Chelsea. Unsurprisingly nothing came of this over-ambitious suggestion.

The FA Cup was kind to Gateshead in their first season. Away to Tranmere in the first round, they drew 4-4 after being 3-1 ahead. On Wednesday afternoon no fewer than 15,000 people absented themselves from work (if they had any) or school to see the replay, when Gateshead won another good game, 3-2. The second round brought visitors all the way from Folkestone. These Southern Leaguers proved to be no pushovers by taking the lead twice before Gateshead eventually won 3-2. A beneficiary of the tie would seem to be Folkestone centre forward Jack Vinall who signed for Sunderland the following year, presumably having been spotted by them in this match.

To be drawn at home to the reigning First Division champions in the third round of the FA Cup is a small club's dream, but as Newcastle and Sunderland were also at home the attendance for Sheffield Wednesday's visit numbered a mere 12,490. Despite Wednesday's 6-2 victory Gateshead acquitted themselves well and their performance merited praise from the press. A rather interesting little Cup run for the League's new boys.

The rest of the season consisted of a good home record – Gateshead won nine and drew two of their remaining 11 games at Redheugh – but poor away form. A second away victory was achieved at Rochdale in March but there were defeats of 6-2 at Crewe and 5-1 at Wrexham, then on 25 April Chesterfield celebrated promotion by defeating Gateshead 8-1.

It was still too early to assess Gateshead's long term prospects. Credit was due to the directors for liaising with local bus operators to provide services to the ground from outlying districts. However, the high attendances at Redheugh (pronounced *Red-yoof*) Park were not maintained throughout the season and this was to become a consistent pattern with crowds dwindling as the season progressed. Gateshead's highest scorer in their first season had been Bill McNaughton, a Londoner, who had been signed from Northampton Town the previous summer. He had found the net 23 times with former South Shields player Robert Kennedy coming second with twelve.

1931-32

Gateshead's second season proved to be one of their best with a good team drawing high crowds. They began with a visit to the seaside and a 3-1 victory over now equally forgotten opponents New Brighton. This *"wonderful display"* was followed by a 2-1 win at Walsall. Centre forward Bill McNaughton scored both goals but this was just a foretaste of what was to follow, for the first two home games were won 4-0 and 6-0 with the McNaughton scoring four in both matches, the opponents being Barrow and York City respectively.

Crowds for these two games exceeded 11,000 and 14,000. A fifth consecutive win ensued at Hull but was followed by the first defeat – at York by 3-2 after Gateshead squandered a 2-0 lead. Lincoln City were chasing Gateshead at the top of the Division and their visit on 19 September drew the season's highest crowd. Lincoln managed to inflict Gateshead's first home defeat by 3-2.

Gates remained high and the home victory over Hartlepools United proved to be the first of six consecutive victories. That statement does need to be qualified however. On 10 October, Gateshead visited Wigan Borough where they lost 2-1 before a crowd of 600, a statistic which caused the Lancashire club to bow to the inevitable and resign from the League. The three goals from this match no longer meant anything but the game had been a rough one and the bruises no doubt remained real enough.

The Third Division (North) continued minus one club despite the unsuccessful attempts of two others, Manchester Central and Merthyr Town to take over Wigan Borough's unplayed fixtures. Doubts were expressed as to whether the whole ramshackle Division would last much longer. But why should such considerations trouble a successful club like Gateshead with their regular five figure crowds? If things got much better they might even rival the gates of Newcastle United reserves!

Gateshead returned to the top of the Division by default as four points which rivals Lincoln City had gained at the expense of Wigan were forfeited. They exulted in their good fortune with a run of victories at home to Southport, Rochdale and Carlisle United and away to Doncaster Rovers and Crewe Alexandra.

Wrexham ended Gateshead's winning run but a week later Gateshead gained their revenge by removing the Welsh club from the FA Cup at Redheugh Park before a crowd of 9,136, although many people no doubt preferred to attend the Sunderland v Newcastle match that day. In the second round an obscure Birmingham and District League side Burton Town (who were managed by former Newcastle Cup-winner Neil Harris) defeated Gateshead 4-1 in the Midlands. The non-Leaguers had been drawn against Wigan Borough in the earlier round but had received a bye when their Third Division opponents folded.

League form was still good and another run of six consecutive victories followed the embarrassing Cup defeat. Gates were no longer in five figures and when Hull City visited on 23 January the crowd fell to 4,490.

A mile away 50,000 were gathering at St. James' Park despite the fact that Newcastle's Cup-tie visitors were only Gateshead's rivals Southport.

Gateshead attracted Lincoln City's highest crowd of the season for the top of the table clash a week later. The result was a Lincoln victory by the only goal of the game but Gateshead remained in good spirits and, although the next game was also lost, they then embarked on an unbeaten run of twelve games which included four away victories. Thus Gateshead kept in the neck and neck race for the one promotion place, but in the end the four points which Lincoln had taken from Gateshead meant that City were promoted on goal average over their only serious challengers. This was only fair as Lincoln had lost the four points they had won from Wigan Borough who had beaten Gateshead.

This had been an exciting and worthwhile season for Gateshead who had begun well with five consecutive victories and whose late season unbeaten run was only ended in the last away game at Rotherham, on a day when Tyneside's attention was elsewhere with Newcastle United beating Arsenal in the FA Cup Final. On 30 April Third Lanark, highly placed in the Scottish First Division, visited Redheugh Park and Gateshead beat them 2-0 in a friendly match.

Stan Seymour was unimpressed with the 2-0 win over Walsall a week later describing the game as *"the worst yet"*. He had been rather critical of the club's affairs during the season, pointing out that early Saturday morning starts for some of the more distant away games were not beneficial to players' form and he was not pleased about the press box, especially when it was moved to the back of the grandstand, as far away from the pitch as it was possible to be.

The South Shields connection was still strong, for many of the directors and players of the old club were still to be found at Redheugh. But it was unlikely that the frequently high attendances in this relatively successful season would have been matched if the club had stayed at Horsley Hill.

South Shields supporters cherished memories of the Second Division which Gateshead narrowly failed to reach that season and never would aspire to. Two former South Shields players were heard from in 1931-32, but not good news in either case. Henry Higginbotham, an Australian born Scotsman who had played briefly on the wing for South Shields when they entered the League in 1919, had fallen on evil days and was suffering from sleeping sickness which prevented him from working. Another of his old clubs, Luton Town, had been trying to raise funds to help his family. And South Shields' notorious bully boy centre half Cyril Hunter, who had been suspended for six months after injuring three Middlesbrough players in 1927, was up to his old tricks.

His career had ended when he was suspended for a whole season for violent play in minor North Eastern football.

1932-33

Mr Ernest E.Douglass who had been manager of the South Shields club during their last three seasons, and had occupied the same position at Gateshead, resigned because of ill health in October 1932. His successor was Bill McCracken the former Newcastle defender whose mastering of the offside trap had necessitated a change in the rules of the game in 1925.

Mr McCracken inherited a side which had made a more than useful start to the season, having won four and drawn three of their first seven games. A midweek double had been achieved at the expense of Darlington, whilst Doncaster and Halifax had been well beaten at Redheugh Park. In drawing 2-2 at Hartlepools on 17 September, Gateshead had benefited from an own goal by home defender Stephen Bowron, who seems to have been an obliging chap as he once did the same thing whilst playing against South Shields.

Hopes that Gateshead would mount another promotion challenge seemed high and an attendance of 10,000 at the first home game against Hull City gave cause for optimism. But when Wrexham visited on 8 October, bitterly cold weather kept the crowd down to 2,000. Those who braved the conditions saw a fine match with eight goals shared after Gateshead had led 3-0. A mascot sporting a goat's head (thought to be the origin of the name of the town) made his first appearance in the match against Southport, which was won 4-1, and up until Christmas victories and defeats came in roughly equal proportions.

There were big crowds for both home and away matches against Carlisle United over Christmas and Gateshead took maximum points. For some reason Gateshead's matches against Carlisle seem to have been regarded as 'local derbies' more so than those featuring Darlington and Hartlepools United. The Gateshead and Carlisle Supporters Clubs entertained each other to tea on these occasions.

The FA Cup trail began with a visit to Barrow. Many Gateshead supporters made the trip and carried goalkeeper Newton shoulder high from the pitch after a 1-0 victory. It had been a poor match however, and a much better one awaited them in the second round. For the second time a South country non-League side (and again from Kent) visited Redheugh Park – this time Margate who brought 200 supporters by a special train. As with Folkestone two years earlier, Gateshead found Margate to be no pushover – quite the reverse as they scored twice in the first seven minutes and kept Gateshead at bay until the tenth minute of the second half. Eventually, however, Gateshead inside forward Kennedy scored a hat-trick and centre forward Ranson another couple to make the final score 5-2. The gate of 11,491 was the highest of the season, the highest of the round and for the only time in history a Gateshead home crowd exceeded that at Roker Park where Sunderland entertained Leicester City before a mere 9,000.

When First Division giants Manchester City came to Gateshead in the Third Round Kennedy scored again but was injured and absent for much of the match. Gateshead goalkeeper Clark, a local man making his debut, played a fine game as City were held 1-1. Clark's second game was less impressive; alas Gateshead lost the replay 9-0 at Maine Road. A number of First Division managers attended this match to see if any Gateshead players showed promise, but unsurprisingly no deals were struck. Nothing at all was done to allay the suspicion that major clubs playing away to small fry were happy with a draw and a big gate for the replay. (Four years earlier City had beaten Swindon Town 10-1 in a similar "replay").

Those disappointed managers should have been at Barnsley four days later when Gateshead put their bad experience behind them and recorded an impressive 4-2 victory. But results over the next few weeks were patchy and promotion hopes disappeared after a home defeat by Tranmere Rovers on 11 February.

In the spring a rumour circulated that Gateshead were about to sign an International player – and so they did. A Belfast-born winger named William Gowdy was signed from Sheffield Wednesday and made his debut on Good Friday at home to Stockport County. His career was an odd one. A former Hull City regular he had only made a single First Division appearance in two years at Hillsborough but had played for Northern Ireland. It's tempting to think that this bold signing is what doubled the gate to 6,848, but a 3-0 defeat by Stockport meant a sharp drop the next day when only 1,929 watched the match against Accrington Stanley.

Gowdy only played four games for Gateshead, returning home to play for Linfield in the close season, and he subsequently made further appearances for Northern Ireland. So by a slight stretch of the imagination Gateshead could boast to have had a current International playing for them, even if all he did for them was to bring in some extra (and welcome) gate money on a single occasion.

The novelty of League football in Gateshead had worn off. The club's finances were never strong and a reduction in players wages hardly inspired optimism.

The club finished the season in seventh position. Champions that year were Hull City for whom centre forward Bill McNaughton had been scoring even more prolifically than he had for Gateshead the previous season. Gateshead were clearly unable to hold on to players like him.

The ability of other clubs to pay higher wages was undoubtedly the reason manager Bill McCracken left in April to take up the same post at Millwall. He took full back Robert Turnbull and free scoring centre forward J.G. Ranson with him.

1933-34

The new season opened with wealthy businessman William Tulip installed as honorary manager. This remarkable man devoted his life to Gateshead Football Club and almost single-handedly kept it in existence during its many dark years.

Across the Tyne Newcastle United's second string had succeeded in gaining admission to the Central League so, with more famous visitors than before on view, their regular large crowds of four and (often) five figures could be expected to continue to the detriment of little Gateshead. This was especially so as the admission charge for these reserve games at St. James' Park was half of that at Redheugh.

Clubs who won the championship of the Third Division (North) did not usually stay in the Second Division for very long, Chesterfield soon returned to the fold, and it was to that Midland town that Gateshead travelled for their first match. A 6-2 defeat did little to inspire optimism but some better results followed. At Darlington a hat trick by Jack Wesley salvaged a point after Gateshead had been 3-0 down. The same player scored four in a 6-3 win over Hartlepools and another hat-trick when New Brighton were beaten 6-0 in November.

Despite these encouraging results the financial crisis at the club was becoming acute. The Mayor of Gateshead appealed to the townspeople to support the club and invitation tickets were issued to schoolboys for one match – a good choice as it resulted in a 4-0 victory over Halifax Town.

Two FA-Cup ties which finished as victories of 5-2 over Darwen of the Lancashire Combination and 1-0 over nearby North Shields, drew comparatively high crowds – the operative word being comparatively. There were 7,757 against Darwen when many Gateshead residents must have been among the 21,000 watching Newcastle and Aston Villa's reserve teams.

Central League games at St. James' Park had been drawing crowds of 16-17,000 all season. What chance did Gateshead have of surviving? Few people thought they would last much longer. The reason the South Shields club had moved was to avoid having to compete with Sunderland. A case of out of the frying pan into the fire.

One of the greatest disappointments to befall a club of Gateshead's stature is to reach the Third Round of the FA Cup and be drawn against another minnow. Even more so to be drawn away – and even worse to be drawn away to a non-League side. Such was Gateshead's fate. If there was a more depressed area than industrial Tyneside in the 1930's it was West Cumberland and the largest town in that region was Gateshead's destination. Workington FC had defeated two League clubs, Southport and Newport County, in the earlier rounds and on New Year's Day they had beaten Wallsend 15-1 in a North Eastern League game. Gateshead beware.

A Sunderland man by the name of Bill Charlton, who had played for the old South Shields club and several other League teams (including Newport), was scoring goals galore for Workington at that time. He and former Gateshead player Andy Lincoln both netted twice as Workington comprehensively defeated Gateshead 4-1. A mercy perhaps that Gateshead had not been playing First Division opponents (with memories of Maine Road)!

Several coachloads of Gateshead supporters had travelled to the West coast for this match, yet a huge crowd gathered at Redheugh Park that day – greater than any which had ever attended a Gateshead home match. But they hadn't gone there to see a soccer match. Record books of that era state that the record attendance at Redheugh Park was that for the opening game against Doncaster Rovers in 1930, but this is incorrect. On 13 January 1934, when Newcastle, Sunderland and Gateshead were all away playing FA Cup-ties a crowd of 18,000 had assembled at the ground to watch a match between English and Australian representative Rugby League sides. This semi-professional sport was trying to extend its horizons beyond its heartland of Yorkshire and Lancashire, and this attendance for a game on Tyneside was encouraging to say the least.

No money, no hope of promotion, out of the Cup. Could things possibly get worse for Gateshead? They certainly could, but there was a little light relief from the dismal story. Veteran Scottish inside forward Robert Kennedy (a true Gateshead star) scored four against Mansfield Town in a 5-3 victory. And not a bad performance a week later at Hartlepools where Gateshead fought back from 3-0 down to draw 3-3.

Then a little bit of sadness at the sight of an ageing First Division star completely out of his depth even in the Third Division (North). Cardiff City's Cup Final captain of a few years earlier, Fred Keenor, played for Crewe Alexandra at Redheugh Park on 17 March. Stan Seymour noted that Keenor .... *"is finding the pace getting too fast for him nowadays and must have been relieved when the final whistle blew"*.

On 24 March the following sequence began:

| New Brighton | 3 | Gateshead | 1 | |
| Carlisle United | 6 | Gateshead | 0 | (Good Friday) |

Then a tonic the next day....

| Gateshead | 4 | Rotherham United | 1 |

Followed by...

Gateshead	2	Carlisle United	3
Walsall	5	Gateshead	1
Gateshead	0	York City	2

(Described by a newspaper as *"an off day"* – among off days)
But it got worse...

| Chester | 4 | Gateshead | 0 |
| Gateshead | 1 | Chester | 3 |

(Gate receipts of £46-1-11)

| Gateshead | 2 | Doncaster Rovers | 4 |

Before a crowd of 515, paying twenty-two pounds eighteen shillings and five pence (£22-92p)

Surely it couldn't possibly get any worse – not much, it couldn't!

At least Gateshead weren't the only people suffering, as Newcastle United had been relegated for the first time in their history. Slightly west of Newcastle and Gateshead lay the (then) coalmining village of Chopwell, nicknamed *'Little Moscow'* because of its political militancy. The Chopwell Institute team had somehow found their way into the First Division of the North Eastern League, and on 5 May they were beaten 16-0 at Workington.

Gateshead were in those parts that day and if they saw those Chopwell men on the road they might have consoled themselves that somebody else was even worse off than they were, for at Barrow the number of goals that Gateshead conceded was 12 (TWELVE). But on a rare visit to the other end of the field Neilson made no mistake from the penalty spot. And hats off to Halifax Town for having lost 13-0 at Stockport on 6 January thereby keeping Gateshead out of the record books. It's a good job nobody noticed.

Digressing somewhat – something strange seems to have been happening in the Third Division (North) regarding high scores in the first few months of 1934. Between that 'Stockport County 13 Halifax Town 0' result on 6 January and 'Barrow 12 Gateshead 1' on the last day of the season, the Division's record away win occurred on 3 February when Barnsley won 9-0 at Accrington – yet a few weeks later Accrington Stanley won 8-0 at home to New Brighton. Barrow had already won a match 9-0 against Chester on 10 February – and had lost 7-0 at Hartlepools, whilst Wrexham had won and lost consecutive games 8-1 and 7-3 at home to Carlisle and away to Stockport. Not to mention an unusual 5-5 draw between Barrow and Walsall. Very strange.

1934-35

Despite the atrocious end to the previous season, Gateshead had remained two places clear of the bottom two who had to apply for re-election. It was now more important than ever that a re-election application should be avoided. The urgent task of finding new players proceeded during the summer. Only three of the team that had lost so heavily at Barrow remained in the line-up for the opening fixture – a 4-2 defeat at home to Chester. A sad loss however, was high scoring veteran forward Robert Kennedy who had returned to Scotland to play for Third Lanark.

New players that day included James McAinsh, a Scot signed from Hull City, at centre forward, James Younger, a winger from Bury, Alec Gray, a schoolteacher with much Third Division (North) experience as he had played for Tranmere, Rotherham, Chester, Southport and Carlisle, and George Mathison, a half back formerly of Newcastle United and Lincoln City. Later in the season a London born winger named William Hales arrived. He had played for the short-lived Thames Association Club and Clapton Orient, and also in French football.

Gateshead had done well to hold on to high scoring Jack Wesley for so long and when he was transferred to Bradford (Park Avenue) in September they received Joe Robson in part exchange. Joe Meek followed Wesley to Bradford a week or two later after he had scored a hat-trick against Crewe Alexandra.

Full back Neilson was now the only former South Shields player still at Redheugh. If any South Shields people were still making the trip they were not making much impression on the attendances which were frequently below 2,000. Newcastle United's relegation didn't seem to benefit Gateshead much either, although gates for reserve matches there had now fallen to around the 2,000 mark. (Even first team games at St. James' Park sometimes drew less than 10,000 to watch United take on their less illustrious opponents).

Despite the influx of new players the season was a poor one with Gateshead again finishing fourth from bottom. The defence remained a weak one conceding six goals at Rochdale and five on no fewer than five occasions away from home. The only away win was at Hartlepools, a happy hunting ground seemingly as Gateshead had now won there three times and drawn twice in five League visits. When Gateshead completed the double in January there was a little bit of crowd trouble with spectators running onto the pitch after the referee had turned down a Gateshead penalty appeal; the official was protected by the players.

The other short distance trip – to Darlington – was made twice with Gateshead losing both the League match and the first round FA Cup-tie. Despite the low crowds, the management announced in March that they were confident that the club would continue.

1935-36

Oldham Athletic's historian Garth Dykes, profiling the career of goalkeeper George Talbot, tells of how in his one season at Boundary Park the player helped Oldham Reserves to attain bottom position in the Central League (21 points behind their nearest rivals) by conceding 122 goals in 33 games. A typical performance of the 'keeper's seems to have been at St James' Park, for the *Sunday Sun* report of Newcastle Reserves' 8-0 victory ends with the terse sentence *"But Oldham really were hopeless"*.

Such is the calibre of player whose services are available to clubs with no money, and the summer of 1935 saw George Talbot return to his native Tyneside to become Gateshead's goalkeeper. He played in the first thirteen games, comparatively successfully, and managed to keep a clean sheet in one of them (against Wrexham). His old club had dropped into to the Third Division (North), and Talbot had the satisfaction of helping Gateshead extract a point from them at Boundary Park. He then went back to Lancashire and played for Southport.

Gateshead lost their first two away games but had the good fortune to entertain Carlisle United in the first home match. Many came from Carlisle, to swell the gate for this ever popular fixture to 8,000. The match was drawn 1-1 with Carlisle's goalscorer being one Bill Shankly. Although the next game against Tranmere drew a crowd of more than 5,000 it wasn't long before attendances fell to around the 2,000 mark. This season was an improvement on the previous two with Gateshead maintaining a mid-table position and - creditably – an unbeaten home record. An unusually high number of 35 players were called upon – more than any other League club.

In January three players – Cull, Rivers and E.Robson – were all transferred to another League club, but as that club was Aldershot the combined fee cannot have been a high one. A few days earlier when Gateshead had played at Carlisle, the directors had been approached by Newport County manager Louis Page who offered £1,000 for each of two players. These two poorest and smallest Southern Section clubs, must have been unusually flush with money at the time.

Early in 1936 the Football League cancelled the rest of the season's fixtures in order to prevent the Football Pools companies from using them. Replacement lists were only issued each Friday and this resulted in considerable inconvenience with clubs having to make hasty travel arrangements. When Gateshead were informed on 28 February that they must travel to Crewe the following day they were unable to contact amateur goalkeeper Goodfellow, with the result that he missed the train from his home town of Alnwick. Gateshead trainer Tommy Dawson (a former full back with Stoke City, Clapton Orient and Gateshead in the 1933-34 season) donned the goalkeeper's jersey at Gresty Road and must have put up a good performance as he played in goal again a few weeks later in the home match against Rochdale. Gateshead won both games.

1936-37
This proved to be the only season in which Gateshead had to apply for re-election to the Third Division (North). After a 3-0 defeat at Rotherham on the opening day crowds in the region of 4,000 watched home games against Stockport County and Port Vale with unexciting scorelines of 0-0 and 0-1. The Port Vale game on 5 September was, as usual, overshadowed by a Newcastle United reserve game with an 11,000 attendance, but more potential customers may have been watching a new competitor.

A crowd of similar size to those present at Redheugh saw the newly formed Newcastle Rugby League club lose their first home game against Huddersfield by 33 points to 12. Their home ground was the Brough Park greyhound stadium which had once interested South Shields FC as a possible new home when they were thinking of leaving town. Naturally they did not want to clash with Newcastle United's home games so anybody seeking an afternoon's sporting entertainment on Tyneside could choose from Newcastle Reserves, Gateshead's Third Division (North) match or this new venture.

To fight off competitors it is necessary to produce an attractive product namely a winning team and Gateshead were unable to supply one. The first victory came in the twelfth match, at Rochdale, on 31 October.

JOE McDERMOTT
(Gateshead, Forward)

Although on the small side, this clever Gateshead forward makes up for his lack of inches by his stylish play and wholehearted endeavour. A native of Fencehouses, and first came into prominence with Bishop Auckland, which club he assisted as an amateur. Was fixed up on professional forms by Middlesbrough in season 1932-33, and after a short spell with the Teessiders moved to Gateshead in June, 1933. Although originally an inside right, McDermott has figured in every forward position for the Redheugh Park club. He stands 5 ft. 6 ins. and weighs 10 st. 10 lbs.

ALBERT OXLEY
(Gateshead, Inside Left)

A product of local football, Oxley is looked upon as one of the most promising players on the books of the Redheugh Park club. An attacking forward who has a particular fancy for soft going, Oxley has been on the Gateshead playing staff since December, 1934. He made his League debut against Southport on January 5th, 1935. Learned his football with Windy Nook, Co. Durham.

JOE INSKIP
(Gateshead, Centre Half)

One of the cleverest centre half backs in the Northern Section is Inskip, who can now be looked upon as one of the long-service members of the Gateshead team. Joined the Redheugh Park club on a free transfer from Sunderland on August 9th, 1933, after he had served the Roker Park side for two seasons. Is a native of South Shields, and a product of that well-known nursery club, South Shields St. Andrews. A sound player in any of the three half back positions, but with a preference for the middle berth, Inskip stands 5 ft. 8 ins. in height and weighs 11 st. 7 lbs.

LESLIE GALLANTREE
(Gateshead, Outside Right)

A native of East Boldon, half-way between Newcastle and Sunderland. Started his career with Harton Colliery, from whom he went to Newcastle United in 1931 at the age of 17. Small in stature, but strong and plucky, he made good progress at St. James's Park and finally earned a place in the first team. He was on the casualty list for some time with a broken leg, but made a good recovery and spent the season 1936-7 with Aldershot. Now he has returned to his native North to join Albert McInroy at Gateshead.

ANGUS LIVINGSTONE
(Gateshead, Full Back)

One of the most reliable full backs in Third League (Northern Section) is this Gateshead defender, who, like many more players at Redheugh Park, is a local product. Claims Wallsend as his birthplace, but learned his football at Walker, joining Gateshead in November, 1935, from Celtic. He made his League debut with the Redheugh club on Xmas Day, 1935, and since then has been one of their most regular and consistent performers.

No. 45.
ALBERT McINROY
(Gateshead, Goalkeeper)

Believe it or not, but Albert used to be an outside left—at school. His native place was Preston, and, as a youth, he signed amateur forms for Preston North End. Played for Leyland, in whose ranks his goalkeeping attracted the attention of Sunderland. Went to Roker Park in 1923, and six years later was transferred to Newcastle United, with whom he gained a Cup Winners' medal in 1932. Later Albert returned on a free transfer to Sunderland, from whom he was secured by Leeds United. Now he is a Gateshead player.

~ Six players of the 1936/37 season ~

The home crowd had to wait another three weeks for a victory and up till then Redheugh gates were smaller than those at both of their rivals.

By a quirk of fate Gateshead then produced a peak performance in the FA Cup and League form showed a dramatic improvement. The draw for the first round could not have been kinder as it paired Gateshead with Notts County. The home crowd of 11,454 was not all that much smaller than that at Newcastle United's first team match against Burnley, and many must have decided that the Cup-tie was the more attractive option. The reason for this choice was to be found in the person of Hughie Gallagher, the former Newcastle legend, who was now a Notts County player. If there was ever a time to impress people and gain new friends it was now. The opportunity was seized and in a fine performance the bottom club of the Northern Section defeated the Southern Section's top club by two goals to nil.

The unpredictability of football; Gateshead now seemed to be on a winning streak. Following the Cup victory the next League match was won 5-4 against Southport – surely a result to tempt the curious to visit Redheugh Park. Then a jarring reminder that Gateshead were the Northern Section bottom side when they visited Millwall in the second round Cup-tie. *"The Millwall attack was brilliant"* read the Sunday Sun headline as if trying to soften the blow for Gateshead's 7-0 defeat. Consolation, perhaps, that Millwall were on their way to a famous Cup run that saw them reach the semi-final.

After a home defeat by Halifax Town, Gateshead enjoyed a happy Christmas by taking four points from fellow strugglers Darlington, with these 5-0 and 2-0 victories being separated by a win over Rotherham. Gateshead had now won four of their last five home games after failing to win any of their earlier six. The victory at Darlington was marred by an incident in which Gateshead's half back Neilson and the home club's centre forward Brallisford were sent off for fighting.

December had been a good month for Gateshead except for the heavy Cup defeat, for eight points had been gained from five League games. But January was a different matter with five more games yielding only a single point. When this team was on song however, anything could happen. On 13 February Gateshead led Hull City 5-0 at half time eventually winning 6-3, and three more home wins followed. But the last eleven games brought only one victory – albeit an impressive one of 4-0 over Tranmere Rovers – and the away form was particularly poor with Hartlepools, Wrexham, Chester and Tranmere all scoring six against this weak defensive side. Worse still, perhaps, was Lincoln City's 5-0 victory at Redheugh before a sparse Wednesday afternoon gathering of 1,224.

33

As well as having to apply for re-election for the first time, Gateshead suffered a further indignity. This was the first season in which their attendances were the lowest in the League, the average of 2,835 being almost a thousand less than any other club.

So who would vote for Gateshead and their North Eastern rival Darlington at the Football League's Annual General Meeting in June? New Chairman William Tulip produced a winning card from up his sleeve by announcing that Redheugh Park was going to be transformed into a greyhound racing stadium during the summer. As well as providing far more covered accommodation than already existed the greyhound racing company would be paying the rates and ground rents.

This bold scheme obviously impressed the club chairmen who gave a resounding vote of confidence in the North East's two minnows. Darlington polled 47 votes and Gateshead 34, comfortably ahead of applicants Shrewsbury Town who only received 12. Two other clubs who hoped to enter the Division fared very badly. Only four votes were gained by eternal optimists South Liverpool. (How could they ever have survived in the League in the shadow of two giant clubs? Even Gateshead's situation looked comparatively favourable). Only one vote was cast for Wigan Athletic. Everybody remembered what happened to that town's last Football League club.

Also discussed at the Annual General Meeting was a proposal to merge the regional Third Division into two national Third and Fourth Divisions. A local journalist opined that clubs in Gateshead's financial situation would not relish costly trips to places like Exeter. That day would eventually arrive but very much water was to pass under the bridge before then. And of course the front pages of the newspapers were discussing far more weighty matters as that grim decade neared its terrible end. The North East's gloom was lifted a little by Sunderland's Cup Final victory over Preston North End on 1 May.

1937-38

Work on transforming Redheugh Park proceeded throughout the summer. The greyhound racing company, as well as surrounding the pitch with the track, installed a huge totalisor board at one end of the ground. More importantly, covered accommodation was provided on the other three sides. Although the club had made a loss of £500 on the previous season secretary/manager Bill Tulip managed to secure a number of new players, of whom the most notable was goalkeeper Albert McInroy from Leeds United.

Although a native of Lancashire McInroy had the rare distinction of having played for both Newcastle United and Sunderland, and had won an International Cap whilst with Sunderland, plus a Cup winner's medal with Newcastle.

Gateshead began the season optimistically. A fair sized crowd watched the opening game against Crewe Alexandra who were beaten 2-0 despite the best efforts of two former South Shields/Gateshead players, Bob Turnbull and John Scott. Then came three points from two games with Port Vale, plus a draw before a 12,000 home crowd against Wrexham and maximum points from two short trips to Darlington and Hartlepools. The transformation of the ground seemed to be matched by that of the club's fortunes, Gateshead were now top of the table and the visit of Lincoln City drew an unbelievably high crowd of 20,752. Local journalists thought the crowd would have been even larger had not the ground been altered and one described the game as being *a rare example of the best Third Division brand of football* with Gateshead drawing 1-1 after being briefly behind.

As so often happened the club's fortunes seesawed dramatically throughout the season. Crowds remained high as October brought three home wins and two away defeats. The home victory over Carlisle United earned a Sunday Sun headline of *Gateshead Gleam* and in winning 5-1 at Accrington they were described as playing *like champions*.

IT NEVER HAPPENED BUT – if the League positions of 16 October 1937 had remained unchanged Gateshead would have reached the Second Division. There would have been no local derby game in 1938-39 however as Newcastle United would have been relegated to the Third Division (North).

The transformation of Redheugh Park met with universal approval as this cartoonist makes clear. Gateshead had now abandoned their claret and blue strip for the less glamorous white shirts and black shorts which served them for the rest of their history.

Gateshead had relinquished the top position and, not for the first time, they were trying to sign Hughie Gallagher, but they played badly in the first round of the FA Cup, losing 4-0 at Walsall (who had been transferred to the Southern Section of the Third Division). December was a bad month financially as only three games could be played and only one point was gained. A 5-1 defeat at York looked ominous but in January Gateshead gained nine points out of a possible 10 and after beating Hartlepools United 2-1 on the 29th they were now back in first place.

Any hopes of promotion soon proved to be a pipedream as only three of the next fifteen games were won. At the end of the season, however, Gateshead bowed out in style with three fine home wins of 3-0, 5-0 and 5-2 over Bradford City, Southport and Darlington respectively.

A season of contrasting fortunes, fifth position in the table was a tremendous improvement for the previous year's re-election seekers, and this was reflected in the attendances which had more than trebled. However, the much increased revenue had to be spent in paying off old debts and when this duty had been attended to the club had a surplus of four pounds to play with.

There were changing fortunes elsewhere as the War clouds gathered. Across the Tyne, Newcastle United only escaped relegation to the Third Division (North) on goal average. They had the weather to thank as they had looked unlikely to win a match at Stockport on 27 December when it was abandoned at a late stage with the scores level at 2-2. Newcastle won the re-arranged fixture 3-1.

Mention of Stockport County serves as a reminder of the limited potential of Gateshead's rivals. Of the 21 seasons Gateshead were to spend in the Third Division (North) this was the only one in which they did not meet Stockport who were now returning 'home' after a single season in higher company. The same fate awaited the 1937-38 champions, Tranmere Rovers. If Gateshead had ever won promotion could they have expected to fare any better in the Second Division? It would seem highly unlikely. Although the converse was not always true, for Bradford City had visited Gateshead for the first time in 1937,-38 and would continue to do so until the Division ended in 1958.

Things could be worse as Newcastle Rugby League club had given up the ghost after two seasons. They had finished second off bottom each time and had won seven, drawn five and lost 62 of their League games. Their last season had been spent at the White City Stadium, a newly build dog track situated in 'No Mans Land' on the Durham side of Scotswood Bridge. The most ambitious thing they ever did was to invite the Australian touring side there on 25 September 1937, but not many people saw Australia win 37-0. Many potential customers were elsewhere. The biggest game in this club's short career was played on the only day in history when Redheugh Park drew a crowd of over 20,000. Gates must have decreed that Rugby League didn't belong on Tyneside.

A similarly unsuccessful soccer club was City of Durham who finished bottom of the North Eastern League. They had conceded 189 goals in 38 games and their goalkeeper was Norman Harbottle. A year before, when he had been Gateshead's goalkeeper, he had let in six goals on four separate occasions. It was fortunate that he went to Durham though, as when he was leaving a match there in October 1937, he rescued a nine-year-old boy from drowning in the River Wear.

Whatever Bill Shankly may or may not have said, football was never as serious a matter as life and death. A thought which must have occurred to many on the terraces as they wondered whether the imminent War would be as bad as the last one or worse.

Casting such gloomy thoughts aside there was still plenty going on in the local football scene. South Shields had a team again and they were doing well in the North Eastern League and sometimes drawing five figure crowds at the old Horsley Hill ground which their predecessors had left in 1930. And on 12 June Gateshead boss Bill Tulip realised a longstanding ambition and signed Hughie Gallagher from Grimsby Town.

1938-39

The Football League celebrated its Fiftieth Anniversary by arranging a "Jubilee Fund" day a week before the season began in earnest. Every League club played a match against a local rival and this gave Gateshead an unprecedented chance to play Newcastle United at St. James' Park. Newcastle won 2-1 and the 30,000 crowd appreciated Hughie Gallagher's first appearance as a Gateshead player. Of course the 35-year-old Gallagher was far past his best and the day when he had single-handedly broken the St. James' Park attendance record on his first return as a Chelsea player was only a memory now (like Newcastle's First Division days).

Be that as it may, this famous old 'has been' was a very welcome sight on Third Division (North) grounds and he proved to be of more than sentimental value by scoring five goals (one a penalty) before a 12,000 crowd in the third home match against Rotherham United. He scored two more in the next home match against York City but finished on the losing side, and it was already apparent that this Gateshead side would not be playing in the Second Division next season. Events elsewhere already indicated that there might not be a 'next season'. When Gallagher missed seven games through illness, attendances plummeted and remained low after his return.

After Gainsborough Trinity (a League club themselves once) removed Gateshead from the FA Cup, in Lincolnshire, prospects for the rest of the season seemed bleak and six consecutive defeats in December did little to inspire confidence. The worst of these was a 5-0 home defeat by Crewe Alexandra, though it should be noted that Crewe had acquired a useful habit of scoring heavily that season, with victories of 6-0 over Lincoln and 7-1 against New Brighton behind them, and further wins of 8-2 v York City and 7-1 v Carlisle United still to come. Darlington had little difficulty in extracting four points from Gateshead in two games over Christmas.

Yet again Gateshead's fortunes changed unaccountably, for of the twenty League games played in 1939 only two were lost, those at Lincoln and Hartlepools. Hughie Gallagher's career ended usefully, though unspectacularly, scoring a single goal in several matches and twice at Halifax. Other clubs seemed to be reaping as much benefit from his presence, as Lincoln City's attendance for Gateshead's visit in March was estimated to include 2,000 who had come especially to see him. Attendances at Redheugh remained low and Gateshead finished this last pre-War season in tenth position.

The world was in turmoil. In August Gateshead paid a second visit to Newcastle, losing another Football League Jubilee match 3-0 before a much smaller crowd of 18,092. With an optimism which now appears quite staggering, the Football League season began on 26 August, though each club eventually only managed to play three games. Gateshead lost a very poor home match 3-0 against Crewe Alexandra, beat Hartlepools United 3-0, and then said goodbye to peacetime by losing 4-3 at Lincoln. Each side had a player called Callender (they were cousins) and Gateshead's John scored against his former club. He was to play very many games for Gateshead in the dim and distant future, but for now his football career had to be put on hold. Would that it could have continued.

SECOND DIVISION	P	W	D	L	F	A	Pts		THIRD DIVISION NORTH	P	W	D	L	F	A	Pts
Luton	3	2	1	0	7	1	5		Accrington	3	3	0	0	6	1	6
Birmingham	3	2	1	0	5	1	5		Halifax	3	2	1	0	6	1	5
West Ham	3	2	0	1	5	4	4		Darlington	3	2	1	0	5	2	5
Coventry	3	1	2	0	8	6	4		Chester	3	2	1	0	5	2	5
Leicester	3	2	0	1	6	5	4		Rochdale	3	2	0	1	2	2	4
Nottingham F	3	2	0	1	5	5	4		New Brighton	3	2	0	1	4	5	4
Plymouth	3	2	0	1	4	3	4		Tranmere	3	1	1	1	6	6	3
Tottenham	3	1	2	0	6	5	4		Rotherham	3	1	1	1	5	6	3
WBA	3	1	1	1	8	8	3		Wrexham	3	1	1	1	3	2	3
Bury	3	1	1	1	4	5	3		Lincoln	3	1	1	1	6	7	3
Newport	3	1	1	1	5	4	3		Crewe	2	1	1	0	3	0	3
Millwall	3	1	1	1	5	4	3		Oldham	3	1	0	2	3	5	2
Manchester C	3	1	1	1	6	5	3		Doncaster	3	1	0	2	4	5	2
Southampton	3	1	0	2	5	6	2		Gateshead	3	1	0	2	6	7	2
Swansea	3	1	0	2	5	11	2		Southport	3	0	2	1	4	5	2
Barnsley	3	1	0	2	7	8	2		Hull	2	0	2	0	3	3	2
Chesterfield	2	1	0	1	2	2	2		Hartlepool	3	0	2	1	1	4	2
Newcastle	3	1	0	2	8	6	2		Barrow	3	0	2	1	4	5	2
Sheffield W	3	1	0	2	3	5	2		Carlisle	2	1	0	1	3	3	2
Bradford	3	0	1	2	2	7	1		York	3	0	1	2	3	5	1
Fulham	3	0	1	2	3	6	1		Bradford C	3	0	1	2	3	6	1
Burnley	2	0	1	1	1	3	1		Stockport	2	0	0	2	0	5	0

Although of little relevance,
the 'final' league tables for the 1939/40 'season'.

WORLD WAR 11
1940/41 TO 1944/45
(Gateshead did not compete in seasons 1939/40 and 1940/41)

Notes: The War seasons were generally run on the basis of clubs playing a limited number of games against relatively local opponents, i.e. each club did not play each other on a home and away basis as normal. Consequently composite league tables with multiple numbers of clubs were derived. In addition some 2nd Championship matches were 'double-headers', with results being used for the League Cup competition. N.B. The 1940/41 to 1944/45 statistical Wartime details (other than actual match details) have been taken from independent sources and have not been verified by the Author. Players (Appearances with 1st Championship goals scored in first brackets and 2nd Championship in second brackets. * Indicates guest player)

1941/42 Season

(North League: 1st Championship, first part of season)

	P	W	L	D	F	A	Pts
Blackpool	18	14	3	1	75	19	29
Lincoln City	18	13	2	3	54	28	29
Preston N.E.	18	13	4	1	58	18	27
Manchester Utd.	18	10	2	6	79	27	26
Stoke City	18	12	4	2	75	36	26
Everton	18	12	4	2	61	31	26
Blackburn Rovers	18	10	2	6	40	24	26
Liverpool	18	11	3	4	66	44	26
GATESHEAD	18	9	4	5	39	35	23
Sunderland	18	9	5	4	50	30	22
Huddersfield Town	18	10	7	1	48	33	21
Bradford P.A.	18	8	5	5	33	28	21
Grimsby T.	18	7	5	6	41	31	20
Barnsley	18	8	6	4	39	31	20
Newcastle Utd.	18	7	5	6	46	39	20
Sheffield Wed.	18	7	5	6	53	37	19
Manchester City	18	8	7	3	48	54	19
Sheffield Utd.	18	7	7	4	39	38	18
Burnley	18	6	6	6	36	40	18
Halifax Town	18	7	8	3	29	41	17
Oldham Athletic	18	6	8	4	40	49	16
Rochdale	18	6	8	4	28	52	16
Chesterfield	18	5	8	5	27	31	15
Chester	18	6	9	3	45	53	15
Middlesbrough	18	6	9	3	44	56	15

(Top 25 clubs shown only)

(2nd Championship - Second part of season)
22 clubs qualified for the Championship - only those playing 18 or more games qualified (the rest, 29 clubs, did not qualify)

GATESHEAD	13	4	7	2	23	36	10	(30th)

League Cup Qualifying Competition. An average figure, dependant on number of matches played was calculated, with the top 32 clubs qualifying. The bottom 19, including Newcastle who finished 38th, and Gateshead, 44th, did not qualify.

GATESHEAD	10	2	6	2	15	30	6	Ave. 6.66	(Northampton - Top - Ave. 16.66).

Players (appearances and goals):

Agar W	3 (0) (4)
Barron J *	31
Black WF *	5
Bohills J	1
Cairns JG	1
Callendar TS *	6
Cassidy W	26 (1)
Conroy T	12
Coyde N *	2
Curry R *	2
Devlin E	1
Dudgeon A	28
Forster LJ *	23 (5) (1)
Gale T	5
Glease R	2
Harrison R	6
Johnson T	26 (7) (5)
Lamb GH	1
Lansbury R *	1
Livingstone A *	31
Makepeace R *	3
McCormack CJ	25 (15) (4)
Musgrove TD	1
Nesbit A	1
Oxley A	4
Park W *	2
Scott HF *	18 (5) (2)
Scott WR *	4
Spelman I *	26 (1) (1)
Spooner PG	13
West N *	5
Wilbert GN *	14 (0) (4)
Wilson J *	12 (3)
Own Goals:	(2) (1)

1941/42 War-time League

1	Aug	30	Bradford	2-2	Scott, Forster	1253
2	Sep	6	BRADFORD	2-2	Forster, Scott	4000
3		13	LEEDS UNITED	3-2	Wilson(pen), McCormack(2)	4000
4		20	Leeds United	1-5	Wilson(pen), McCormack(2)	2500
5		27	Middlesbrough	1-1	Johnson	5900
6	Oct	4	MIDDLESBROUGH	4-1	McCormack(2), Scott, Martin(og)	7000
7		11	NEWCASTLE UNITED	1-1	Scott	12000
8		16	Newcastle United	1-3	McCormack	12000
9		25	Bradford City	2-1	McCormack(2)	1849
10	Nov	1	BRADFORD CITY	1-1	Whittingham(og)	3700
11		8	HUDDERSFIELD TOWN	3-2	McCormack, Wilson, Forster	4700
12		15	Huddersfield Town	1-3	McCormack	1716
13		22	York City	4-3	McCormack(2), Spelman, Forster	4000
14		29	YORK CITY	1-0	Johnson	
15	Dec	6	DONCASTER ROVERS	6-2	Johnson(4,1pen), Cassidy, Forster	3000
16		13	Doncaster Rovers	1-5	McCormack	1783
17		20	SUNDERLAND	2-0		6000
18		25	Sunderland	3-1		
19		27	NEWCASTLE UNITED	2-2	Wilbert(2)	10000
20	Jan	3	Newcastle United	2-4	Wilbert, McCormack	17000
21		10	YORK CITY	3-0	McCormack, Scott, Johnson	3404
22		17	York City	3-3	McCormack(2), Forster	4161
23		31	SUNDERLAND	1-2	Johnson	6500
24	Feb	14	Middlesbrough	1-3	Johnson	2500
25		21	BRADFORD CITY	1-0	Black	1500
26		28	Bradford City	0-2		2000
27	Mar	14	MIDDLESBROUGH	1-7	McCormack	3500
28		21	Sunderland	1-5	Johnson	
29	Apr	4	NEWCASTLE UNITED	4-0	Johnson, Agar, Scott, Wilson	2774
30		6	Newcastle United	2-0		4658
31	May	9	Newcastle United	2-6		3500

1942/43 War-time League

1	Aug	29	York City	2-1	Barrett(2)	3200
2	Sep	5	YORK CITY	1-4	McCormack	3000
3		12	LEEDS UNITED	3-1	Scott(2), Cassidy	2500
4		19	Leeds United	2-1	McCormack	3000
5		26	Bradford City	7-3	Ross(3), Barrett(3), Harrison	3033
6	Oct	3	BRADFORD CITY	2-2	McCormack, Agar	4000
7		10	HUDDERSFIELD TOWN	3-4	Wilbert(pen), McCormack, Johnson	3000
8		17	Huddersfield Town	1-2	Johnson	2252
9		24	Bradford	0-6		1850
10		31	BRADFORD	1-1	Johnson	2600
11	Nov	7	NEWCASTLE UNITED	4-1	Johnson, Spelman, McCormack, Wilbert	6644
12		14	Newcastle United	4-7	Forster(2), Wilbert, Barrett	10000
13		21	Sunderland	4-3	Johnson(2), McCormack(2)	
14		28	SUNDERLAND	1-0	Oxley	7150
15	Dec	5	MIDDLESBROUGH	5-0	Johnson(3), Forster, Wilbert	
16		12	Middlesbrough	3-2	J.Callender, Forster(2)	
17		19	NEWCASTLE UNITED	3-1		5300
18		25	Newcastle United	6-6	?,?,?,?,?,?,?	15000
19		26	Sunderland	1-7	Johnson	
20	Jan	2	SUNDERLAND	5-4	McCormack(3), J.Callender, Johnso	5900
21		9	BRADFORD CITY	2-3	Johnson, McCormack	2700
22		16	Bradford City	3-2	McCormack, Wilbert	2000
23		23	Middlesbrough	3-2	J.Callender, McCormack, Johnson	3500
24		30	MIDDLESBROUGH	6-0	Wilbert(4), McCormack, Forster	3800
25	Feb	6	YORK CITY	3-2	Forster, J.Callender, Johnson	4026
26		13	York City	0-2		5065
27		20	Newcastle United	0-2		17100
28		27	MIDDLESBROUGH	2-6	Johnson, McCormack	9500
29	Mar	6	Sunderland	2-1	McCormack, Wilbert	
30		13	SUNDERLAND	1-2	Park	3700

Gateshead FC emerged from a two year spell of hibernation in 1941, and Chairman William Tulip expressed gratitude to a number of wellwishers who donated clothing coupons to help provide the team strip. It has been said that War brings together people who would not associate otherwise and this was certainly the case on the football field. In happier circumstances Gateshead would never have competed with, much less defeated, Newcastle United, Sunderland, Middlesbrough, Leeds United and Huddersfield Town.

The goalkeeper's art seems to have been neglected in those dark days. No games ended goalless. Scores of five and six and more were commonplace, sometimes by both sides in the same match. Obviously little or no importance can be attached to these surreal scorelines and frequent 'giantkillings' when most players were in the Forces and made guest appearances for several teams as opportunity dictated.

Two League tables were issued in each of the Wartime seasons. The First referred to matches played between August and Christmas and the second to the remainder of the season. These tables are complex and scarcely comprehensible, involving very large numbers of clubs, but have been included, at least in part form (taken from Jack Rollin's book 'Soccer at War').

1942/43 Season

(North League 1st Championship)

	P	W	L	D	F	A	Pts
Blackpool	18	16	1	1	93	28	33
Liverpool	18	14	3	1	70	34	29
Sheffield Wed.	18	12	3	3	61	26	27
Manchester U.	18	12	4	2	58	26	26
Huddersfield T.	18	10	2	6	52	32	26
Stoke City	18	11	4	3	46	25	25
Coventry City	18	10	3	5	28	16	25
Southport	18	11	4	3	64	42	25
Derby County	18	11	5	2	51	37	24
Bradford PA	18	8	3	7	46	21	23
Lincoln City	18	9	4	5	58	36	23
Halifax Town	18	10	5	3	39	27	23
GATESHEAD	18	10	5	3	52	45	23
Aston Villa	18	10	6	2	47	33	22
Everton	18	10	6	2	52	41	22
Grimsby T.	17	8	4	5	42	31	21
York City	18	9	6	3	47	36	21
Blackburn R.	18	9	6	3	56	43	21
Barnsley	18	8	5	5	39	30	21
Sheffield Utd.	18	7	5	6	45	35	20

(Top 20 clubs shown only)

(2nd Championship)

	P	W	L	D	F	A	Pts
Halifax Town	18	7	9	2	30	39	16
Chester	20	6	11	3	40	49	15
Northampton T.	17	6	9	2	30	37	14
Wolves	17	5	8	4	38	45	14
Swansea Town	18	4	8	6	36	52	14
Grimsby Town	13	4	4	5	30	27	13
Bury	16	5	8	3	44	42	13
Doncaster R.	17	5	9	3	27	41	13
Rotherham U.	18	4	9	5	28	43	13
GATESHEAD	13	6	7	0	29	36	12
Stockport C	19	4	11	4	37	76	12
Southport	18	4	11	3	38	58	11
Leeds United	16	5	10	1	32	50	11
Oldham Ath.	18	4	11	3	28	47	11
Middlesbrough	18	5	13	0	31	69	10
Lincoln City	10	4	5	1	23	18	9
Burnley	14	3	8	3	17	31	9
Walsall	16	3	11	2	22	35	8
Cardiff City	17	2	12	3	22	47	7
Mansfield Town	10	1	8	1	12	41	3

(Bottom 20 clubs shown only)

Players (appearances and goals):

Agar W	3 (1)
Barrett P	22 (5) (4)
Callendar J	13 (3) (4)
Callendar TS *	26
Cassidy W	26 (1) (1)
Casson J	3
Clarke JH	1
Dawson E *	30
Devlin E	16
Dryden H	2
English A *	1
Farrington R *	2
Forster LJ *	15 (10) (2)
Forster W *	5
Gale T	13
Gray R	1
Harrison R	11(1)
Johnson T	22 (6) (6)
Livingstone A	27
Makepeace R *	1
McCormack CJ	29 (14) (9)
Mills H.	1
Oxley A	4 (1)
Park W *	2 (0) (1)
Ross J *	1 (2)
Scott FH *	4 (2)
Shanks R *	1
Simpson R *	2
Smith R *	1
Spelman I *	19 (1)
Wands A	10
Wilbert GN	24 (5) (2)
Young G	3

League Cup Qualifying Competition. 9 or 10 matches were 'double-headers', and on a points system, the top 32 clubs qualified. The bottom 22 did not qualify. Gateshead finished 35th.

GATESHEAD	10	5	5	0	25	30	10

(Manchester City and Rochdale were top with 16 points each)

1943/44 Season

(North League 1st Championship)

	P	W	L	D	F	A	Pts
Blackpool	18	12	2	4	56	20	28
Manchester U	18	13	3	2	56	30	28
Liverpool	18	13	4	1	72	26	27
Doncaster R.	18	11	2	5	45	25	27
Bradford PA	18	11	3	4	65	28	26
Huddersfield T.	18	12	4	2	48	25	26
Northampton T.	18	10	3	5	43	25	25
Aston Villa	18	11	4	3	43	27	25
Sunderland	18	10	5	3	46	30	23
Hartlepool	18	10	5	3	44	31	23
Everton	18	9	5	4	60	34	22
Blackburn R.	18	10	6	2	47	32	22
Rochdale	18	10	6	2	43	41	22
Sheffield U.	18	8	5	5	30	26	21
Lincoln City	18	8	6	4	51	40	20
Birmingham	18	8	6	4	38	31	20
Manchester C	18	9	7	2	38	35	20
Mansfield T.	18	9	7	2	32	33	20
Derby County	18	8	6	4	43	45	20
Chester	18	9	7	2	40	43	20
Grimsby T.	18	8	7	3	32	36	19
WBA	18	8	7	3	42	44	19
GATESHEAD	18	8	8	2	40	51	18
Burnley	18	5	6	7	24	22	17
Walsall	18	5	6	7	27	31	17

(Top 25 club shown only)

(2nd Championship)
(Top 20 not shown, next 10 only shown)

	P	W	L	D	F	A	Pts
GATESHEAD	21	9	8	4	45	53	22
Doncaster R	17	9	5	3	42	33	21
Derby C.	21	8	8	5	33	28	21
Rochdale	20	8	7	5	40	36	21
Barnsley	17	8	5	4	34	30	20
Halifax T	20	8	8	4	44	42	20
Chester	20	9	9	2	65	65	20
Hartlepools U	20	8	8	4	49	50	20
Stockport C.	19	10	9	0	44	49	20
Sheffield W.	20	8	8	4	32	36	20

League North Cup Qualifying Competition
GATESHEAD   10 5 4 1   27 28   11
(Top 32 qualified, Gateshead finished 28th)
League Cup 1st round:
1st leg: Gateshead 1   Darlington 2
2nd leg: Darlington 1   Gateshead 1
(Aggregate 2-3)

Players: (appearances and goals)

Barrett P	7 (3) (1)
Barron J *	1
Batey R *	2
Bohills J	3
Callender J	13
Callender TS *	38
Cassidy W	24
Clarke J	5
Dawson E *	4
Devlin E	35 (0) (1)
Dryden H	5 (1)
Gale T	17
Gibson W	7
Gray R	21
Easten W	5
Embleton E *	1
Forster LJ *	6 (2)
Forster WB *	25
Harper A	3 (0) (3)
Harrison R	24 (3) (3)
Hetherington TB*7	
Johnson J	1
Johnson T	35 (11) (9)
Lancaster W	18 (2) (1)
Livingstone A	25 (1) (5)
McConnoy JE *	4
McCormack CJ	29 (16) (9)
Middleton W	1
Park W *	2
Robson R	2
Tulip J *	1
Turnbull F	18 (1) (3)
Wands A	21 (0) (1)
West N *	1
Wilbert GN	2
Wilson JJ	1
Wort F	15

1943/44 War-time League

#	Month	Date	Opponent	Score	Scorers	Att
1	Aug	28	DARLINGTON	4-3	Johnson, McCormack, L.Forster	2000
2	Sep	4	Darlington	2-2	McCormack, L.Forster	5000
3		11	YORK CITY	3-0	McCormack, R.Harrison, Johnson	2000
4		18	York City	1-5	Johnson	4036
5		25	HARTLEPOOLS UNITED	3-3	McCormack(3)	3000
6	Oct	2	Hartlepools United	0-5		4649
7		9	Leeds United	2-5	Johnson, McCormack	3000
8		16	LEEDS UNITED	3-4	McCormack, Harrison	300
9		23	Middlesbrough	0-3		2000
10		30	MIDDLESBROUGH	5-3	McCormack, Johnson	3000
11	Nov	6	BRADFORD CITY	2-1	Johnson(2)	2500
12		13	Bradford City	4-1	Dryden, Johnson(2), Lancaster	2200
13		20	SUNDERLAND	2-3	Johnson, Livingstone	
14		27	Sunderland	3-2	Barrett, Johnson, Lancaster	
15	Dec	4	DARLINGTON	2-1	Johnson, Barrett	4000
16		11	Darlington	1-7	Turnbull	6233
17		18	NEWCASTLE UNITED	1-3	Harrison	6000
18		25	Newcastle United	2-0	McCormack(2)	15635
19		27	Darlington	0-5		8268
20	Jan	1	DARLINGTON	2-1	Barrett, Livingstone(pen)	5000
21		8	MIDDLESBROUGH	2-1	Livingstone(pen), Johnson	2500
22		15	Middlesbrough	2-4	Clark, Livingstone(pen)	4500
23		22	Newcastle United	1-2	Harrison	13681
24		29	NEWCASTLE UNITED	1-3	McCormack	8859
25	Feb	5	SUNDERLAND	7-4	Johnson(2),Harper(2),Wands,McCormack,Turnbull	5000
26		12	Sunderland	4-1	Forster(2), Lancaster, Livingstone(pen)	4000
27		19	Hartlepools United	6-5	Forster(2),Johnson(2),Harrison,Turnbull	7000
28		26	HARTLEPOOLS UNITED	2-2	Forster(2)	2000
29	Mar	4	DARLINGTON	1-2	Johnson	4000
30		11	Darlington	1-1	Johnson	9994
31		18	MIDDLESBROUGH	2-1	McCormack, Turnbull	2000
32		25	Middlesbrough	1-4	Harper	2000
33	Apr	1	HARTLEPOOLS UNITED	3-1	McCormack(2), Devlin	2000
34		8	Hartlepools United	3-3	Johnson(2), Forster	5419
35		15	DARLINGTON	1-0	Forster	1500
36		22	Darlington	0-4		5101
37		29	HARTLEPOOLS UNITED	3-1	Forster,McCormack,Livingstone(pen)	500
38	May	6	Hartlepools United	2-6		2000

1944/45 War-time League

#	Month	Date	Opponent	Score	Scorers	Att
1	Aug	26	NEWCASTLE UNITED	2-2	J.Callender(2)	8109
2	Sep	2	Newcastle United	1-3	McCormack	3320
3		9	Middlesbrough	1-4	Thompson	4000
4		16	Middlesbrough	5-5	Johnson(2),McCormack,Dudgeon(p),Behills	2000
5		23	HARTLEPOOLS UNITED	1-3	McCormack	2000
6		30	Hartlepools United	5-2	McCormack, Bohills	6000
7	Oct	7	Huddersfield Town	0-4		4263
8		14	HUDDERSFIELD TOWN	2-6	Johnson(2)	3000
9		21	YORK CITY	4-2	McCormack(3), og	1500
10		28	York City	2-10	Dudgeon(pen), McCormack	4100
11	Nov	4	Darlington	6-1	McCormack(3), Forster(3)	6701
12		11	DARLINGTON	3-1		3500
13		18	Hull City	3-1	Thompson, McCormack(2)	5000
14		25	HULL CITY	5-2	McCormack(2),Thompson,Hays,Forster	3000
15	Dec	2	BRADFORD	1-2	Cairns	4220
16		9	Bradford (at York)	4-1	Hays, McCormack(3)	2250
17		16	Sunderland	1-2	Cairns	8500
18		23	SUNDERLAND	1-0	Johnson	12700
19		25	Middlesbrough	1-1		7614
20		30	DARLINGTON	2-1	McCormack, Cairns	5000
21	Jan	6	HARTLEPOOLS UNITED	1-2	McCormack	3000
22		13	Hartlepools United	1-1	McCormack	6756
23		20	Newcastle United	4-2	Johnson(2), Cairns(2)	11688
24	Feb	3	SUNDERLAND	2-1	Johnson, Thompson	
25		10	Sunderland	0-3		14700
26		17	Middlesbrough	3-2	Hays, Cassidy, Thompson	4000
27		24	MIDDLESBROUGH	1-2	McCormack	5100
28	Mar	3	Sunderland	2-0	McCormack, Cairns	7300
29		17	NEWCASTLE UNITED	0-3		14300
30		24	Sunderland	2-2	Cairns, Tweedy	3200
31		31	SUNDERLAND	4-2	McCormack(4)	3800
32	Apr	2	Middlesbrough	1-3		
33		7	Darlington	4-2	Cairns(2), Howden, Hays	4195
34		14	DARLINGTON	3-4	McCormack, Johnson, Wharton(og)	2000
35	May	5	Huddersfield Town	3-3	Cairns(2,1pen), McCormack	2929
36		12	Huddersfield Town	3-2	Johnson, Cairns, Dryden	3412
37		19	NEWCASTLE UNITED	3-0	Cassidy, McCormack(2)	9977
38		21	Newcastle United	1-3		18000
39		26	Sunderland	6-3	Johnson, Cairns(2), Thompson(3)	13187

Gateshead's wartime exploits ended with a Cup Final victory. Their aggregate wins over Huddersfield and Newcastle in May 1945 earned them the right to play Sunderland in the final of the Tyne Wear Tees Cup at Newcastle. Gateshead won handsomely by 6-3.

Newcastle United often made the short (walking distance) trip to Redheugh Park during the War. Gateshead 'keeper Clark is seen here on the 17th March 1945.

1944/45 Season

(North League 1st Championship)
(Top 10 not shown, next 25 only shown)

	P	W	L	D	F	A	Pts
Stoke City	18	9	5	4	37	25	22
Birmingham	18	8	4	6	30	21	22
Barnsley	18	10	6	2	42	32	22
Rotherham U.	18	9	5	4	31	25	22
WBA	18	9	5	4	36	30	22
Liverpool	18	9	6	3	41	30	21
Grimsby Town	18	9	6	3	37	29	21
Halifax Town	18	8	5	5	30	29	21
Chester	18	9	6	3	45	45	21
Blackpool	18	9	7	2	53	38	20
Burnley	18	8	6	4	39	27	20
Leeds Utd.	18	9	7	2	43	42	20
Sheffield W.	18	9	7	2	34	30	20
Chesterfield	18	8	7	3	30	19	19
Darlington	18	9	8	1	52	45	19
Wolves	18	7	6	5	31	27	19
Rochdale	18	7	6	5	35	33	19
Crewe Alex.	18	9	8	1	43	41	19
Blackburn R.	18	7	7	4	30	29	18
Manchester U.	18	8	8	2	40	40	18
Preston NE	18	7	7	4	26	28	18
Walsall	18	5	7	6	27	29	16
GATESHEAD	18	7	9	2	45	53	16
Northampton T	18	5	7	6	30	38	16
Newcastle U	18	7	10	1	51	38	15

(2nd Championship)
(Top 10 not shown, next 20 only shown)

	P	W	L	D	F	A	Pts
Bristol City	22	13	7	2	55	33	28
Blackburn R.	24	13	9	2	62	51	28
Huddersfield T.	27	12	11	4	52	49	28
Wrexham	22	10	5	7	55	36	27
Bolton Wands.	23	11	7	5	52	35	27
Blackpool	24	12	9	3	58	42	27
Stoke City	23	12	9	2	67	42	26
Lovell's Ath.	19	12	5	2	44	27	26
Cardiff City	20	12	6	2	41	27	26
Grimsby T.	21	10	5	6	51	37	26
Birmingham	24	9	8	7	38	34	25
Crewe Alex.	23	11	9	3	50	50	25
Doncaster R.	20	11	7	2	44	26	24
Bradford PA	22	10	8	4	49	39	24
Accrington St.	24	9	9	6	39	41	24
Barnsley	24	11	11	2	39	42	24
Rotherham U.	20	10	7	3	41	37	23
GATESHEAD	21	9	7	5	46	42	23
Preston N.E.	25	9	12	4	41	56	22
Sheffield U.	24	9	12	3	56	48	21

Players: (appearances and goals)

Bell JH	2
Bohills J	4 (2)
Cairns WH	25 (2) (12)
Callendar J	34 (2)
Callendar TS *	37
Carr GM *	1
Cassidy W	21 (0) (2)
Casson J	1
Clark J*	10
Devlin E	31
Down G	9
Dryden H	4 (0) (1)
Dudgeon A	36 (2)
Farrington R *	1
Forster A	2
Forster LJ*	13 (3)
Gale T	2
Gascoigne W	1
Gray R	22
Hays CJ *	36 (2) (3)
Howden J	5 (0) (1)
Johnson T	36 (3) (6)
Lancaster W	2
Livingstone A	1
McCormack CJ	34 (23) (15)
Nesbit A	3
Park W *	8
Thompson W	21 (5) (5)
Turnbull FE	1
Tweedle J *	1 (0) (1)
Wands A	12
Wilbert GN	3
Wilson A	7
Wort JF	3
Own Goal: (0) (1)	

League Cup Qualifying Competition. 10 matches were 'double-headers', and on a points system, the top 32 clubs qualified The bottom 28 did not qualify. Gateshead finished 35th.

GATESHEAD	10	4	4	2	15	18	10 (Derby C. and Aston Villa were top with 17 points each)

THE END OF THE WAR
1945- 46 SEASON

1945/46 was an interim season when each team played each other on a home and away basis, but the various leagues were regionalised.

With the War over the football world's return to normality was only partial. Gateshead's opponents in the 1945-46 season had a more familiar look. All were old Third Division (North) rivals. The Pennines were not crossed until a Cup-tie took Gateshead to Oldham late in the season.

The Eastern section of the Third Division (North) consisted of ten clubs. There were two League tables and a knockout Cup competition. By attaining third position in the first half of the season and fifth position in the second Gateshead qualified for the knockout stage. After defeating Oldham and Carlisle on aggregate Gateshead were beaten by Rotherham in the semi-final.

The FA Cup returned but in a rather different format. Uniquely to this season all rounds up to the Quarter Finals were played on a two leg basis. Gateshead met three familiar opponents. They had little difficulty in disposing of Hartlepools United and seemed to be safe when they won 4-2 at Darlington. However, some anxious moments were experienced when Darlington raced to an early 2-0 lead at Redheugh before highscoring Cecil McCormack saved the day with a goal five minutes from the end.

Gateshead were drawn to play the first leg of the tie against Rotherham at home but, anxious to avoid a clash with a Newcastle match, they requested that the first leg be switched to Rotherham. Gateshead drew 2-2 at Millmoor but lost the home game 2-0 in midweek.

1945-46 3rd in Division (North - East Region) First half of season

5th in 3rd Division (North Cup) Second half of season

	Date	Opponent	Result	Scorers	Att	Gray	Devlin	Callender T	Callender J	Dudgeon	Cassidy	Forster	Johnson	McCormack	Thompson	Hays	Cairns	Cant	Bell	Bentley	Howden	Wilson	Robinson	Rutherford	Dryden	Birchham	Brown	Callon	Lancaster	Oxley	Atkinson	Render	Dawson	Clark	McDermott
1	Aug 25	Darlington	4-2	McCormack(2), Thompson(2)	5000	1	2	3	4	5	6	7	8	9	10	11																			
2	Sep 1	DARLINGTON	4-2	T.Callender, Thompson	3000	1	2	3	4	5	6	7	8	9	10	11																			
3	8	YORK CITY	1-3	Johnson	5364	1	2	3	4	5	6	7	8	9	10	11																			
4	15	York City	1-2	Cairns	5825	1	2	3	4	5	6		8	7	10		9	11																	
5	22	Halifax Town	4-1	Cairns(3), Thompson		1	2			4	5	6		8	7	10	9	11	3																
6	29	HALIFAX TOWN	3-3	Cassidy, Cairns(2)		1	2			4	5	6		8		10	9	11	3	7															
7	Oct 6	LINCOLN CITY	6-1	Cairns(4), McCormack, Johns	5273		2			4	5	6		8	7	10	11	9	3		1														
8	13	Lincoln City	4-1	Cairns(4)	5768		2			4	5			8	7	10	9		3			11	1								6				
9	20	Hartlepools United	2-0	Forster, Howden	6000		2	5	4			6	7	8		10	9		3			11	1												
10	27	HARTLEPOOLS UNITED	3-1	Forster, Cairns, Johnson	5613		2	5	4			6	7	8		10	9		3			11	1												
11	Nov 3	DONCASTER ROVERS	3-1	Atkinson(2), Howden	4860		2	5	4			6	7	8		10			3			11	1								9				
12	10	Doncaster Rovers	2-2	McCormack, Forster	5959		3	5	4			6	7	8	9	11			2			10	1												
13	Dec 11	ROTHERHAM UNITED	4-1	Johnson, Cairns(2)	7981		2	5	4				8	7	10		9					11	1	3							6				
14	22	BRADFORD CITY	3-2	T.Callender, McCormack(2)	4000		2	6	4	5			7	8	9							11	1	3	10										
15	25	CARLISLE UNITED	3-1	McCormack, Cairns, Howden	8000																														
16	26	carlisle United	2-3	Forster(2)																															
17	Jan 1	Rotherham United	1-3	McCormack	4500		2	6		5			7	4	9	10			3			8	1	11											
18	12	HALIFAX TOWN	2-2	T.Callender(pen), Ruecroft(og)		1	2	5	4	5	6	7	8	9			10						3		11											
19	19	Halifax Town	1-0	Cairns			2	3	4	5	6	7	8				9		3			10		11	1										
20	26	Doncaster Rovers	2-4	T.Callender, McCormack	8000		2	3	4	5	6	7	8	9								10		11	1										
21	Feb 2	ROTHERHAM UNITED	6-4	Cairns(5), T.Callender(pen)	4500		2	3	4	5	6	7	8				9					10		11	1										
22	9	Darlington	1-3	Dryden	8000		2	3	4	5	6	7	8				9					10	1	11											
23	16	DARLINGTON	3-1	Howden, Cairns, T.Callender(i)	4000		2	3	4	5	6	7	8				9						1	11		10									
24	23	Carlisle United	0-3				2	3	4	5	6		8				9			7	1			11		10								
25	Mar 2	CARLISLE UNITED	0-2		4000		2	6	4	5			7	8			9		3				1	11		10									
26	9	DONCASTER ROVERS	3-3	Cairns(3)	4261		2	6	8	5			7				9	11	3			10	1					4							
27	16	Rotherham United	3-1	Forster, Cairns, Johnson	6252		2	3		5		6	7	8			9	11				10	1					4							
28	23	Oldham Athletic	2-2	Cant(2)			2	3		5		6	7	8			9	11				10	1					4							
29	30	OLDHAM ATHLETIC	3-0	Lancashire, Howden, Johnsor	5000		2	5						10	8				11			9	1	3					4	7		6				
30	Apr 6	Carlisle United	2-1		12000		2	5	8				7				10	11				9	1	3					4		6				
31	13	CARLISLE UNITED	2-1	Cairns(2,1pen)																														
32	19	ROTHERHAM UNITED	2-2	Forster, Johnson																														
33	20	Bradford City	1-5	McCormack					2			7	8	9	11				3			10	1					4			6	5		
34	22	Rotherham United	1-3	McCormack			5	4			7	8	9			10		3					2	11				6				1	
35	27	Barrow	3-2	Howden, Cairns, Oxley	1762		5	2			7			11		9		3		8								4		10	6	1	
36	May 4	BARROW	4-2	Callow, Cairns(2), Cant			4	5								9	11	3			1	2				10	8			6			7

Not all line ups available from Newspaper sources   One Own Goal

F.A. Cup

	Date	Opponent	Result	Scorers	Att	Devlin	Callender T	Dudgeon	Forster	Johnson	McCormack	Thompson	Cairns	Bell	Howden	Wilson	Robinson	Rutherford	Brown	Atkinson	Dawson	Clark	McDermott
1/1	Nov 17	Hartlepools United	2-1	Cairns(2,1pen)	5148	5		4			8	9	11		10		3		1	2		6	7
1/2	24	HARTLEPOOLS UNITED	6-2	Howden, Cairns(2), McCorma	6152	5		4			8	7	10	9		3		11	1	2		6	
2/1	Dec 8	Darlington	4-2	Rutherford,Cairns,J.Callender,McCormack	9765	2	6	4	5		8	7		9		3		11	1		10		
2/2	15	DARLINGTON	1-2	McCormack	8000	2	6	4	5		8	7		9				11	1	3	10		
3/1	Jan 5	Rotherham United	2-2	Atkinson, Thompson	13744	2	5	4			8	9	11			10		1	3			7	6
3/2	9	ROTHERHAM UNITED	0-2		10952	2	5	4		10	8	9	11			3		7	1				6

Third Division North - East Region (First Half Season)						
	P	W	L	D	F	A	Pts
Rotherham U.	18	12	4	2	56	28	26
Darlington	18	12	4	2	61	36	26
GATESHEAD	**18**	**11**	**5**	**2**	**51**	**34**	**24**
Doncaster R.	18	8	6	4	34	35	20
York C.	18	6	6	6	34	34	18
Halifax T.	18	7	7	4	39	46	18
Bradford C.	18	6	8	4	45	40	16
Carlisle U.	18	5	10	3	34	58	13
Lincoln C.	18	4	12	2	34	54	10
Hartlepools U.	18	3	12	3	22	45	9

Third Division North - East Region (Second Half Season-Third North Cup)						
	P	W	L	D	F	A	Pts
Doncaster R.	10	6	1	3	24	15	15
Carlisle U.	10	7	3	0	30	17	14
Bradford C.	10	4	3	3	27	22	11
Hartlepools U.	10	4	3	3	25	21	11
GATESHEAD	**10**	**4**	**4**	**2**	**21**	**23**	**10**
Darlington	10	5	5	0	26	31	10
Rotherham U.	10	3	5	2	24	26	8
York C.	10	2	4	4	16	18	8
Halifax T.	10	2	4	4	15	18	8
Lincoln C.	10	2	7	1	21	38	5
(Top 8 only qualified for Cup)							

1946-47

On 31 August 1946 a Hartlepools United full back named Fred Gregory missed a penalty in a match against Barrow at the Victoria Ground. Of what relevance is that a mundane fact in a history of Gateshead FC? Merely that had his aim been surer, and had Hartlepools won that game instead of drawing it 1-1, then that first Saturday of the post-War era would have gone down in history as the only day on which all six of the North Eastern teams won. There were other days on which Newcastle, Sunderland, Middlesbrough, Gateshead, Darlington and Hartlepools amassed eleven points but a 100% Saturday never dawned (though, on 7 February 1953 all six of them lost).

The fixture lists for the abandoned 1939-40 season had been recycled (appropriately for those austere times), and crowds were generally high though not noticeably so at Gateshead. Brothers Jack and Tom Callender began their long post-War careers with the club. The only player credited with appearances in 1938-39 who was still around was half back Bill Cassidy.

After Gateshead's 2-1 home victory over Crewe Alexandra on the opening day their next win was in the fifth match when they visited the much bombed city of Hull. Centre forward Cecil McCormack scored both goals on that occasion and on 28 September he joined the sad 'losing side hat-trick scorers club', when Chester won 4-3 at Redheugh. McCormack was becoming a consistent marksman, so he obviously wouldn't be staying long. Finances were tight as always and the only home League attendances of over 7,000 occurred when popular visitors Carlisle United won 3-1 in October, and when League leaders Doncaster Rovers did the same a month later (Doncaster won 18 of their 21 away games that season).

Patchy results, a lower half League position, and modest crowds were the order of the day, but the FA Cup brought some success with home victories over Bradford City and Lancaster City. In the first round match Bradford City's 38 year old player coach Jack Milburn suffered a suspected broken leg. His nephew and namesake was on the verge of becoming a household name nearby. The Third Round took Gateshead to meet Manchester City at Maine Road. They put up a good performance, but their Second Division opponents scored three times in the last eleven minutes to win comfortably. Gateshead were more fortunate than many clubs as they managed to play all but one of their January and February fixtures as the notorious winter of 1947 caused widespread postponements and consequent lack of income. Less lucky were New Brighton whom Gateshead visited on 8 March. That club's heavy backlog of postponed games influenced the referee's decision to proceed with the match which Gateshead won 3-2 on a hazardous pitch.

Stanley

Rock Bottom Touched in Home Defeat

[By "JASON"]

Gateshead 3, *Stanley 0

Alice, wandering around in Wonderland, found things getting "curiouser and curiouser" as time went on. Stanleyites are finding events getting worse and worse these days at Peel Park. The tragedy is that Stanley's displays are not happening in the rosy romanticism of the fairy-tale, but in the stark and material present.

Those who on Boxing Day saw the "Reds'" worst display since the club restarted operations in 1944 fear for the future. The slide down the slippery re-election path is gaining momentum. It was given a hearty shove in that direction by Gateshead, who scored three times without reply and were unfortunate not to have been able to take a bigger bag of goals back with them to the North-east.

There is no excuse for the defeat. Stanley were poor and made a moderate visitors' team look good by contrast. There was no plan, co-ordination, understanding, speed or snap. There was not even the punch to take advantage of two golden chances which might have acted as face-savers in the closing minutes from point-blank range. In fact, there was not a redeeming feature about the display throughout, unless one credits Briggs with keeping the score down by his almost lone shouldering of the considerable defensive burden. Even he blotched his copy-book by slicing a centre into his own net, and slipped several times.

With Malcolm unable to cope with the right wing problem set by Clark, the former Stanley winger, and his partner Johnson, Webster found himself invariably facing two quick-moving players who interchanged positions dizzily and had him running vainly between them. And the rest of the forwards showed an intelligent grasp of the fundamental principle of soccer—putting the ball into the open space in front of a colleague.

That was an example which Stanley might have copied, but didn't. Instead, they could not find their men, were slow to take advantage of any opportunities and were generally outclassed.

And while the defence were not helped by the lack of covering, the forwards suffered by lack of support. Even when the ball ran for them the attack was never smooth. In fact, the team might have been complete strangers to each other, so marked were the individual operations of the players.

The spectators were not prepared for the general breakdown when Stanley showed promise in the first ten minutes. Then, at least, there was some show of smoothness. Several juicy passes were slid along the wings by Hudson and Keeley, and once a hanging Bond centre was punched off Robinson's head.

But it didn't last long. Gateshead showed how the game should be played; there was always a man in the open to collect the ball. In fact, it seemed as though there were two white-jerseyed teams on the field. The writing was on the wall when Clark crashed a shot against the Stanley bar and the ball was scrambled into the net—only for the referee adamantly to disallow the goal. Rose was knocked down by a shot from McCormick, while Conroy might have been penalised for fouling Rutherford in the penalty area.

QUICK GOALS

After 29 minutes the first blow fell. Briggs was drawn out of position and the ball was slipped up the middle. McCORMICK was left unchallenged by a spreadeagled defence and he tapped the ball past the advancing Rose. A minute later, BRIGGS sliced the ball into his own net after Johnson, interchanging position with Clark in a clever bout of passing, had centred. Rose covered himself with glory—and mud—when he brilliantly kept out still another McCormick effort from a right wing centre. Even Cassidy had time to run in and flick the bar with a shot which had Rose helpless.

The best goal of the trio, however, came within ten seconds of the restart. Gateshead kicked off and, in a series of quick moves, had the Stanley defence tangled. McCORMICK slashed the ball home—a lovely goal, which had come without a "Red" touching the ball.

DETERMINATION

From that point onwards, the game deteriorated into nothing. Gateshead, sitting pretty, were content to carry steadily on. Stanley went from bad to worse, and could do little that was right. This was one of the dreariest 45 minutes it has been my misfortune to see, and the less said about it the better. Apart from the straight shots which Dawson easily held in the dying minutes from Hudson and Bond, the only time he was in action was when he collected back passes from his defensive colleagues.

Midway in the second half, heavy rain came on, making the pitch unpleasantly heavy and adding to the general misery. Whether it was the rain or the game which caused a mass drift away from the uncovered sides of the ground is problematical. I think it was a combination of both.

Attendance (at the start), 5,000.

Teams:—

Stanley: Rose; Conroy, Webster; Hutton, Briggs, Malcolm; Bond, Hudson, Robinson, Keeley, Keating.

Gateshead: Dawson; Thompson, McDougal; J. Callender, T. Callender, Cassidy; Clark, Johnson, McCormick, Small, Rutherford.

Referee: Mr. A. C. Denham, Preston.

The small army of researchers who have scoured newspaper files to record the history of football should never forget the debt they owe to reporters of by-gone years. Although their job was an easy one compared to the ways many of their readers earned a crust the chronicling of the local clubs doings was not always a pleasure.

This anonymous scribe from the Accrington Observer did not enjoy Gateshead's 1946 victory at Peel Park one little bit. Elsewhere in the same edition he was totally pessimistic about his club's chances of gaining re-election. As it turned out Accrington Stanley had some good years ahead (relatively speaking) and their League career lasted slightly longer than Gateshead's.

Gateshead goalkeeper Edward Dawson in action at Darlington on Good Friday of 1947.

The heaviest defeat of the season and the biggest victory came in consecutive home games. Twice before the War Gateshead had lost home matches 5-0 (against Lincoln and Crewe), so Barrow's victory by that score was not unprecedented. It seems difficult to account for Barrow's late surge which brought all their goals in the last seventeen minutes when the game had been evenly contested before that. The same opponents had, of course, inflicted Gateshead's heaviest ever defeat on an embarrassing occasion thirteen years earlier. Two weeks later Gateshead beat Halifax Town 6-1.

This account of the first post-War season began at the Victoria Ground, West Hartlepool, and ends there on the unusually late date of Monday 26 May. On a ground where they often did well, Gateshead won 3-1 thanks to an impressive hat trick by centre forward Martin Small. Less pleasing was the performance of Tom Johnson whose rough play provoked some hostility from the home crowd.

1947-48
Gateshead's mid-table position in the previous season meant a low gate for the first home game of the new one, though this was a Monday evening match against Darlington, and even in August these games were always a problem at Redheugh. The preference for Saturday games was illustrated by the appreciably increased gate for the Saturday match against Carlisle. Gateshead lost both these encounters.

Home form continued to be poor and by the end of November they had lost three times at Redheugh, but only twice away, whilst four of their five victories had been on their travels. This anomalous situation continued in the FA Cup. For the second year in succession Bradford City were the first round visitors and the Yorkshiremen won 3-1 this time.

On Christmas Day, however, Gateshead won 7-0 against Hartlepools United though they failed to complete the double two days later when they lost 3-2 at the Victoria Ground. Between these games Hartlepools had signed a new goalkeeper (unsurprisingly) and this ex-Barnsley man, Rimmington, made a dramatic dash from West Yorkshire to West Hartlepool arriving just in time to frustrate Gateshead. Thereby hangs a tale.

When Gateshead had played at Halifax on 22 November, centre half Tom Callender had to move into the forward line to replace Harry Hawkins who had failed to show. The latter was unaware that the train on which his team mates were travelling was routed via Stockton (close to his Teesside home), and he planned to join them at the more usual boarding point of Darlington. Realising his error he caught the train to Leeds but missed the connection for Halifax. A bus which took him the rest of the way was delayed, and he arrived at the Shay just as the match was kicking off.

What a host of travellers' tales must have gone untold by players rushing to matches in those days of steam trains, first and third class carriages and cavernous, gloomy stations. Several players were still in the Forces and had to make long journeys to play. The previous season Gateshead's high scoring Cecil McCormack had failed to arrive at Oldham from an RAF station in the South. McCormack was now performing quite well for First Division Middlesbrough to whom he had been transferred for £6,000 in the Summer. Like all small clubs Gateshead had to sell players to survive though it was all but unknown for an ex-Redheugh player to shine in the top division.

After the big win on Christmas Day there was another good victory of 3-0 over Tranmere on New Years Day. Gateshead had to compete with a Newcastle first team crowd of 61,000 and – not for the only time – the match at Redheugh was not reported in the local morning paper, *The Journal*. (On 27 December, there had been a crowd of 15,000 at St. James' Park for a match between Newcastle Schoolboys and North of Scotland Schoolboys – an annual fixture but hardly an International).

Life must go on whatever the handicaps and a series of good results at home resulted in a crowd of 9,718 bracing a gale force wind to watch another victory against Mansfield. The club was now in third position and there was talk of promotion. When Oldham won 5-3 at Redheugh the crowd was disappointingly low but increased again when eventual champions Lincoln City were beaten 3-2 on Easter Monday.

The Callender brothers Tom (an ever-present in those first five post-War seasons) and Jack were not the only long service players to emerge in that era. Goalkeeper Bob Gray had made his debut at Tranmere in September, after being rejected by Newcastle. When Gateshead won 3-0 at Wrexham late in the Season the *Sunday Sun* reporter said the result was a travesty as Wrexham's relentless pressure was frustrated by Gray who worked wonders, and that Gateshead owed this undeserved victory as much to him as they did to the scorers of the three breakaway goals. Between them Gray and the Callender brothers would eventually make 1,341 League appearances for Gateshead.

The club made a profit of £2,035 over the 1947-48 season – doubtless thanks to McCormack's transfer – but at the Annual General Meeting reference was made to the transport problem with spectators having long waits for buses to take them home after matches. The writer remembers that problem a decade later when crowds were small, but it must have been chronic with crowds of ten thousand and more, and a cause of anxiety for visiting supporters wishing to catch trains home from Newcastle Central Station.

1948-49
A crowd of just over 6,000 saw Gateshead start the season with a 3-0 victory over New Brighton. The race for the single promotion place fizzled out early as Hull City won their first nine games and virtually disappeared over the horizon. Doncaster Rovers, who had amassed a record number of point two years earlier, were already back (which speaks volumes about the standards of football in the Division) and they won 3-0 at Gateshead in October as they mounted a vain challenge to their Yorkshire rivals.

Despite the absence of any hope of promotion Gateshead maintained a high position and drew reasonably large crowds although the chief interest in the season was in the FA Cup. Two non-League clubs from picturesque places visited less-than-pretty industrial Gateshead in the earlier rounds. Netherfield from Kendal in the Lake District were beaten 3-0 in the first round, with Scarborough suffering an identical fate in the Second. It was some time since South country opposition had been faced and unpretentious Aldershot were the Third Round visitors. A crowd of 11,266 was quite satisfactory for a game which even the Aldershot manager – old friend Bill McCracken – admitted was hardly the tie of the round.

Gateshead won 3-1 and this time their wishes came true, for they were drawn at home to a leading Second Division side.

The 17,000 who gathered to see Gateshead play West Bromwich Albion were not disappointed. *"No praise can be too high for Gateshead "* noted the *Sunday Sun* describing how Tom Callender's goal in the 41st minute came after much pressure had been applied to the Albion defence. The second half was four minutes old when Albion equalised and the score remained 1-1 at 90 minutes. In those bleak post-War days the Government discouraged midweek afternoon matches with the absenteeism they engendered, so extra time was played in (first time) drawn Cup-ties. The Midlanders scored twice in extra time and were worthy winners over the two hours. There had been enough giantkilling for one day with Sunderland having lost to Yeovil Town.

The biggest League attendance thus far had been 11,674 for the still popular Carlisle fixture in October, but Hull City's runaway championship side were drawing large crowds everywhere, and when Gateshead played Raich Carter's side over Easter there were gates of 43,795 at Hull and 17,538 at Gateshead. Hull City won both matches 2-0.

The Gateshead reserve side, playing in the North Eastern League, deserve a rare mention for their achievement on 18 December when they won 5-4 at Workington after being 4-0 down at half time. Their hosts were not yet a Football League side though they shared their grounds with a recently elected Rugby League club. Die-hard supporters of the old Newcastle Rugby League club were reported to be travelling west to watch their sport at Workington that season, presumably with a forlorn hope of trying to resurrect it locally.

Matchday programme for the Accrington game

Two last notes concerning the 1948-49 season. When Gateshead won 4-1 at Wrexham in October there was some anger among the Welsh crowd concerning refereeing decisions; Gateshead seem to have been unpopular visitors to the Racecourse with rough play and raised tempers appearing in a number of match reports over the years. And the limitations of lower Division clubs employing mostly part-time players were revealed one Tuesday in April, when no fewer than five of Gateshead's first team squad were unable to travel to Oldham because of their work commitments.

1949-50

There were four good seasons during Gateshead's League career and this was to be one of them. (The previous two had been 1931-32 and 1937-38 and there was another yet to come). A good 3-1 win at Rochdale on the opening day was marred by an injury to Bobby Gray who had to miss a few games. Ernie Passmore scored four in a 7-1 home victory over Halifax Town on Monday evening, a result which swelled the crowd to more than 13,000 when Gateshead beat Bradford City 4-2 the next Saturday.

(Below) Passmore in the process of scoring his second.

(Above) Hartlepools United goalkeeper Rimmington managed to foil Ernie Passmore on this occasion but the Gateshead centre forward beat him five times in this match at the Victoria Ground in 1949.

Strangely Halifax then overcame Gateshead 5-2 at The Shay, but the next two away games, at Chester and Hartlepools, were won, the latter by 5-3 with centre forward Passmore scoring all five of them. There was another home win over Southport but a very bad patch followed comprising a run of thirteen games of which only one was won.

As promotion hopes seemed to have faded the FA Cup provided a resurgence of interest with a home win over York City followed by an away tie at Newport County. Sixty or so Gateshead supporters made the long trip to

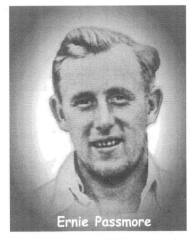

Ernie Passmore

Monmouthshire to witness a drawn game, and 14,000 saw Gateshead lose the replay 2-1 in extra time. By now home defeats had become commonplace, and after twenty League games Gateshead had fallen from first to 12th position.

But on Boxing Day there began a second transformation of Gateshead's fortunes, with victory at Darlington, and a third point taken from them the next day, that elusive home victory gained at the expense of Chester on the last day of the decade, then Gateshead marched on triumphantly winning the remaining ten home games.

There is a long standing suspicion that many lower division clubs never wanted promotion (as distinct from those who never looked to be in any danger of it). This suspicion is strengthened when the results tables of certain clubs are studied and it is noted how some frontrunners suffer surprising defeats when the money gained from their earlier efforts is safely in the bank. But Gateshead's results from New Years Day to the end of the season suggest the very opposite. Here was a team who began the season well, faltered and then took the Division by storm.

Gateshead's best ever away win occurred on 25 March when they beat York City 5-1. Tranmere Rovers were beaten by the same score at Redheugh a week later then, after a 1-0 setback at Mansfield, a 5-0 win over Accrington Stanley proved to be the first of seven consecutive victories. Wrexham were beaten away, Oldham at home, New Brighton away, Rotherham away, then New Brighton and Carlisle at home. But points lost earlier in the season proved fatal to Gateshead's promotion hopes and on Wednesday 19 April Doncaster's victory at Crewe assured the Yorkshire club their second post-War championship.

Gateshead's disappointment was evident when they visited Crewe themselves on the Saturday. The Alex beat them 3-1 with the Gateshead defence described as being *"all at sea"*. The gate for the last home game against Barrow, which Gateshead won 3-1, was less than half of that for the previous home match against Carlisle.

1950-51

The year 1950 saw the number of clubs in the Football League increased from 88 to 92. The Southern Section of the Third Division welcomed Gillingham (who had been there before) and Colchester United, whilst the Northern Section was enhanced by the election of Scunthorpe United and Shrewsbury Town. Both had been trying to get into the League for a long time. Whether or not this extension was a good move, it made for a crowded fixture list especially with midweek games in August and September.

Gateshead could not have got off to a better start as they beat Accrington Stanley 7-0 in the first match with inside forward Jim Kendal scoring four of them. That's the sort of result to arouse interest and after losing at Carlisle in midweek they then won 1-0 at Crewe, in what a journalist described as *"a grand game"*. Gates for the next seven games topped the 10,000 mark (easily), the first being a thriller, with Carlisle taking the lead three times, only for Gateshead to win 4-3.

New Brighton and Halifax were beaten 4-0 and 5-0 on the following Saturday and Monday. The high attendance figures were maintained up to and including Rotherham United's visit on 21 October. Up to then, Rotherham had been a team who did not relish trips to Tyneside. They had not won in thirteen previous visits to Redheugh and before 1930 they had lost all their six matches at South Shields (by 10-1 on one occasion). The then current Rotherham side were pushing for promotion, and demonstrated that history counted for nothing by ending Gateshead's 100% home record with a convincing 3-0 victory. This result signalled the end of five figure attendances at Redheugh that season.

Oddly, Gateshead were excused from playing in the first (and second) round of the FA Cup because of their high League position the previous season. New boys Shrewsbury Town had not entered the FA Cup (they would have had to play through from the qualifying rounds and reasoned that financially it was not practical to enter the competition), so the two clubs arranged to play their League fixture at Shrewsbury on the date of the first round. Shrewsbury won 1-0, and they transferred to the Southern Section the following season. Gateshead's third round tie was away to Sheffield United where they were unlucky to lose by the only goal of the game.

Gateshead had occupied first and second position in the table for much of the season but when it became clear that they were not going to catch Rotherham interest waned and attendances fell dramatically, eventually reaching 2,736 for the match against Barrow on 31 March. This sort of gate was to become the norm later in the decade.

The best performance of the season was a 2-1 victory over high-flying Rotherham at Millmoor on 10 March but – as usual – Gateshead were upstaged by Newcastle United who were playing Wolves in the semi-final of the FA Cup at nearby Hillsborough.

On 28 April that other team from across the Tyne played in the Cup Final. Gateshead were scheduled to meet Southport at Redheugh that afternoon. Television had not reached Tyneside then and radios, though commonplace, were heavy and unportable (and needed plugging in), so Gateshead thought it might be best to postpone their match to Monday evening. On the Saturday afternoon Newcastle beat Blackpool 2-0. On Monday evening another Tyneside team met one from the Lancashire coast; this time Lancashire was avenged by 3-1 - but not many noticed.

This mid-Century season had seen many breaks from tradition for Gateshead Football Club. There had been more matches and two new opponents and no first round Cup tie. They had seemingly got into a good habit of scoring seven goals in the first home match (but it wasn't maintained).

A less welcome innovation was that Hartlepools United had completed the double over them at Christmas for the first time. That had been Gateshead's prerogative – they had previously taken maximum points from the 'Pools' on five occasions. And in the stagnant Third Division (North) with its mostly unchanging cast, Gateshead bade farewell to two of their opponents whom they had met every season and would never see again. Rotherham United broke all the rules by remaining in the Second Division for a full seventeen years and, indeed, coming close to promotion to the First on one occasion.

At the other end of the table New Brighton disappeared. Gateshead might have shed a tear for this small club, not because they would miss travelling to that little known location on the Wirral to pick up a paltry share of a small gate, but because they were usually good for a few easy points. In the ten post-War meetings of these clubs Gateshead had won nine and drawn one. New Brighton had only won once and drawn once on fourteen visits to Redheugh. They failed to be re-elected and were replaced by Workington.

1951-52

In this season Gateshead's usual pattern continued of high attendances following a useful start, falling to very low ones as promotion hopes dwindled, and reaching a highly embarrassing three figure tally for a weekday afternoon match. The situation was alleviated somewhat by a good Cup run.

Five victories in the first seven games found the club in top position but a bus strike in September kept crowds down. Only 7,501 witnessed a good 4-1 win over Tranmere on 8 September though the figure improved when Hartlepools were beaten two days later. There were no complaints about, or from, the crowd of 13,132 who saw old favourites and promotion rivals Lincoln City beaten 3-1 in a match in which Gateshead supplied *'top grade'* football to maintain the top spot. Crowds remained in five figures for the 4-1 defeat of newly elected Workington, and a 1-1 draw against Grimsby Town who were also paying their first visit after having fallen from the First Division.

In the first round of the FA Cup Gateshead drew 2-2 at Stockport and the replay was also drawn before a Redheugh crowd of 7,769. A sensible suggestion was made that the second replay should be played close to one of the clubs, i.e. either at St James' Park or Maine Road. However, the two clubs declined to toss a coin as both considered that if they lost the toss their opponents would virtually have home advantage. This obstinacy caused the FA to insist that the game be played at Hillsborough in neutral Sheffield, convenient to neither and losing revenue to both. Gateshead won 2-1.

The second round saw Guildford City of the Southern League visiting Redheugh Park and an anomalous situation regarding Gateshead's high scoring centre forward Ernie Passmore. He was now domiciled in the South and playing for Guildford City but was technically still a Gateshead player. What subsequent disputation Gateshead would have submitted had a Passmore goal removed them from the Cup is a matter of speculation, but the eventuality did not arise as Gateshead won 2-0 before 13,927. Thousands overcame transport difficulties by walking to Redheugh.

The third round saw Gateshead make a long journey to Ipswich where they squandered a deserved lead by giving away a penalty in the last minute enabling Ipswich to level the score at 2-2. The Wednesday afternoon replay at Redheugh was a memorable one with 13,733 present, including many Newcastle and Sunderland players. Gateshead's forwards dominated most of the game but a 'deadly' Ipswich Town forward line sometimes sailed through an unsteady defence and they went ahead after seventeen minutes through Dobson.

Eleven minutes later Jack Callender equalised with a header but further defensive blunders presented Roberts of Ipswich with the easiest of chances to regain the lead. Another Gateshead equaliser – a second header, this time by Buchan on 59 minutes - was cancelled out seven minutes later by Dobson again when, taking advantage of a hesitant defence, he fired a shot that gave Bob Gray no chance. With crowds streaming out of the ground and the referee about to blow for time Jack Callender passed to John Johnson who headed past Ipswich goalkeeper Parry to make the score 3-3. Pandemonium ensued as those leaving the ground returned for an extra half hours football, though darkness was setting in, and a white ball was substituted for the earlier one. There were no further goals in extra time.

Defensive lapses notwithstanding, this was probably the best game that was ever seen at Redheugh Park. For the second replay it was Sheffield again, Bramall Lane this time, and a Gateshead victory ensued, though Ipswich were poor in this game. Gateshead won 2-1, again after extra time, with John Ingham scoring both goals.

West Bromwich Albion were the fourth round visitors and the suggestion that the match be played at St James' Park was welcomed by the Gateshead directors. Bad weather on 2 February resulted in a postponement to Wednesday afternoon. It was surprising that Cup-ties were played that day as King George the Sixth had died early in the morning, but the match went ahead and Gateshead were beaten 2-0. They were considered to be rather unlucky as West Bromwich Albion's first goal was disputed, but there was a good crowd of 39,287 which could technically be regarded as Gateshead's record 'home' attendance.

The old old story. Out of the Cup and the Third Division (North) Championship heading elsewhere (to Lincoln again). Five figure attendances were just a memory from early season Saturdays and light evenings. The Wednesday afternoon headache followed; who was going to take time off work to watch Gateshead play Accrington Stanley? Not many. Embarrassingly few. The Football League's official attendance record give the figure as 622, though newspapers recorded it as 484. Either way this number was not good enough for League football (Gateshead won 1-0). Tyneside's morning paper *The Journal* carried no match report, but there was a front page cartoon showing a Gateshead player asking a lone spectator if he fancied a game of cards!

Two weeks later there was another midweek match when Oldham Athletic were the visitors. Gateshead scheduled this game to kick off at 5.30pm – but still not very convenient for anybody leaving work at five o'clock.

The attendance of 2,548 was a great improvement, though still not much to write home about. No wonder Gateshead were among the first clubs to make tentative enquiries about floodlights.

At Redheugh Park on Good Friday, when the first team was away at York, there was a reserve team attendance of 1,455 for a North Eastern League game. The visitors were Sunderland Reserves who were beaten 2-0. A generation earlier Sunderland's second string used to attract more people to the old South Shields ground at Horsley Hill than came to see Football League games. There was another South Shields club at a new ground, and they had occasionally drawn crowds of over ten thousand, as had Gateshead quite often. But in December 1951 the South Shields Supporters Club found it necessary to make a donation to enable the club to pay the players' wages. Was the decision to leave South Shields in 1930 a right one? Apparently it was!

1952-53
This was to be Gateshead's season of seasons – one in which the local and national newspapers did take notice. The League season began with a fine 2-0 win over Carlisle United with the press enthusing over the display of Ken Smith, a new inside forward who had been signed from Blackpool. 11,390 spectators attended this game but crowds fell as the next six games yielded only one victory – albeit a 6-1 triumph over Crewe Alexandra.

Results improved somewhat and the next time a five figure crowd assembled at Redheugh they were rewarded with a *"promotion form"* display, and a 2-0 victory over Grimsby Town on 8 November.

However, it was in the FA Cup that Gateshead were to exceed all expectations and when Crewe Alexandra returned to Redheugh in the first round, the match proved to be a more even one – *"hard and entertaining"* was the verdict of one journalist – resulting in a 2-0 victory. A visit to Bradford followed in the next round. This was described as *"A game which had everything from stylish football to goalmouth thrills galore"*, and Gateshead returned home from Park Avenue with a 2-1 victory to their credit.

Gateshead were rewarded for these two solid performances against familiar opponents with a home draw against famous Liverpool. A capacity crowd might have been expected, had not both of Gateshead's giant neighbours been drawn at home, though to rather less glamorous opposition.

The 56,507 who went to Roker Park were disappointed as Sunderland were held to a draw by Scunthorpe United, whilst the 63,499 who went to Newcastle wasted their money (lots of it) as the match against Swansea Town was abandoned after eight minutes because of fog which was blanketing Tyneside. Those who opted to visit Redheugh Park were the wise ones though it must be said that the fog did rather lessen the enjoyment of the 15,193 who saw Gateshead's historic 1-0 victory – or at least saw part of it.

Weather nowithstanding, this result was no fluke as, apart from a spell in the early stages, Gateshead dominated the game and mounted relentless pressure against a Liverpool defence which was described as *"mediocre even by Third Division standards"*. On 73 minutes Gateshead had the ball in the net but this was disallowed after the referee consulted a linesman. But it was still one way traffic, and after 84 minutes Campbell placed a corner kick and the ball *"disappeared into the thick fog"*. Inside forward Ian Winters headed what must have been the most muted giantkilling goal in history, as it was seen by neither crowd nor press. Gateshead continued to attack but there was no further score.

A notable scalp, and the first time Gateshead had beaten a team from a higher division. The goalscorer, Scotsman Ian Winters, made himself scarce immediately after the match as he had to find his way through the fog to Newcastle Central Station and his train home to York (presumably keeping a low profile among Liverpool supporters).

In the fourth round Gateshead were drawn away to Hull City of the Second Division and more than 4,000 supporters made the 100 mile trip to cheer them on. Gateshead stayed at the East Yorkshire resort of Hornsea for a day or two and clearly the see air agreed with them.

Despite having to play against a gale, Gateshead went ahead after four minutes when Campbell's accurate corner landed in the goalmouth, appearing to strike a Hull defender and ending up at the feet of Ingham who fired between two full backs to score. Gateshead continued to attack and after 29 minutes Winters tried a powerful shot which Hull City defender Phillips tried to intercept but only managed to deflect it into his own net. The home side scored three minutes later and they attacked relentlessly in the second half, but Gateshead's resolute defence proved impregnable. Gateshead's worthy victory meant that they were now the North East's last representative in the FA Cup.

Again Gateshead were paired with a Second Division club, but much further away, at Plymouth. Again the Gateshead players enjoyed a pleasant hotel break, this time at Okehampton in Devon, and again this unaccustomed gracious living paid dividends. *The Sunday Sun* report appeared under the headline:-

PLYMOUTH HOE! HO HO SAY GATESHEAD

And it gets worse! We are told how Plymouth Argyle *"launched a barrage which would have done credit to Drake's gunners but, unlike the Armada, the Gateshead defence did not wilt"*.

Ian Winters

Although Gateshead came close to scoring at the onset, they had goalkeeper Bob Gray to thank for surviving this almost constant pressure. In the 53rd minute, however, Ingham won a contest with a Plymouth player and passed a high ball to that useful man Winters who leapt into the air and headed home from ten yards out. Pymouth Argyle's historian who was there, seemingly, grumbles about Gateshead's *"spoiling tactics"*, but nothing alters the fact that Gateshead scored and Plymouth didn't. Plymouth should be pleased with their distinction of being the only club to have been dismissed from the FA Cup by both the old South Shields club and Gateshead.

Gateshead were now in the last eight and were drawn at home to First Division Bolton Wanderers. A crowd of 17,692 thronged Redheugh Park and throughout the first half the quick-tackling Gateshead defence thwarted the Bolton forwards.

FA Cup Quarter Final day at Redheugh.
Tom Callender (right) shakes hands with Bolton Wanderers captain Willie Moir.

In the fifty fifth minute Nat Lofthouse put Bolton ahead with a goal *"brilliant in its execution yet simple in conception"*. Bolton looked a good side thereafter. Although Gateshead missed a good scoring chance their impressive run was now at an end. Bolton, of course, went on to play Blackpool in the most famous of Cup Finals.

Back to League action!
Wearing Newcastle United's colours to avoid a clash with their hosts, Gateshead defenders Bobby Cairns and Tom Callender watch as Bobby Gray is unable to prevent Stockport County scoring in February 1953.

On a Wednesday afternoon in April, Workington drew 1-1 at Redheugh before a three figure attendance. Where were those 4,000 *"Gateshead supporters"* who had travelled to Hull for the Cup-tie a few weeks earlier? On their way home from work probably. This was an exceptionally low crowd of course, but Saturday afternoon attendances remained low for League games and the last match of the season – a cheering 5-0 victory over Accrington Stanley – was played before fewer than 2,000.

1953-54

Changing times meant that the 1953-54 season began with a full programme of games in midweek. The powers-that-be had cottoned on to the fact that the televising of the FA Cup Final meant that it was no longer wise to play League matches on that day. From now on the scheduled fixture lists would end a week before Cup Final day. Games planned for 5 May 1954 were brought forward to Wednesday 19 August 1953, when Gateshead travelled to Halifax and drew 0-0. They won impressively at Southport on the Saturday but a tolerably high crowd at the first home game had to be content with a goalless draw against Scunthorpe United.

Home wins over Chester and York City followed, and the only five figure attendance of the season saw Gateshead's best performance when they beat leaders Port Vale 1-0. As per always crowds up to Christmas and New Year far exceeded those in the first months of 1954. Gateshead's once-in-a-lifetime Cup run had been and gone, and this year there wasn't even the novelty of a non-League or Southern Section opponent. Old familiar rivals Tranmere Rovers won 2-1 at Redheugh in the first round before 9,701 spectators.

Yet despite their parlous financial situation this was quite an encouraging season for Gateshead. An unbeaten home record was maintained until February when Darlington beat them. They were the only team to take three points from runaway champions Port Vale, and one of only three teams to beat them. (The other two were Hartlepools and Workington – well done the North!). Gateshead played before a crowd of over 20,000 when they visited Vale Park in February. Incidentally Port Vale (who had been transferred from the Southern Section) not only won promotion but went one better than Gateshead had the previous season by reaching the FA Cup semi-final.

The highlight of the season was the home game against Grimsby Town on 27 February. At half time Gateshead led 1-0 through a goal by Johnson, but the small crowd were to get good value for their money in the second half. Haley, an impressive young amateur, scored shortly after the interval, but things started to hum when William Watkin put Gateshead 3-0 ahead at 60 minutes. Grimsby scored in the 62nd, but then Watkin scored in the 63rd, 65th and 66th minutes with Campbell adding a seventh at 76 minutes.

Four goals in seven minutes should have won Watkin (who was a native of Grimsby incidentally) rather more fame than it did. Middlesbrough noticed and immediately signed him but their hopes that he might save them from relegation were not realised. Any of those spectators who returned to Redheugh a week later would see another good performance with Don Robson scoring five for Gateshead Reserves in an 8-3 victory over North Shields.

Gateshead were now in second position but a 5-1 defeat at Wrexham signalled the beginning of a weak run with attendances sinking in the customary manner. They finished the season in fourth place.

1954-55
A midweek double over Southport compensated for a home defeat by Chesterfield on the opening day. Crowds were in the region of 6-7,000 as the early stages of a rather uneventful League season progressed.

There was some excitement in the FA Cup, however, with Gateshead's only high score of the season occurring when Chester were beaten 6-0 in the first round on 20 November. This easy victory over the Division's bottom side was followed by a home pairing with top club Barnsley. There were six goals in this game too – but they were evenly divided. This was a great improvement on the League match just a month earlier when Barnsley had won 4-0 at Redheugh. Few people gave Gateshead much chance in the replay at Oakwell but – with a glamorous home tie against Tottenham Hotspur at stake - Gateshead defended resolutely and a goal by Ken Smith was enough to secure victory.

'Spurs played at Sunderland on New Years Day, and the local press criticised them for not taking a look at Redheugh Park while they were in the vicinity, or sending somebody to observe Gateshead as they played Crewe Alexandra. They would not have seen much to worry them as Gateshead won a poor game 1-0. The season's highest League crowd attended, taking advantage of the opportunity to purchase Cup-tie tickets.

In the event a rather moderate 'Spurs side progressed to the next round as, although Gateshead managed to pen them in their own half for 60 minutes, the Tottenham goalkeeper Reynolds was rarely troubled and their centre forward Brooks settled the game with two *"lightning raids"* and two *"unstoppable shots"*.

Johnny Ingham in action at Redheugh Park. This long serving player scored 109 goals in 431 games between 1947 and 1958.

The only bright spot that remained in Gateshead's season was a run of four consecutive victories in March, but this was followed by a run of eleven games without a win before the Cumbrian pair Workington (home) and Carlisle (away) were beaten in the last two games. The unsuccessful run caused Gateshead to fall to seventh place after being slightly higher for most of the season.

1954-55 could be regarded as the end of Gateshead's good years (relatively speaking). In the nine seasons since football re-commenced they had been a better than average Third Division (North) side, had come close to promotion once and had played in the Third Round of the FA Cup on six occasions; of the 16 clubs who had spent that entire era in that Division only Gateshead and Stockport County had finished in the lower half of the table in only one season (1946/47 in Gateshead's case), Accrington Stanley and Hartlepools United had been lower half sides in seven of those seasons, Chester and Darlington in eight of them whilst Halifax Town had the dubious distinction of being a lower half club in all nine.

In the FA Cup too Gateshead's record compared favourably with all but one of their fifteen 'eternal' rivals. In those nine post-War seasons they had played in the third round six times – once fewer than Stockport but more than anybody else. Accrington Stanley had not reached the third round at all in nine attempts, and three clubs had only managed to do so once; Southport, ex-First Division Bradford City and Halifax (though their single Cup run had been a good one with two First Division 'scalps').

Yet none of Gateshead's less successful rivals had had the humiliation of playing home League games before crowds of three figures. This had happened twice more in the season just concluded when a series of postponements in January and February had meant that matches against Stockport and Chester had to be played on weekday afternoons.

Gateshead were destined to spend five more seasons as a Football League club. In all five of them they would finish in the lower half of the table and never once would they win – or even draw – an FA Cup-tie. The match against Tottenham Hotspur in January 1955 was the last time a crowd of more than 10,000 ever assembled at Redheugh Park, and the average for the next five seasons was to be less than half of that.

Of course nearby Newcastle United were on the crest of a wave, having won the FA Cup for the third time in five years.

1955-56

Gateshead opened the season by drawing 2-2 at Accrington. The first two home games drew crowds of less than 4,000 as Tranmere Rovers held Gateshead to a 3-3 draw and Barrow were beaten 3-2. Barrow's manager was Newcastle's recent captain and Cup Final hero Joe Harvey. Another former Newcastle and Sunderland star, Ivor Broadis, was now player manager of Carlisle United and dominated play as his team won 3-2 at Redheugh in September.

As was often the case this fixture drew the season's highest crowd 6,400, though this figure was nearly equalled a month later against Derby County who had fallen on evil days and were slumming it in this lowly company for a while. Crowds of even 4,000 could not be maintained and they sank much lower as Gateshead remained in the bottom half of the table. How Gateshead must have envied Derby whom they visited in February, when the crowd of 19,203 was close to Gateshead's record attendance back in 1937. Derby defeated Gateshead easily - 4-2 at Gateshead and 4-1 at Derby.

Thereafter the only comparatively high home crowd was for the visit of Hartlepools United on Good Friday. Hartlepools had removed Gateshead from the FA Cup in the first round in November.

A departure from tradition occurred in the penultimate home match when a penalty was converted successfully by Alan Oliver against York City. This was the first time since the War that a Gateshead penalty had not been taken by near-ever-present Tom Callender. In the final home game, against Crewe Alexandra, which was won easily enough 4-1, two different players – Ken Smith and Alan Oliver – both missed a penalty. How often has that ever happened?

1956-57

Times were changing at both first team and reserve level. Since before the War there had been talk of the amalgamation of the Third Division's Northern and Southern Sections. In September a meeting of the Northern Section clubs voted against this proposal by 14 votes to 10 but it was felt that the move was not far off.

Jack Callender
in 1957

And the North Eastern League in which Gateshead Reserves played was coming to an acrimonious end. Sunderland and Middlesbrough should really have been playing their second teams in the Central League along with Newcastle United, Manchester United, Aston Villa and clubs of similar stature. Instead they had to be content with games against small town/large village sides such as West Stanley and Ashington, as well as the reserve sides of minnows like Gateshead, Hartlepools and Workington.

People connected with both Middlesbrough and Sunderland made less than complimentary remarks about the smaller North Eastern League clubs and their facilities and this drew angry responses. The North Eastern League's days were numbered though the two big clubs ended up little better off.

Gateshead started the season like a house on fire by going two goals ahead in the first six minutes before another near 20,000 crowd at Derby. This proved to be a flash in the pan as County eventually won 5-3 with only an *"international display"* by long serving goalkeeper Bobby Gray saving Gateshead from a heavier defeat.

There was a good crowd of over 7,000 on 1 September for the home game against Hartlepools United who had won their first four games. Gateshead beat them 4-3 with three of the seven goals (one for Gateshead and two for Hartlepools) being penalties.

The Football League now allowed matches to be played under floodlights, and the Gateshead v. Workington match on Monday 17 September was billed as being floodlit in the second half. However, referee Arthur Ellis instructed the club to switch on the lights at the kick-off, so Redheugh Park hosted a floodlit League match before many First Division clubs ever did. No more embarrassing afternoon games at an empty ground.

The month of September saw a much sadder event concerning the club, namely the death through injury of a young player, John Haley. Haley had been injured in a reserve game at Ashington on 8 September but had felt well enough to resume his employment at a colliery. He then played against Middlesbrough Reserves at Redheugh on 22 September but left after feeling ill. He was admitted to Newcastle General Hospital suffering from concussion and died there on the 29th. John Haley made his League debut against Workington three years earlier and had scored in the 7-1 victory over Grimsby Town in 1954, probably his most enjoyable game. He lived at Grangetown, Sunderland and was 24 when he died, leaving a widow and child.

Life goes on and Gateshead's season was not a good one. There were two heavy defeats – 6-0 at Chesterfield and 7-0 at Darlington - and to add insult to injury four of Darlington's goals were scored by Bill Tulip, a relative and namesake of Gateshead's chairman/manager.

Something of a rarity occurred just before Christmas when a Gateshead player was sent off in a volatile game at Wrexham. Gateshead had been losing 4-0 despite another fine goalkeeping display by Bobby Gray which had earned Welsh applause.

The game was nearing its end in near darkness (something which no longer happened at Redheugh) and long serving centre forward Bill Brown had managed to reduce the arrears. Wrexham goalkeeper Waters had just dropped the ball when uproar broke out in the penalty area. When the ruck of players cleared Wrexham half back Green was seen to be lying on the pitch. Clearly there had been a fight between Brown and Green and the referee ordered this colourfully named pair from the pitch.

In April there was an incident at Halifax when a director of the home club received a permanent ban for making an ungentlemanly remark to a linesman during a match which Gateshead won 1-0.

Gateshead's average attendance this season was 3,875, a slight improvement on the previous year but was still the lowest in the Football League. Their League position of 17th was their lowest since the War. In the season that was to follow there was a unique incentive to finish in the top half, for promotion of a sort, was on offer.

1957-58
At the Annual General Meeting of the Football League in June 1957 the club chairmen voted to end the Northern and Southern Sections of the Third Division and replace them with a non-geographical Third and Fourth Division. The Third Division was to comprise the two relegated Second Division clubs and the top half of the old geographical divisions (excluding of course the two promoted clubs).

The clubs had been canvassed and, generally speaking, the Northern clubs were less enthusiastic than their Southern counterparts. Travelling costs were an obvious worry and the Lancashire and Cheshire clubs would not find local Derby games coming round so often. However, the Third Division (North) had led a precarious existence since it was hastily thrown together in 1921. Several smaller clubs had dropped out and few would be sorry to see the end of it. Many of its members had never won promotion, unlike the Southern Section, some of whose clubs had eventually reached the First Division.

It was hoped that the new arrangement would engender increased interest in the last season of the old geographical sections. The chase for the championship usually involved only a handful but everybody would be struggling to keep in the top half of the table. Gateshead got off to a good start with a home victory over Crewe Alexandra, followed by a draw at Bradford, then a 2-1 win at Wrexham. This victory was marred by an injury to long serving goalkeeper Bobby Gray after he clashed with the home club's centre forward.

An untypical shot of Gateshead's long serving goalkeeper Bobby Gray who seems well out of position as Accrington Stanley's George Stewart eludes defenders Eric Oldham (left) and Bobby Dawson to score at a muddy Peel Park in November 1957. Gateshead lost 3-0 but whilst at Accrington they agreed terms for the transfer of full back Armour Ashe from the home club.

The game was stopped for several minutes as Gray received attention and, after further treatment at half time, he continued making several good saves despite being in obvious pain. (Gateshead had been leading 2-0 at the time of the incident). The 'keeper was kept in hospital overnight and missed the next five games.

Bobby Gray's absence may have proved crucial as two home defeats ensued at the hands of Bradford and Scunthorpe. When he returned he was not in top form as he conceded five goals at both Stockport and Chesterfield. A flu epidemic caused the postponement of the match against Mansfield, scheduled for 28 September.

A lean spell followed and by New Year Gateshead had only won seven of their 25 games and with crowds low, the prospect of finishing above the half way line seemed remote. Fellow strugglers Chester had knocked Gateshead out of the Cup in the first round.

There were new visitors on 4 January when relegated Bury won 2-1 at Redheugh. This was the day of the third round of the FA Cup, and sadly it was the day that Bobby Cairns, who played left back in the victory over Liverpool five years earlier, died in a mining accident in Northumberland.

With only one victory in each of January and February it is rather surprising that a brief revival in March and April should have lifted Gateshead into ninth position.

However a ten match run with only one defeat was sufficient to increase attendances significantly. Four consecutive home victories over Carlisle, Mansfield, Rochdale and Oldham found Gateshead in the position of needing two points from their last two away games to win the limited form of 'promotion' that was uniquely on offer. But they never looked like getting them as they lost 2-1 at Tranmere and 3-0 at Mansfield.

So the Third Division (North) came to an unlamented end in those Spring days of 1958. It had been 'home' to Gateshead FC since the move from South Shields in 1930, although they had twice come within a whisker of promotion and had only once had to apply for re-election. The club had been a fairly large fish in a small pond and had finished in the top half of the table in 13 of their 21 season with their average position being ninth. 13 out of 21 is also the number of times that they had been among the five worst supported teams and they had been bottom of this 'league' on three occasions.

Early in the season a journalist noted the inadequate bus service to the ground and observed that *'Gateshead's support will never materially improve unless this problem is addressed'*. The low crowd for the home game against Mansfield Town on Monday 14 April was partly because of an early kick-off due to Mansfield's refusal to play under Gateshead's floodlights, and partly because of a Newcastle v Manchester City match later that evening that was watched by more than 56,000. (Only the keenest and most resourceful could have attended both but could not Gateshead's management have shifted this already re-arranged game to another date?).

Rather oddly Gateshead and Carlisle United were the only clubs in the Division whose attendances had increased significantly, thanks to the 'top half means a higher status' incentive. Crowds were well up at Tranmere and at the Division's last championship winners Scunthorpe, but these clubs had markedly better results over the previous year to thank for the increase. At most places the attendances were lower than in 1956-57.

The prospect of being founder-members of the new Fourth Division was not an enticing one despite the novelty of meeting Southern opponents. The new arrangements were to bring Gateshead no joy at all, merely a swift end to their Football League career.

1958-59

The Football League's smaller clubs began their new adventure with some trepidation. How would old Northern Section sides based in towns the size of Barrow and Crewe fare against Millwall or Crystal Palace who could draw support from such an enormous area? Would the share of gate receipts from away matches in the South cover increased travel costs? Quite probably. In the last season of the old geographical divisions half of the Southern Section clubs had averaged gates of over 10,000. Only four Northern Section sides equalled this figure and they had all finished above the half way line.

Of ten clubs with average gates of less than 7,000 only Aldershot were in the Southern Section. Needless to say Gateshead were on this list as were old rivals Halifax Town and Rochdale, who had both managed to reach the new Third Division.

Given the apparent difference in potential would it be long before the Fourth Division resembled the old Third Division (North)? Saturday 23 August 1958 saw the old Division sides pitted against each other en masse for the first time.

Third Division results included:-
BRENTFORD 4 BRADFORD CITY 0 and
MANSFIELD TOWN 1 SOUTHAMPTON 6
Whilst Gateshead's new division saw
CRYSTAL PALACE 6 CREWE ALEXANDRA 2 and
WATFORD 5 SOUTHPORT 1

Not very encouraging. Seven former Southern Section clubs defeated ex-Northern Division sides but Bury (who had only been in the Northern Section in its last season) won at Colchester and Carlisle United scrambled a single goal home victory over Aldershot. The highest score that day however, was in the Second Division where Middlesbrough beat the last Southern Section champions Brighton & Hove Albion 9-0. So Southern clubs had their limitations too.

Gateshead began brightly with a 3-0 away win against old familiar rivals Barrow but on Monday evening Shrewsbury Town (paying their second visit) beat them 2-1. After this match goalkeeper Bob Gray was dropped for the first time ever. His replacement, a young amateur named Alan Stalker, played well in a 2-1 home victory over Oldham Athletic though he failed to save a penalty which he had given away himself after fouling an Oldham forward.

After three more games (two draws and a 4-1 home defeat by Bradford) Bob Gray was recalled for the visit to Aldershot. How would Gateshead fare on their first visit to a completely strange Southern ground? The scoreline:-
ALDERSHOT 5 GATESHEAD 0... was not an encouraging one – and that was only after 20 minutes! The final score was 8-1.

Poor Bob Gray after all his good performances over eleven years. He kept a clean sheet on his next trip when Gateshead won at Walsall but was unable to travel to Gillingham because of work commitments and this fine servant of the club never played again.

Gateshead had not had a paid manager since before the War but Ron Batty, a tough ex-Newcastle full back and Cup medallist who had been with the club since March, was appointed player-manager in October; Gateshead played six games that month and lost all of them.

Southern clubs were finding Gateshead to be easy meat. No points had been gained at Aldershot, Coventry, Gillingham, Crystal Palace or Watford, whilst Shrewsbury, Millwall and Exeter had all won at Redheugh (as had Bradford, Darlington and Chester). Being in 92nd position in the Football League had not been possible before this season but that was Gateshead's situation now.

Late 1950's arrival from Oldham Athletic - Wilf Hobson

Things improved in November with a home win of 3-0 against Hartlepools United, two drawn games at Southport and Crewe and – best of all – a convincing victory over a new opponent when Northampton Town were beaten 4-1 at Redheugh. A fly in the ointment was Bradford's repeat 4-1 win when they visited in the FA Cup.

Gateshead were becoming used to having the weekend off on the day of the second round but this season they did something rather unusual, when they played a League match on a Friday evening. Workington had also been eliminated and the two clubs agreed to bring forward their League match (at Workington) and play it under floodlights. This was not the first time this had happened – Accrington Stanley had played two Friday night games earlier in the season - and it was far from being the last. In the next decade it was to become the norm for a few lower Division clubs.

Gateshead lost this match at Workington 4-2 but then won two home games against York City and Barrow. They faced Port Vale over the Christmas/New Year period and these eventual Fourth Division champions beat them 8-0 at home and 4-0 at Redheugh – results which speak for themselves. After further defeats at Oldham by 3-0 and Bradford by 4-1 (a scoreline which was becoming monotonous), the club was now at its lowest ebb.

Again Gateshead were bottom of the Fourth Division and now that four clubs had to apply for re-election what were their chances of escaping that indignity? Remote, surely. For that matter what were their chances of being re-elected?

All was not lost however, and a run of three consecutive victories at home to Aldershot and Walsall and away to Millwall inspired new confidence. What on earth got into Gateshead at The Den on 7 February? Not only did they have a London crowd marvelling at their skill as they won 2-0 but they had the ball in the net on no fewer than five occasions, only to have all five efforts disallowed. Strangely Millwall also had three 'goals' disallowed.

Two defeats followed, but in early March Gateshead began a run of ten games of which only one was lost. The club was not in the habit of paying transfer fees (though they had a pretty good record of staying out of debt), but they managed to scrape together £3,000 or so and signed George Aitken, Sunderland's Scottish International half back who had interested them all season.

Aitken's first game for Gateshead was at Chester on 7 March and this match also saw the League debut of young goalkeeper Brian Williamson. The latter played well after starting nervously and Gateshead won 1-0.

A feature of the early days of the Fourth Division was an arrangement of fixtures whereby clubs could play two games in distant parts of the country within two or three days of each other. Gateshead's players had already had a short 'working holiday' at Margate in October between two pointless games at Gillingham and Crystal Palace. In April there was another short stay in Devon to take in games at Exeter and Torquay, and this time Gateshead returned home with three points.

The double was completed over Torquay a week later and when Gillingham were beaten 2-0 at Redheugh a week after that Gateshead vanquished all fears of having to apply for re-election. Well done, little Gateshead! What an improvement since January when they were bottom of the League and all seemed lost following those awful defeats by Port Vale.

The four clubs beneath them – Oldham Athletic, Aldershot, Barrow and Southport – were all re-elected but Peterborough United, an exceptionally eligible applicant, polled 26 votes. Best keep out of the bottom four the following season! The previous season's 12 Northern Section clubs all finished in the bottom half of the Fourth Division in 1958-59, except Carlisle United and promoted York City (though the other three promoted clubs were all Midlanders who had set foot in the Northern Section in the past).

The eleven Northern Section clubs who had reached the Third Division experienced mixed fortunes. Hull City won promotion and four others ended up in the top half of the table. Rochdale sank like a stone (as would surely have been Gateshead's fate if they had finished a couple of positions higher in 1958), and Stockport County were returning to the fold. The two other relegated clubs were doubly unfortunate. Notts County and Doncaster Rovers were both suffering that fate for the second consecutive season.

The best performance by an old Northern Section team was the double victory achieved by Hartlepools United over Crystal Palace in two midweek games early in the season. Neither Gateshead nor Darlington won a single point from that London club whose average attendance exceeded that of the three North Eastern minnows put together.

1959-60

This proved to be Gateshead's last season in the Football League but it began brightly enough. The four goals that were scored at far away Gillingham on the opening day proved insufficient to gain even one point with the home team scoring five. Three games against old rivals Barrow and Southport yielded five points with Gateshead being unlucky not to win at Barrow after being twice ahead in a fine match.

A 4-0 defeat at Millwall rather took the gloss off things, but then Notts County paid their first and last League visit to Redheugh: *"A 5-0 win for Gateshead would have been fair. Gateshead almost took a sensational five second lead straight from the kick-off. Their inside trio tore through the County defence and Stephenson's shot from centre forward Smith's pass was deflected desperately by County full back Butler for a corner"*. Gateshead were well on top playing attractive football and County had to defend for the whole 90 minutes. Who tells us all this? The reporter from the Nottingham Journal. Poor unlucky Gateshead, for the match ended goalless.

Torquay won at Redheugh on the Saturday, then the same Nottingham reporter had a different story to tell when County beat Gateshead 4-0 at Meadow Lane. This result was not an accurate one either – but only because Notts County should have scored double figures. Unusually this game was played on a Thursday, presumably to assist Gateshead as they embarked on a little Midland/South tour which then took them to Northampton and Aldershot and from which they returned without a single point. Full back Ken Moffitt became the third and last Gateshead player to be sent off after becoming embroiled in a loud argument with a linesman at Aldershot.

Two consecutive home games resulted in impressive victories of 5-0 and 4-1 over Doncaster Rovers and Aldershot and there was another good match a few weeks later when Crewe Alexandra were beaten 4-3 after Gateshead had led 4-0 at half time. Rochdale, however, took four points from them in two midweek games.

These results notwithstanding, it was nice to see Rochdale again after their year in higher company but Gateshead must have been a little put out to think that Accrington Stanley and Halifax Town were now their betters. The latter visited in November and removed Gateshead from the FA Cup by the odd goal in seven.

On the day of the second round, Gateshead travelled to Clydeside and beat Morton 2-1 in a friendly match. In those days the Scottish Second Division had an odd number of teams so every Saturday one of them was free. Gateshead had an ulterior motive in forging links with Scottish clubs.

The last eight games of 1959 brought only one League victory, although Gateshead did manage to hold League leaders Walsall to a draw on their own pitch (which the *Sunday Sun* reporter described as resembling the Tyne with the tide out). Two consecutive victories in the New Year were followed by a run of nine games without a win. A freak goal ended the sequence as Workington goalkeeper Newlands held a powerful shot from a corner by Moffitt, but leaned backwards over the goalline and was adjudged to have conceded.

In late March the club dispensed with the services of manager Ron Batty and trainer Tommy Rigg. Long serving employee Bob Keen took over temporarily as applications for the post of manager poured in. Among these gluttons for punishment was the Ashington manager David Davidson, who was offered the job but then thought better of it. With only four games to go and the necessity to apply for re-election a certainty Scotsman Charlie Ferguson was appointed.

The last two home games were both fine ones with Oldham Athletic and promoted Walsall being well beaten, but a comprehensive 4-0 defeat at Carlisle brought down the curtain on a fateful season.

Although there had been a few bright moments, Gateshead had experienced a poor season and their final placing was third from bottom. They had not won away from home and once again had achieved few successes against Southern opponents; Torquay United, Northampton Town and Watford had taken maximum points from Gateshead, and so had Rochdale, Chester, Bradford (again) and Darlington.

Redheugh shock for the leaders

By JOHN HOBBS

Gateshead 3, Walsall 0

IF mighty Walsall lose the Fourth Division championship they can blame eleven re-election candidates from Gateshead.

Last night they crashed—and I mean CRASHED—to the best team of opportunists and tacticians seen at Redheugh Park for months.

The uncrowned champions were never in the hunt against a home attack which produced 90 minutes of concentrated pressure.

The 2,366 crowd who watched this last home game of the season, must have gone home wondering why their club have to apply for re-election.

Gone was that failure to make full use of goal-scoring potential; gone those lapses when victory was snatched from their grasp in the dying minutes.

Aitken the star

Gateshead played football which promises well for the future—if they are re-elected.

Man of the match—and possibly of the season—was veteran George Aitken, who gave a faultless display.

And some bouquets must go to young Peter Stephenson, Bobby Lumley and Ken Murray for great displays against a defence of no mean quality.

Gateshead took the lead in the seventh minute.

With Walsall defenders appealing for offside, Lumley dashed through and kicked the ball nearly out of goalkeeper Christie's hands into an open goal.

After this early success, there seemed no holding the home attack. They always looked the more dangerous.

After the interval, they continued their onslaught on the Walsall goal.

In the 50th minute, Murray added a second goal from a Stephenson cross.

The home inside-right was beautifully positioned to head into the net with Christie helpless.

Murray got a second in the 75th minute, with a first-time volley, which Christie never saw.

Fate sealed

That sealed the Midlanders' fate.

They must have felt relieved at not having met this Gateshead side earlier in the season!

Gateshead left the field to the cheers of their supporters . . . and, I am sure, a pat on the back from new manager Charlie Ferguson.

● FOOTNOTE. There is only an outside chance that Walsall will lose the title—only Torquay can beat them, but it is a remote possibility.

GATESHEAD. — Williamson; Dawson, Armstrong; Redhead, Lackenby, Aitken; Stephenson, Lumley, Wilson, Murray, Steele.

WALSALL. — Christie; Haddington, Billingham; Dudley, Jones, Rawlings; Askey, Faulkner, Richards, Hodgkisson, Taylor.

When Watford beat Gateshead 5-0 on 16 April their high scoring centre forward Cliff Holton became the only player in history to score a hat trick on consecutive days. (The previous day had been Good Friday). Two of Holton's goals were penalties and oddly there had been four penalties when Watford won 3-1 at Gateshead earlier in the season. On that occasion Gateshead scored with theirs but goalkeeper Brian Williamson had saved one of Holton's thus preventing him from scoring a hat trick.

On 28 May at the Football League's Annual General Meeting, Gateshead's application for re-election was rejected. Oldham Athletic (applying for re-election for the second successive year) gained 39 votes, whilst second came newly elected Peterborough United with 35. Nobody could deny the claim of this Midland League dominating and FA Cup giant killing club. Safely re-elected were Hartlepools United with 34 votes (this was the fourth time they had had to apply) and Southport (their seventh application and their third in succession) with 29. Far behind with only 18 votes came Gateshead whose only previous application had been 23 years earlier. An injustice.

League Football at Redheugh Park had ended. The team that nobody noticed had slipped further into oblivion.

A North Eastern reporter relishes Gateshead's last ever home League game. Would that Gateshead could have produced this form earlier in the season.

GATESHEAD'S POST-FOOTBALL LEAGUE
VENTURES INTO THE FA CUP

A feature of Gateshead's last five seasons in the Football League was their failure to progress beyond the first round of the FA Cup. Hartlepools United, Hull City, Chester, Bradford and Halifax Town all eliminated them at this stage. As soon as they left the League, however, Gateshead's FA Cup performances showed a marked improvement, raising hopes that they might be able to regain their lost status. In their first season in the wilderness they were drawn at home to Barnsley who had been Gateshead's most recent Cup 'scalp' back in 1954-55. The match resulted in a goalless draw before a Redheugh crowd of 5,552. Barnsley (a club still without floodlights) won the replay 2-0 on the Wednesday afternoon and went on to reach the last eight of the competition.

In the 1961-62 season Gateshead had the indignity of having to play in the last qualifying round of the competition and an away replay was needed to beat Selby Town 3-0 after this Yorkshire side had held Gateshead 1-1 at Redheugh. The first round produced a welcome result when Gateshead defeated Tranmere Rovers 3-2 in an impressive display at Prenton Park. The second round tie was awaited with optimism but Workington proved to be too good for Gateshead, winning an entertaining game 2-0 before a large Redheugh crowd.

In 1962-63 after victories over West Auckland (2-0 away after a 2-2 draw) in the qualifying round and 2-1 over Wigan Athletic at home in the First Round. Gateshead travelled to meet another old League rival Bradford City. This match was lost 3-2 but the Gateshead players drew the referee's attention to the fact that one of the Valley Parade floodlight pylons was not operative and part of the pitch was in darkness for the later stages of the game. Any thoughts that Gateshead might have had about protesting to the Football Association were given the greatest impetus two days later. When the draw for the third round was made, Bradford City were drawn at home to Newcastle United. The possibility of their giant neighbours playing at Redheugh was an enticing one but the FA refused permission for the second round tie to be replayed.

Gateshead's Cup exploits in 1963-64 were impressive to say the least. South Shields were defeated 5-3 in the qualifying round then Gateshead travelled to Darlington where they staged a remarkable performance. Captained by the former Newcastle and Scotland star Bobby Mitchell and playing fast entertaining football, they led 4-0 at half time and were content to spare their Fourth Division hosts further punishment with the final score standing at 4-1.

The Second Round pairing could not have been tougher. They were drawn away to Fourth Division promotion candidates Carlisle United who were prolific goalscorers that season. Gateshead were rather unlucky to lose 4-3.

1964-65 was the first season in which Gateshead had already been eliminated before the competition proper began. The little known Lake District side Netherfield paid their second visit to Redheugh Park in the qualifying round. Fifteen years earlier Gateshead had beaten them 3-0 but on this occasion Netherfield gained their revenge with a 4-1 victory.

8 December 1965, a Wednesday afternoon and a second round FA Cup-tie at Redheugh Park. Horden Colliery Welfare and top amateurs Crook Town have been defeated in the earlier stages but today's visitors are Hull City, old Third Division (North) rivals and now pushing hard for promotion to the Second Division. The crowd is a good one, 5,935, and it might have been more had the match not been postponed from Saturday or had it been an evening game. Hull City having refused to play under Gateshead's floodlights.

The end of an era. Never again will a large crowd make their way to this inconveniently situated ground. Never again will Gateshead FC play an FA Cup-tie, home or away, beyond the qualifying stages. Hopes of rejoining the Football League have faded. The Scottish League idea was a worthy and commendable one but doomed to failure. There are quite probably several people here today who attended the first Football League match against Doncaster Rovers in 1930. But this match is the last occasion on which Gateshead FC can claim to be anything but the most minor of clubs. In the event Hull City experienced no difficulty in defeating their semi-professional opponents by four goals to nil.

Thereafter FA Cup involvement ended at a very early stage. In 1966-67 Blyth Spartans won 3-1 at Redheugh in the fourth qualifying round. In subsequent seasons the one time conquerors of Liverpool had to play in the first qualifying round. Only those scanning the small print in the sports pages would notice Gateshead's early elimination each year by small North Eastern opponents. In 1967-68 their conquerors were Blyth Spartans and over the next few years Bishop Auckland, Spennymoor United, Ferryhill Athletic, North Shields and Spennymoor again, were the victors.

And when the draw for this earliest stage of the FA Cup was made for the 1973-74 season Bishop Auckland were drawn at home to Gateshead. The Bishops proceeded to the next stage without playing a match. The quarter-finalists of twenty years before had ceased to exist.

Action from the Gateshead v. Hull City Cup-tie.

8 December 1965

THIRTEEN YEARS AND MANY LEAGUES.....

In 1960, rightly or wrongly, Gateshead were no longer a Football League club. This worst case scenario had been anticipated and a bold scheme was put into effect immediately. Less than a month after their rejection Gateshead applied to join the Second Division of the Scottish League. All Scottish clubs had been canvassed and Gateshead offered each prospective opponent a guarantee of £200 for a visit to Redheugh Park. This was an appreciably higher sum than the smaller Scottish Clubs were used to, and there was some support. East Stirlingshire and East Fife pleaded Gateshead's case but the Scottish League chairman would not entertain the idea of admitting an English club.

South Shields FC had also applied to join the Scottish League. Before accusing them of being mere copycats it should be noted that the situation of region's semi-professional clubs was a difficult one. Their natural home, the North Eastern League, had ceased to exist two years earlier and eight former NEL clubs - some of very slender means such as Consett and Horden Colliery Welfare - were making expensive trips to places like Sutton-in-Ashfield and Denaby in the Midland League; the only attraction had evaporated now that Peterborough United had bettered themselves at Gateshead's expense.

What now? A new organisation called the Northern Counties League was hastily brought into being. Gateshead were still awaiting the Scottish League's AGM and the chairman of the new League accused them of 'playing ducks and drakes' by asking them to wait before deciding to join.

The 1960-61 season began with Gateshead established as a Northern Counties League club and a home win of 3-0 against Stockton was recorded on the opening day. The Scottish League still held its attraction and very often in that season the odd team in the 19 strong Second Division spent their spare weekend entertaining or visiting Gateshead. Results were good and relations with the clubs from north of the border mutually beneficial. Clearly Gateshead could hold their own in the Division and as most of its clubs regularly played before crowds of under a thousand, there would be no financial embarrassment if Gateshead joined them. There was only one fly in the ointment. When 'Decision Day' came round in the summer of 1961, Gateshead's application to join was rejected by the Scottish League as well as by the English one.

The Northern Counties League didn't look as though it would last for very long. There were only ten clubs who met each other in two separate championship competitions, reminiscent of the Wartime Leagues, and this organisation ceased to exist after its second season. In 1962-63 Gateshead played in a new North Eastern League which only lasted for a single season. The North Regional League was composed of the reserve sides of Football League clubs. Gateshead's first team were welcomed into it and 1963-64 was a good season. Under the direction of player-manager Bobby Mitchell they won the championship of the League and enjoyed a good Cup run. But the Football League still didn't want them back.

By now it was obvious that any desire to return to the Football League was 'whistling for the Moon'. In 1968-69 Gateshead joined the new Northern Premier League. This was comprised of top semi-professional clubs drawn from a wide geographical area similar to that of the old Third Division (North). Gateshead, who were now managed by former Middlesbrough and England star, George Hardwick, finished 11th out of 20 in the first season. A year later, after Hardwick left, Gateshead ended in bottom position and were replaced by old Football League rivals Bradford who had just suffered the fate which befell Gateshead ten years earlier.

No money, no future, no hope. Now it was the Wearside League for a season. In 1971 the club left crumbling old Redheugh Park (not even a greyhound stadium anymore) for the town's International Stadium. Two years were then spent in the Midland League where the only event of note was a 13-0 victory over Loughborough United; although Gateshead's opponents had played another match earlier the same day at Stockton. An earlier Loughborough had been a Football League club 73 years before, who set up a record for the fewest number of victories and points in a season. They would have been proud of their footsore descendants.

Come to think of it, it seemed rather a long time since Gateshead played in the Football League. Since then they'd been in the Northern Counties League, the North Eastern League, the North Regional League, the Northern Premier League, the Wearside League, the Midland League, and in League with the Devil. In August 1973 the club's directors, who were probably suffering from League Fatigue drafted a letter to the Midland (that word again) asking them to instruct their clubs not to send a team to Gateshead anymore.

It was a long time since anybody noticed.

FINAL LEAGUE TABLES
1960/61 ~ 1972/73

1960/61 season

Northern Counties League Cup							
Gateshead	17	11	3	3	50	20	25
Blyth Spartans	18	10	5	3	42	19	25
North Shields	18	10	3	5	52	30	23
Consett	18	9	5	4	35	23	23
Ashington	18	7	4	7	46	40	18
South Shields	18	7	3	8	46	30	17
Horden Colliery	18	7	2	9	36	43	16
Stockton	18	6	2	10	29	68	14
Scarborough	18	5	2	11	33	46	12
Annfield Plain	17	2	1	14	25	75	5

(Top 4 qualified for semi-finals.
North Shields beat Consett 3-0 in final)

Northern Counties League							
North Shields	18	11	5	2	59	28	27
Ashington	18	12	2	4	50	20	26
Blyth Spartans	18	8	5	5	27	23	21
Consett	18	10	0	8	47	40	20
Gateshead	18	8	3	7	33	25	19
Scarborough	18	9	1	8	33	28	19
South Shields	18	8	3	7	32	30	19
Stockton	18	6	4	8	42	44	16
Horden Colliery	18	6	2	10	25	42	14
Annfield Plain	18	0	1	17	15	51	1

1961/62 season

Northern Counties League Cup							
South Shields	12	7	4	1	27	12	18
North Shields	12	8	1	3	30	15	17
Scarborough	12	6	4	2	23	13	16
Consett	12	6	3	3	27	18	15
Carlisle United Res.	12	7	1	4	22	20	15
Ashington	12	6	1	5	23	20	13
Darlington Res.	12	6	1	5	23	23	13
Gateshead	12	3	5	4	18	22	11
Annfield Plain	12	3	3	6	24	27	9
Stockton	12	3	3	6	16	19	9
Horden Colliery	12	3	3	6	17	28	9
Workington Res.	12	3	0	9	10	31	6
Blyth Spartans	12	1	3	8	10	24	5

Northern Counties League							
Consett	24	16	3	5	77	44	35
South Shields	24	16	2	6	67	30	34
Ashington	24	14	5	5	63	36	33
Horden Colliery	24	13	4	7	57	50	30
Gateshead	24	13	3	8	42	34	29
Scarborough	24	11	5	8	48	31	27
North Shields	24	10	5	9	61	42	25
Darlington Res.	24	8	5	11	55	57	21
Blyth Spartans	24	7	6	11	52	61	20
Carlisle United Res.	24	6	7	11	31	43	19
Stockton	24	6	3	15	41	82	15
Annfield Plain	24	5	3	16	34	72	13
Workington Res.	24	5	1	18	36	82	11

1962/63 season

NORTH REGIONAL LEAGUE

	Pld.	Won	Drn.	Lost	Goals For	Agst.	Pts.
Rotherham United	32	23	5	4	89	32	51
Middlesbrough	32	20	4	8	80	49	44
Crewe Alexandra	32	16	9	7	69	45	41
Bradford Park Avenue	32	17	6	9	88	52	40
Scunthorpe United	32	16	8	8	58	43	40
Sunderland	32	17	6	9	65	54	40
Doncaster Rovers	32	16	5	11	62	55	37
Grimsby Town	32	16	3	13	68	53	35
Lincoln City	32	14	7	11	54	58	35
Oldham Athletic	32	12	6	14	49	60	30
Gateshead	32	10	9	13	60	55	29
Hull City	32	11	7	14	57	61	29
Hartlepools United	32	10	8	14	53	62	28
York City	32	6	6	20	35	80	18
Stockport County	32	6	5	21	33	64	17
Halifax Town	32	4	9	19	34	67	17
Bradford City	32	3	7	22	45	109	13

1963/64 season

NORTH REGIONAL LEAGUE

	Pld.	Won	Drn.	Lost	Goals For	Agst.	Pts.
Gateshead	32	21	3	8	79	47	45
Middlesbrough	32	19	6	7	74	37	44
Hull City	32	20	4	8	67	43	44
Rotherham United	32	18	8	6	76	47	44
Scunthorpe United	32	19	4	9	85	53	42
Grimsby Town	32	15	9	8	57	49	39
Lincoln City	32	15	7	10	77	69	37
Sunderland	32	12	11	9	69	62	35
Crewe Alexandra	32	16	3	13	51	51	35
Port Vale	32	13	7	12	63	65	33
Carlisle United	32	12	8	12	49	53	32
Oldham Athletic	32	12	5	15	85	65	29
Doncaster Rovers	32	11	7	14	50	63	29
Darlington	32	10	7	15	60	59	27
Halifax Town	32	8	11	13	57	82	27
Bradford Park Avenue	32	11	5	16	63	74	27
York City	32	8	10	14	38	59	26
Bradford City	32	8	7	17	83	88	23
Workington	32	8	6	18	53	76	22
Stockport County	32	4	10	18	34	79	18
Hartlepools United	32	3	9	20	44	93	15

1964/65 season

NORTH REGIONAL LEAGUE

	Pld.	Won	Drn.	Lost	For	Agst.	Pts.
Hull City	32	24	4	4	95	26	52
Sunderland	32	23	5	4	105	33	51
Middlesbrough	32	19	8	5	102	45	46
Gateshead	32	17	7	8	80	43	41
South Shields	32	18	4	10	79	61	40
Port Vale	31	15	8	8	60	39	38
Rotherham United	32	15	8	9	72	54	38
Lincoln City	32	15	6	11	61	54	36
Carlisle United	32	15	5	12	68	43	35
Scunthorpe United	32	14	7	11	65	58	35
Oldham Athletic	32	15	5	12	75	72	35
Grimsby Town	30	14	4	12	60	63	32
Doncaster Rovers	32	11	9	12	59	59	31
Bradford City	32	11	5	16	65	76	27
Workington	32	11	5	16	56	90	27
York City	32	8	6	18	48	69	22
Bradford Park Avenue	32	9	4	19	46	74	22
Crewe Alexandra	31	8	4	19	37	78	20
Darlington	32	5	6	21	45	99	16
Hartlepools United	32	4	7	21	32	95	15
Halifax Town	32	3	3	26	32	111	9

1965/66 season

NORTH REGIONAL LEAGUE

	Pld.	Won	Drn.	Lost	For	Agst.	pts.
Hull City	32	23	4	5	89	30	50
Middlesbrough	32	21	5	6	79	41	47
Carlisle United	32	22	3	7	75	39	47
South Shields	32	21	4	7	115	46	46
Sunderland	32	20	2	10	99	64	42
Ashington	32	15	8	9	70	55	38
Rotherham United	32	14	5	13	59	54	33
Workington	32	10	7	15	66	92	27
Oldham Athletic	32	10	7	15	50	66	27
Darlington	32	11	4	17	57	82	26
Gateshead	32	10	6	16	48	67	26
Doncaster Rovers	32	8	9	15	51	65	25
Hartlepools United	32	9	7	16	56	76	25
York City	32	9	6	17	58	78	24
Bradford City	32	10	4	18	36	68	24
Bradford Park Ave.	32	7	5	20	45	90	19
Halifax Town	32	6	6	20	37	77	18

1966/67 season

NORTH REGIONAL LEAGUE

	Pld.	Won	Drn.	Lost	For	Agst.	Pts.
South Shields	20	13	3	4	53	29	29
Hull City	20	11	6	3	37	22	28
Sunderland	20	11	2	7	57	33	24
Ashington	20	9	6	5	53	34	24
Rotherham United	20	11	2	7	44	38	24
Middlesbrough	20	8	3	9	45	42	19
Carlisle United	20	8	3	9	27	44	19
Doncaster Rovers	20	6	4	10	31	36	16
Gateshead	20	6	3	11	29	41	15
Bradford Park Avenue	20	5	4	11	22	43	14
Darlington	20	3	2	15	30	66	8

1967/68 season

NORTH REGIONAL LEAGUE

	Pld.	Won	Drn.	Lost	For	Agst.	Pts.
Hull City	15	11	3	1	42	17	25
Middlesbrough	16	10	3	3	47	27	23
Sunderland	16	9	4	3	45	27	22
South Shields	16	9	3	4	39	18	21
Ashington	16	6	4	6	28	26	16
Gateshead	16	5	6	5	26	37	16
Carlisle United	15	2	4	9	18	30	8
Stockton	16	1	4	11	21	44	6
Workington	16	1	3	12	17	46	5

1968/69 season

NORTHERN PREMIER LEAGUE

	P	W	D	L	F	A	Pts
Macclesfield Town	38	27	6	5	82	38	60
Wigan Athletic	38	18	12	8	59	41	48
Morecambe	38	16	14	8	64	37	46
Gainsborough Trin.	38	19	8	11	64	43	46
South Shields	38	19	8	11	78	56	46
Bangor City	38	18	9	11	102	64	45
Hyde United	38	16	10	12	71	65	42
Goole Town	38	15	10	13	80	78	40
Altrincham	38	14	10	14	69	52	38
Fleetwood	38	16	6	16	58	58	38
Gateshead	38	14	9	15	42	48	37
South Liverpool	38	12	13	13	56	66	37
Northwich Victoria	38	16	5	17	59	82	37
Boston Utd	38	14	8	16	59	65	36
Runcorn	38	12	11	15	59	63	35
Netherfield	38	12	4	22	51	69	28
Scarborough	38	9	10	19	49	68	28
Ashington	38	10	8	20	48	74	28
Chorley	38	8	9	21	46	75	25
Worksop Town	38	6	8	24	34	88	20

1969/70 season

NORTHERN PREMIER LEAGUE 1969-70

	P	W	D	L	F	A	Pts
Macclesfield Town	38	22	8	8	72	41	52
Wigan Athletic	38	20	12	6	56	32	52
Boston Utd	38	21	8	9	65	33	50
Scarborough	38	20	10	8	74	39	50
South Shields	38	19	7	12	66	43	45
Gainsborough Trin.	38	16	11	11	64	49	43
Stafford Rangers	38	16	7	15	59	52	39
Bangor City	38	15	9	14	68	63	39
Northwich Victoria	38	15	8	15	60	66	38
Netherfield	38	14	9	15	56	54	37
Hyde United	38	15	7	16	59	59	37
Aftdncham	38	14	8	16	62	65	36
Fleetwood	38	13	10	15	53	60	36
Runcorn	38	11	13	14	57	72	35
Morecambe	38	10	13	15	41	51	33
South Liverpool	38	11	11	16	44	55	33
Great Harwood	38	10	9	19	63	92	29
Matlock Town	38	8	12	18	52	67	28
Goole Town	38	10	6	22	50	71	26
Gateshead	38	5	12	21	37	94	22

1970/71 season

WEARSIDE LEAGUE

1 Horden Colliery Welfare
2 GATESHEAD
3 Stockton
4 South Shields Reserves
5 Washington
7 Wingate St. Mary's
8 Murton Colliery Welfare
9 Boldon Colliery Welfare
10 Darlington Reserves
11 Hartlepool United Reserves
12 Annfield Plain
13 Silksworth Colliery Welfare
14 Reyrolles
15 Hylton Colliery Welfare
17 Morrison Busty Colliery Wel.
18 Sunderland S.S.
19 Whitburn
20 Thornley Colliery Welfare

Final positions only
detailed records
not traced

1971/72 season

MIDLAND LEAGUE

Grantham	34	25	5	4	106	32	55
Alfreton Town	34	22	5	7	85	39	49
Skegness Town	34	18	8	8	62	34	44
Long Eaton United	34	16	10	8	49	38	42
Belper Town	34	16	9	9	46	33	41
Worksop Town	34	17	7	10	70	53	41
Arnold	34	18	4	12	70	54	40
Gateshead	34	17	5	12	60	53	39
Frickley Athletic	34	13	8	13	46	43	34
Boston	34	13	7	14	44	48	33
Sutton Town	34	10	11	13	47	52	31
Retford Town	34	11	8	15	61	69	30
Eastwood Town	34	9	9	16	50	65	27
Ashby	34	10	7	17	47	62	27
Heanor Town	34	11	5	18	51	68	27
Kimberley Town	34	7	8	19	31	72	22
Stamford	34	5	8	20	33	71	19
Loughborough United	34	5	1	28	27	98	11

1972/73 season

MIDLAND LEAGUE

Worksop Town	34	26	3	5	101	35	55
Frickley Athletic	34	22	6	6	75	26	50
Kimberley Town	34	20	5	9	66	38	45
Alfreton Town	34	17	10	7	80	44	44
Sutton Town	34	16	12	6	55	33	44
Belper Town	34	17	9	8	52	31	43
Boston	34	16	10	8	62	30	42
Long Eaton United	34	14	7	13	51	56	35
Gateshead	34	14	6	14	72	68	34
Arnold	34	12	10	12	57	57	34
Skegness Town	34	13	6	15	67	52	32
Ashby	34	11	8	15	54	52	30
Eastwood Town	34	10	9	15	51	56	29
Bridlington Trinity	34	9	5	20	58	74	23
Hednesford Town	34	11	1	22	49	93	23
Stockton	34	6	10	18	43	50	22
Retford Town	34	7	8	19	36	81	22
Loughborough United	34	2	1	31	24	167	5

Gateshead's matches against Scottish League Clubs
1960-61

In their first season outside the Football League Gateshead played fifteen
games against Scottish League clubs with the following results:-

Aug	13	Stranraer	3-3
Sept	10	Berwick Rangers	1-0
	17	ALLOA ATHLETIC	5-2
Oct	1	Morton	2-1
	8	DUMBARTON	3-0
	28	RAITH ROVERS	2-4
Nov	25	STENHOUSEMUIR	3-1
Dec	23	HAMILTON ACADEMICAL	6-1
	27	FALKIRK	1-0
Jan	2	BERWICK RANGERS	2-4
	7	Alloa Athletic	1-0
	21	MORTON	5-1
Feb	4	Dumbarton	1-4
	24	AYR UNITED	2-3
Apr	15	ARBROATH	2-2

Nine victories, two drawn games and four defeats. Had Gateshead been
playing in the Second Division of the Scottish League this 66.6% success
rate would have seen them in fourth position. Two of Gateshead's
opponents - Raith Rovers and Ayr United were First Division clubs.
Four of the home games were played on Friday evenings under the
Redheugh floodlights, namely those against Raith, Stenhousemuir,
Hamilton and Ayr. Home gates were usually under 2,000 though there
was a crowd of 5,245 on 2nd January.

Some of these games went almost unreported locally. But Gateshead did
not always impress. A Berwick journalist reporting the match on 10th
September said he could quite understand why Gateshead had lost their
League status and he did not think they would regain it. He was critical
of Gateshead's tactics, singling out George Aitken as being particularly
guilty of rough play in what he described as *"the unfriendliest Friendly"*
he had ever seen. Gateshead lost more friends when they won 4-0 at
Ashington in a Northern Counties League game on 10th December.

They were accused of *"rough house"* conduct and were booed off the field at the end. The Ashington goalkeeper that season was old friend Bobby Gray.

Fair play or foul, victories or defeats, Gateshead's contact with new opponents from across the border did not bear fruit. Their application to join the Scottish League in 1961 was as unsuccessful as the earlier one.

Third Division Rivals:
Gateshead dominate the "Going Nowhere League"

Even the Third Division (North) had its aristocrats. There were promotion prone clubs such as Barnsley, Chesterfield, Hull City and Lincoln City and there were clubs who had once been in the First Division - the two Bradford clubs, Oldham and Grimsby. If clubs such as these are excluded as well as Midlanders Mansfield and Walsall who were sometimes in the Southern Section there remains a hard core of eleven clubs who opposed Gateshead in every one of their 21 seasons in that lowly sphere.

When a comparison is made of the League placings of these "Going Nowhere" clubs an interesting fact emerges - namely that Gateshead finished higher in the table than each of them on more occasions than not.

This is most pronounced in the case of Darlington who finished behind Gateshead in 17 seasons out of 21. In 16 seasons Gateshead finished higher than Barrow, Halifax and Rochdale, and 15 times they bettered Accrington, Carlisle and Crewe. They outperformed Hartlepools in 14 seasons, York City in 13 and Southport in 12 with their nearest challenger being Wrexham whom they topped in 11 seasons out of 21.

If this study is extended to include clubs whom Gateshead met in all but one of their Third Division (North) seasons it emerges that Gateshead finished higher than Chester (who joined a year after Gateshead) in 12 seasons out of 20 and ahead of Tranmere Rovers (promoted for one season) in 11 out of 20. Only Stockport County prove to be Gateshead's masters having finished ahead of them in 12 seasons out of 20.

The conclusion to be drawn is that this Division was Gateshead's spiritual home and where they belonged. Certainly they experienced nothing but trouble when the old Division came to an end.

Writing early in the Twenty First Century when the Third Division (North) is a faded memory a number of points are noticeable. Although Accrington Stanley, Barrow and Southport have followed Gateshead into oblivion many of Gateshead's old rivals have managed to keep the flag flying despite average attendances much lower than Gateshead's were even in the Fourth Division. Some have prospered.

The Divisions have been re-classified now and, although it is hard to think of any facet of life that has not altered out of recognition since 1958, references to "First Division Crewe Alexandra" still take some getting used to.

One last point. If Hartlepools United aficionados feel that this book makes only negative reference to the club then mention should be made of one of the earliest floodlit games in the North East on 4th November 1953 when Gateshead met the 'Pools at Redheugh Park.

Both sides had reached the semi-final of the Durham Professional Cup (a modest enough achievement in a competition with four entrants), both clubs played their regular League sides, and there was a good attendance of 7,035.... and the result was Gateshead 2 Hartlepools United 7.

This book only records the history of the Gateshead Football League club. An early Gateshead Town F.C., and later Gatehead Football Clubs including, in 1974, that which arrived from South Shields (again!), are outside the scope of this book.

A LOOK AT SOME GATESHEAD PLAYERS

**High Scorers, Dour Defenders, Long Servers, ex-First Division Men
and Young Hopefuls plus a surprise European.**

There were two instances of Gateshead players scoring five goals in a League game. **Hughie Gallagher**, whose five goals were scored against Rotherham United in 1938, needs no introduction to students of football history. Many people are still alive who can remember his skill and artistry at several clubs and for Scotland. Proving to be too hot a property for small Scottish club Airdrieonians, for whom he had scored 91 goals in 111 games, his record at Newcastle was equally sensational. Shortly after he transferred to Chelsea in 1930 Gateshead made an offer for him but had to wait until 1938, after he had played for Derby County, Notts County and Grimsby Town, before signing him. Gallagher spent the rest of his life in the town and his death on a Gateshead railway line in 1957 is well known.

Ernie Passmore's five goals were scored at Hartlepools in September 1949. Two weeks earlier he had scored four against Halifax Town at Redheugh Park with a hat-trick at Chester thrown in for good measure in an intervening game. Passmore had played six games for Swansea Town before joining Gateshead at the end of the 1946-47 season. It is rather puzzling that he never played at the game's highest level. When he left Gateshead it was for Southern League Guildford City. He scored 51 goals in 55 games for that club and returned to Redheugh Park to play for Guildford in an FA Cup-tie.

Five other players scored four for Gateshead in a League game. **Bill McNaughton** did so in two successive games against Barrow and York City in 1931. This London born player had arrived at Gateshead from Northampton Town. As with Passmore it is surprising that he did not go to a First Division club (there had been an offer of £5,000), instead he transferred to Hull City for whom he created an individual scoring record of 41 goals when City won the

Bill McNaughton

Third Division (North) Championship in 1932-33. His only other club was Stockport County.

Another four goal man was **Jack Wesley** who achieved that feat against Hartlepools United in a 6-3 victory on 30th September 1933. Wesley scored 26 times for Gateshead in the 1933-34 season. The following September he transferred to Bradford Park Avenue where he spent the rest of his career.

In the same season of 1933-34, **Robert Kennedy** scored four goals in a 5-3 victory over Mansfield Town. This Scotsman had been a prolific marksman with Falkirk in the 1920s and had kept up the good work for both South Shields and Gateshead. When he left Gateshead he spent several successful years with Third Lanark in the Scottish First Division.

Two other players netted four in a game for Gateshead after the War. There was **Jim Kendall** from nearby Birtley, who spent his entire career in the Third Division (North). He got off to a good start by scoring a hat-trick on his League debut, though his side, Barrow, lost 4-3 at Rotherham. Another good start (to the 1950-51 season) occurred when Kendall scored four of Gateshead's seven goals against Accrington Stanley. Accrington was where he ended his career after another spell with Barrow.

And finally there was **Bill Watkin**, whose four goals in seven minutes against his home town club Grimsby in 1954 has already been referred to. Middlesbrough signed him on the strength of his performance. The hope that he would help to save them from relegation was not realised but Watkin did score for his new club in an outstanding victory away to the champions, Wolves. He wasn't at Ayresome Park for long and returned to Third Division football with Mansfield Town.

Gateshead players who transferred to First Division clubs rarely made much impression at that level. **William Cairns**, a high goalscorer at Redheugh Park in 1945-46, achieved am impressive tally of 34 goals in 59 First Division games in the first two post War seasons but he returned to the Third Division (North), without changing clubs, as Grimsby Town's fortunes ebbed.

William Cairns   Cecil McCormack

Cecil McCormack scored more than 100 goals for Gateshead during and after the War. His First Division experience with Middlesbrough was brief but useful with his best performance being a hat-trick in a 7-1 win at Blackburn. He left for Southern League Chelmsford City but returned to the Football League to score goals galore for Barnsley and Notts County in the 1950s. He then emigrated to Canada where he died in 1995. A First Division team mate at Middlesborough was goalkeeper **Derek Goodfellow** who had been at Gateshead before the War.

In Gateshead's first season of 1930-31, two players, **Henry Barkey** and **Albert Taylor** transferred to Liverpool and Chelsea, but only played five and one games respectively in the highest division. Two players from Gateshead's last season, also failed to shine there. Winger **Ken Wimshurst** transferred to champions, Wolves but failed to make the first team. He gained much experience as a half-back with Second Division clubs Southampton and Bristol City. Goalkeeper **Brian Williamson** had a spell with Crewe Alexandra and then stepped up to play for Leeds United and Nottingham Forest. He had to be content to understudy better known goalkeepers and his first team chances were few. It is something of a surprise to discover that **Carl Wilson**, who made a few appearances for Gateshead in 1959-60, and a handful for Doncaster Rovers and Millwall, then went on to spend a season with top Dutch club Rotterdam Sparta and a German side.

Apart from Hughie Gallagher top players who ended their careers at Redheugh Park were not numerous. **Jack Allen**, formerly with Sheffield Wednesday but mostly remembered for scoring a disputed goal for Newcastle in the 1932 Cup Final, played for Gateshead in 1935-36 (a part season). Tough tackling full-back **Ron Batty**, who had a Cup Winners medal to show for his years at Newcastle, arrived at Redheugh in 1958.

Jack Hedley

He became player-manager and was joined by Sunderland's ex-Scottish International **George Aitken** plus another player from that club, **Jack Hedley.**

The highest crowd for a club match in Europe was a gathering of 146,433 who saw Celtic play Aberdeen in the Scottish Cup Final in 1937. **Willie Buchan** scored Celtic's winning goal on that occasion. Years later (having been at Blackpool and Hull in the meantime) Buchan was a senior member of the Gateshead team that came close to promotion. Gateshead thought so highly of the player that they bought a house for him to live in, to save him from commuting from Glasgow. In the last season Willie Buchan was at Redheugh - 1951-52 - the crowds for all 23 home League games added together did not equal that Hampden Park assembly that he had entertained in his youth.

Most of Gateshead's players arrived from the network of local youth teams or from higher division clubs where they had not made the grade. Goalkeeper **Bobby Gray**, hero of many a battle, (best of all as Gateshead's saviour when under relentless pressure in the FA Cup at Plymouth) had been rejected by Newcastle while high scoring forward **Ken Smith** had tried his luck at Blackpool without success.

The most famous Gateshead players were **Tom and Jack Callender**. Usually to be found in the half-back line, but versatile too on

Jack (left) and Tom Callender

occasions, their combined scoring total of over 100 seems surprisingly high, even taking into account Tom's many successes from the penalty spot.

Whilst this brief review has only mentioned a few players anybody seeking a flavour of life at a small professional club in the 1950s could do no better than to read **Pat Hewson**'s eloquent foreword to this book.

~ REDHEUGH PARK ~

Early 1950's
Pre-season
Training at
Redheugh:

(Left to right)
Pat Hewson
Billy Brown
Billy March
Bobby Gray

Redheugh Park
1947

A plan of
the ground

(Drawing by Paul Smith)

Redheugh Park as it looked for most of its existence. Apart from the small stand in the top right hand corner, most of the building work dated from 1937 when Greyhound racing began there. The floodlights were on the roof of the stands. In September 1959 the club was instructed to install additional lights to bring the system up to the minimum standard required by the Football League.

The last days - Midland League football in the early 1970's.

By the late 1980's little remained
(Looking towards the Ropery Road end)

TEAMS GROUPS: 1934 ~ 1959

~1934-35 Season ~
Back: Neilson, Spedding, Burgess, Ince, Rivers, Hall, Younger
Middle: W.R.Tulip (Chairman), Ferguson, Mathison, O'Donnell, W.Marsden (Trainer)
Front: McAinsh, Hamilton

~ 1935-36 Season ~
Back: Moore, Spedding, Robinson, Talbot, Allen, Neilson, Inskip, T.Dawson (Trainer)
Front: Cull, Conroy, McKenzie (Capt), Tulip (Sec. Manager), Rivers, Heslop, Webster

~ **1948-49 Season** ~
The Gateshead team that beat New Brighton 3-0 on the opening day of the 1948-49 season.
Back: Wyles, Gray, Cassidy, Callender, Hood, Atkinson
Front: Ingham, Small, Passmore, Weddell, Wilbert

~ **1951-52 Season** ~
The Gateshead team which won 2-0 at Southport on 1 September 1951.
Centre forward George Wilbert scored both goals.
Back: J.Callender, Wyles, Gray, Woodburn, Robinson, T.Callender
Front: Ingham, Buchan, Wilbert, Winters, Campbell

~ 1952-53 Season ~

Very often Third Division (North) teams were photographed when they played at Southport, due to the presence of a sports photography business in that town. Gateshead lost this match 3-2 but were praised for their "crisp clear footwork".
Back: March, J.Callender, Cairns, Turnbull, Brown, Smith
Front: Ingham, Wilbert, T.Callender, Winters, Robinson

~ 1953-54 Season ~

Again Gateshead line up for an early season photograph with the familiar Southport building in the background. This time Gateshead gained an impressive 4-2 victory.
Back: J.Callender, Cairns, Gray, T.Callender, Brown, Hewson
Front: Price, Ingham, Wilbert, Johnson, Watkin

~ 1956-57 Season ~
Full squad lines up for a pre-season practice match.
Back: Cairns, McCready, Moran, Milburn, Robson, Johnson, Coatsworth
Middle: Hewson, March, T.Callender, Oldham, Brown, Beeston, Gray, Hunter, Haley, D.Herron, J.Callender.
Front: T.Rigg (Trainer-coach), Dawson, Davis, Lydon, Ingham, Smith, Oliver

~ 1959-60 Season ~
An uncaptioned photograph of Gateshead's "probables" and "possibles"
on the eve of their final League season.

Players' Who's Who

Name		Date of Birth	Birthplace	Died	First Season	Apps.	Goals	Pos.	Previous Club	Next Club
Aitken GC	George	28/05/1925	Lochgelly		1958	58	0	4	Sunderland	
Alexander DL	Dennis	19/02/1935	Nottingham		1958	18	1	10	Brighton & Hove A.	
Allen JWA	Jack	31/01/1903	Newburn	1957	1935	23	12	9	Bristol Rovers	
Anderson N	Norman	30/11/1930	Hebburn		1953	19	2	0		
Appleton TH	Tom	09/06/1936	Stanley		1958	26	0	4	Burnley	Accrington Stanley
Armstrong JM	Joe	29/01/1939	Newcastle		1959	24	9	10	Leeds United	
Ashe AD	Armour	14/10/1925	Paisley	1968	1957	54	1	0	Accrington Stanley	Southport
Askew J	James		North Shields		1933	30	0	1		
Atkin TL	Tommy		Newcastle		1932	49	16	7	Doncaster Rovers	Darlington
Atkinson FJ	Fred	24/08/1919	Newcastle		1946	32	6	0		
Atkinson T	Thomas				1933	2	0	1		
Baldridge R	Robert	26/11/1932	Sunderland		1956	60	22	8		
Barkas HB	Harry	21/01/1906	Wardley Colliery	1974	1930	19	7	9	South Shields	Liverpool
Barrass RK	Richard				1938	4	1	9		
Batty RR	Ron	05/10/1925	Lanchester	1971	1957	42	0	0	Newcastle United	
Beardshaw EC	Colin	26/11/1912	Crawcrook	1977	1935	12	0	5		Stockport Co.
Beattie T	Thomas	12/03/1921	Sheepwash		1946	18	4	0		
Beeston T	Thomas	26/04/1933	Gateshead		1956	1	0	1		
Bell JH	John	29/08/1919	Morpeth	1996	1946	50	0	0		
Birtley RJ	Bob	1908	Easington		1939	3	2	8	Crystal Palace	
Boland G	George 'Dicky'	06/10/1902	Marley Hill	1977	1931	92	16	11	Fulham	Crewe Alexandra
Bow J	James		Lochore		1936	1	0	10	Clapton Orient	
Brannigan DM	Daniel		Dunasken		1931	55	2	6	Halifax Town	
Brown A	Alex	21/11/1914	Seaton Delaval		1939	1	0	10	Darlington	Mansfield Town
Brown W	William	27/03/1928	Murton		1950	216	7	0		
Buchan WRM	Willie	17/10/1914	Grangemouth		1949	90	16	10	Hull City	
Burgess C	Caleb	1909	Knighton		1934	16	0	3	Aldershot	
Burke JW	Joe	1913	Jarrow		1933	13	0	10		New Brighton
Cairns RL	Robert	25/12/1927	Choppington	1958	1948	140	0	0	Sunderland	
Callender JW	Jack	02/04/1923	West Wylam		1939	472	45	7		
Callender TS	Tom	20/09/1920	West Wylam	2002	1946	439	59	0	Lincoln City	
Campbell J	John	23/07/1928	West Wylam		1949	182	47	11		
Carolin B	Brian	06/12/1939	Ashington		1957	17	0	0		
Carr JJ	John	1909	Gateshead		1933	54	2	3	Chester City	
Cassidy W	William	30/06/1917	Gateshead		1936	133	6	6		
Charlton JA	John				1949	1	0	1		
Charlton T	Thomas		West Sleekburn		1930	91	28	7	South Shields	
Clark H	Harry	30/03/1913	Cloughdene		1946	23	1	0	Accrington Stanley	
Clark RN	Ronald				1932	31	0	1		Manchester Utd.
Coatsworth J	John	21/05/1933	Newcastle		1956	16	4	9		
Conroy T	Thomas		Walker		1934	186	0	2	Darlington	
Conway JG	John	24/01/1931	Gateshead		1953	4	0	0		
Cook W	William		Darlington		1935	3	0	8	Darlington	
Crowther GE	George		Pudsey		1930	62	0	1	Stockport Co.	
Cull JE	Ernie	18/11/1900	Aston		1935	18	5	7	Accrington Stanley	Aldershot
Daglish J	John		South Moor		1934	14	0	6	Darlington	
Davidson DL	Dave	04/06/1905	Aberdeen	1969	1937	15	2	6	Hartlepool Utd.	
Davies J	James	20/11/1901	Northwick		1930	51	0	5	South Shields	Chesterfield
Davis G	Gordon	14/12/1930	Newcastle		1951	87	0	0	Everton	

Name		Date of Birth	Birthplace	Died	First Season	Apps.	Goals	Pos.	Previous Club	Next Club
Dawson R	Bobby	31/01/1935	South Shields		1956	117	1	2	Leeds United	
Dawson T	Tommy	15/12/1901	Springwell	1977	1933	20	0	3	Leyton Orient	
Dickinson S	Samuel				1936	1	0	8		
Doran T	Terry	02/04/1940	Jarrow		1959	1	0	3		
Downie W	William				1936	11	0	6		
Embleton E	Eddie	1916	South Moor		1938	17	9	10	Hartlepool Utd.	Doncaster Rovers
Felton ET	Edward	1906	Gateshead		1937	4	1	7	Darlington	
Ferguson JJ	John	1904	Rowlands Gill		1934	21	5	7	Manchester Utd.	
Firman K	Ken	05/02/1941	Felling		1958	1	0	8		
Forster LJ	Leslie	22/07/1915	Newcastle		1946	15	3	0	York City	
Fowler HN	Norman	03/09/1919	Stockton	1990	1949	65	0	3	Hull City	
Frame WG	William				1931	6	0	1		
Gallacher HR	Hughie	02/02/1903	Bellshill	1957	1938	34	18	9	Grimsby Town	
Gallantree WL	Les	25/12/1913	East Boldon		1937	13	2	7	Aldershot	
Gallon JW	Jack	12/02/1914	Burradon	1993	1946	20	2	0	Swansea City	
Gibson RH	Bob	05/08/1927	Ashington	1989	1956	50	26	9	Lincoln City	
Goodfellow DO	Derrick	26/06/1914	Shilbottle		1934	30	0	1		Sheffield Wed.
Gowdy WA	Bill		Belfast		1932	4	0	6	Sheffield Wed.	Aldershot
Grant K	Ken	13/11/1938	High Spen		1958	5	0	7		
Granville R	Ralph	23/04/1931	Glasgow		1957	1	0	0		
Gray R	Robert	14/12/1923	Newcastle		1947	432	0	1		
Gray RA	Alec	07/10/1903	Cowpen	1954	1934	11	2	10	Carlisle Utd.	York City
Green JH	John		Newcastle		1930	2	0	8	Newcastle United	Doncaster Rovers
Hales W	William				1934	14	4	11		
Haley J	John	24/04/1932	Sunderland	1956	1953	38	2	0		
Hamilton J	Jimmy	1904	Hetton-le-Hole		1934	4	0	9	Hartlepool Utd.	
Harbottle AN	Albert			1997	1935	35	0	1		
Harrison R	Ron	15/05/1923	Hebburn		1947	6	1	0	Darlington	
Hartley TW	Tom	07/05/1917	Gateshead		1935	5	1	8		Bury
Harvey GMH	George				1937	6	0	7		
Hawkins GH	Harry	24/11/1915	Middlesbrough	1992	1947	27	12	0	Southport	Hartlepool Utd.
Hedley JR	Jack	11/12/1923	Willington Quay		1959	10	0	2	Sunderland	
Heron WB	William	29/03/1932	Washington		1954	21	1	0		
Herron J	John	02/03/1938	Widdrington		1957	8	0	0	Leeds United	
Heslop JJ	John				1932	8	0	7		
Heslop R	Robert	05/02/1907	Annfield Plain		1935	94	13	8	Nottm. Forest	
Hetherington H	Harry	07/11/1928	Chester-le-Street		1948	2	1	0	Sunderland	
Hetherington TB	Tom	22/01/1911	Walker		1946	1	0	1	Barnsley	
Hewson PG	Pat	02/06/1926	Gateshead		1953	131	0	0	West Bromwich A.	
Hobson W	Wilf	26/01/1932	Consett		1959	31	1	4	Oldham Athletic	
Hogarth G	Gordon	18/11/1936	Sunderland		1957	12	0	0		
Hogg J	Jack	07/10/1931	Blyth		1957	80	21	0	Portsmouth	
Hogg W	William				1935	1	0	11		
Hood GW	George	27/11/1920	Houghton-le-Spring		1947	30	0	0		
Hornsby S	Stanley				1936	8	0	3		
Howdon S	Steve	01/02/1922	Prudhoe		1946	2	1	0		
Humble G	Geoffrey				1935	3	1	9		
Hunter JD	John	20/09/1934	Backworth		1955	4	0	1		
Hutchinson D	Doug	03/05/1922	Gateshead		1946	3	0	0		
Ince J	John				1934	21	0	1	Darlington	
Ingham RJ	John	18/10/1924	Hebburn		1947	432	110	0		

Name		Date of Birth	Birthplace	Died	First Season	Apps.	Goals	Pos.	Previous Club	Next Club
Johnstone S	Stan	28/10/1940	Shiremoor		1958	5	1	11		
Jones S	Sidney	03/05/1911	Gretna		1935	3	0	7	Carlisle Utd.	Manchester Utd.
Keane J	John		Clydebank		1937	5	0	7	Exeter City	
Kemp SP	Sam	29/08/1932	Stockton		1958	8	1	7	Mansfield Town	
Kendall JB	Jimmy	04/10/1922	Birtley		1948	57	20	0	Barrow	Barrow
Kennedy R	Robert		Glasgow		1930	134	53	10	South Shields	
Kirtley JH	Harry	23/05/1930	Washington		1956	95	14	10	Cardiff City	
Lackenby G	George	22/05/1931	Newcastle		1959	43	2	5	Carlisle Utd.	Hartlepool Utd.
Laird JW	William		Larkhill		1932	2	1	9	Sunderland	
Lawrence W	Walter				1937	10	0	1		
Lincoln A	Andy	17/05/1902	Seaham Harbour	1977	1932	1	0	4	Lincoln City	
Littlewood AJ	Alf	28/01/1902	Esh Winning	1975	1930	3	0	5	South Shields	Southport
Livingstone A	Angus		Wallsend		1935	98	1	3		
Lough JD	John	31/10/1922	Gateshead		1946	1	0	0		
Lumley R	Bobby	06/01/1933	Leadgate		1959	40	6	8	Chesterfield	Hartlepool Utd.
Lydon GM	Micky	25/11/1933	Sunderland		1955	105	24	10	Leeds United	
McAinsh J	James	13/10/1913	Clackmannan	1978	1934	46	6	7	Hull City	
McArdle P	Peter	08/04/1911	Lanchester	1979	1938	20	5	11	Stockport Co.	Crewe Alexandra
McCormack JC	Cec	15/02/1922	Newcastle	1995	1946	27	19	0		Middlesbrough
McDermott J	Joseph		Fencehouses		1933	104	28	10	Middlesbrough	
McDougall L	Laybourne	12/05/1917	Tynemouth		1946	60	0	0	Blackpool	
McInroy A	Albert	23/04/1901	Walton-le-Dale	1985	1937	73	0	1	Leeds United	
McKenzie RR	Roddie	22/05/1901	Inverness		1935	19	1	4	Newcastle United	Reading
McLauchlan R	Bob		Whitburn		1931	6	0	3		Barnsley
McLaughlin JW	John		Newcastle		1938	4	0	1		
McNaughton WF	Bill	08/12/1905	Poplar	1980	1930	63	46	8	Northampton Town	Hull City
Malpass FL	Frank	16/10/1932	Consett		1949	3	0	1		
March W	Billy	28/02/1925	Chester-le-Street		1952	133	0	0	Barnsley	
Marley G	George	22/04/1921	Gateshead		1947	22	2	0		
Mathison G	George	24/11/1909	Walker	1989	1934	81	5	5	Lincoln City	Burnley
Maycock R	Ranson	01/04/1905	Waterhouses	1950	1930	16	4	9	South Shields	Accrington Stanley
Meek J	Joe	31/05/1910	Hazlerigg	1976	1930	135	50	8	Middlesbrough	Bradford
Mellon JM	James		Newcastle		1934	18	0	3	Torquay United	
Milburn WR	William	25/01/1932	Sunniside		1956	2	0	4		
Miller EC	Edward	1917	Percy Main	1969	1936	99	23	11	Fulham	
Milne W	Walter		Arbroath		1937	25	0	3	Blackburn Rovers	
Moffitt K	Ken	02/02/1933	Newcastle		1957	75	2	0	Brentford	
Moon G	George		Blackhill		1930	1	0	2		
Moore JE	John	1912	Newcastle		1935	24	4	8	Hull City	
Moran LF	Lister	24/06/1930	Ryton-on-Tyne		1951	23	0	0		
Morley JF	Joseph	05/11/1916	Felling		1938	1	0	8		
Murphy VJ	Vincent		Limerick		1933	2	0	11	Notts County	
Murray K	Ken	02/04/1928	Darlington	1993	1959	18	6	10	Wrexham	
Myers AW		12/02/1928	Newcastle		1951	1	0	1		
Neilson GH	George	28/08/1908	Thornley		1930	273	15	4	South Shields	
Newton C	Cyril		Hamsterley		1932	44	0	1	Birmingham City	
Nisbet KH	Ken	09/06/1907	Rosyth	1992	1931	1	0	9	Rochdale	
O'Connor RT	Robert	09/08/1940	Gateshead		1958	2	0	11		
O'Donnell W	William		Felling		1932	53	1	2	Blackpool	
Oldham E	Eric	27/06/1933	Newcastle		1956	53	0	3	Bolton Wanderers	Hartlepool Utd.
Oliver G	George	22/01/1919	Houghton-le-Spring	1981	1946	13	1	0	Halifax Town	

Name		Date of Birth	Birthplace	Died	First Season	Apps.	Goals	Pos.	Previous Club	Next Club
Passmore E	Ernie	28/04/1922	Moorsley		1946	41	26	0	Swansea City	
Paterson A	Andy	1909	Leeholm	1989	1931	79	0	6		Oldham Athletic
Patterson RA	Robert	12/03/1935	Newcastle		1958	26	0	1		
Pickard F	Frank	1912	Darlington		1936	4	2	9	Hartlepool Utd.	
Pickard TJ	Thomas	1911	Amble		1930	17	0	1	Sunderland	Bradford City
Price LE	Leslie	26/08/1930	Consett		1952	39	12	0	Sunderland	
Purvis B	Bartholomew	15/10/1921	Gateshead		1946	1	0	0	Everton	Reading
Quigley JA	James				1934	23	3	11		
Ramsay GA	George	24/04/1923	Sunderland		1946	7	1	0		
Ranson JG	Jack	01/04/1909	Norwich		1932	32	21	9	Chester City	Millwall
Reay JC	John				1936	15	2	7	Chesterfield	Hull City
Redhead WS	Bill	10/10/1935	Newcastle		1959	20	0	4	Newcastle United	
Reed G	Gordon	05/1913	Spennymoor		1936	23	2	9	Darlington	
Reilly WJ	Billy	24/12/1902	Lanark		1930	26	1	6	South Shields	Chelsea
Render J	James				1938	2	0	5		
Rivers W	Wally	08/01/1909	Throckley		1934	59	12	10	QPR	Aldershot
Robinson E	Edward	15/01/1922	Bywell		1946	90	7	0		
Robinson JW	Billy	13/04/1932	Chester-le-Street		1958	21	5	7	Hartlepool Utd.	
Robinson R	Ralph 'Robby'	1906	Annfield Plain		1935	19	0	3	Newport County	
Robson E	Ernie		Gateshead		1934	7	4	9		Aldershot
Robson J	James				1935	4	2	9		
Robson J	John				1935	2	1	11		
Robson JD	Don	05/02/1934	Winlaton		1953	34	11	0	Doncaster Rovers	
Robson R	Ron	12/09/1932	Sunderland		1957	7	0	0		
Ross J	John				1937	3	0	7		
Rutherford R	Robert	20/04/1922	South Shields		1946	10	2	0		
Scott J	John	1909	Hamsterley		1930	83	0	6	South Shields	Crewe Alexandra
Short WJ	William				1936	2	0	8		
Sinclair TM	Thomas	13/03/1907	Alva		1930	99	1	2	South Shields	
Sinton L	Leslie				1938	3	0	7		
Skeen G	George	04/08/1920	Gateshead		1946	86	3	0		
Slater R	Ray	22/08/1931	Seaton Delaval		1956	6	2	9	Chesterfield	
Small ML	Martin	02/02/1920	Gateshead		1946	96	29	0		
Smirk AH	Alf	14/03/1917	Pershore		1947	11	4	0	Southend Utd.	
Smith G	George				1936	2	0	4		
Smith JT	John	08/04/1905	Chester Moor		1937	49	33	9	Sheffield Wed.	
Smith K	Ken	21/05/1932	South Shields		1958	41	16	10	Shrewsbury Town	Darlington
Smith K	Ken	07/12/1927	Consett		1952	259	76	0	Blackpool	
Spedding JJ	James	1912	Keighley		1933	88	14	4		Huddersfield T.
Spedding S	Stanley				1936	2	0	1		
Spooner PG	Peter	30/08/1910	Hepscott	1987	1939	3	2	11	York City	
Stalker A	Alan	18/03/1939	Ponteland		1958	4	0	1		
Steele BJS	Bennett	05/08/1939	Seaton Delaval		1959	23	5	11	Chesterfield	
Stephenson P	Peter	02/05/1936	Ashington		1959	35	6	7	Middlesbrough	
Stokoe D	Dennis	06/06/1925	Blyth		1956	13	0	6	Workington	
Storey WCG	Bill		Washington		1937	3	0	10	Exeter City	
Talbot GR	George	15/07/1910	Willington Quay	1990	1935	12	0	1	Oldham Athletic	Southport
Talbot JH	James		Craghead		1930	16	3	11	South Shields	Barrow
Taylor A	Albert	1910	Ashington		1930	27	3	11	South Shields	Chelsea
Taylor GS	Gordon	10/06/1936	Stanley		1957	3	0	1		
Temple JL	Jimmy	16/09/1904	Scarborough	1943	1933	18	4	7	Sunderland	

Name		Date of Birth	Birthplace	Died	First Season	Apps	Goals	Pos.	Previous Club	Next Club
Thompson KH	Ken	24/04/1926	Sunderland		1946	9	0	0		
Thompson W	William	23/12/1921	Ashington		1946	3	0	0		
Traynor JW	John				1934	2	0	3	Crystal Palace	
Trewick A	Alan	27/04/1941	Blyth		1959	10	1	9		
Trewick G	George	15/11/1933	Stakeford		1956	110	0	5		
Turnbull GF	George	04/02/1927	Gateshead		1952	3	0	1	Accrington Stanley	
Turnbull JM	Jimmy		Ashington		1934	13	6	9	Barnsley	
Turnbull RA	Bob		Allenvale		1930	120	1	3	South Shields	Millwall
Turnbull T	Thomas	11/06	Morpeth		1934	5	0	11	Bristol Rovers	
Turnbull WJ	Billy	21/12/1900	Blyth		1932	10	0	2	Brighton & Hove A.	Oldham Athletic
Turner AE	Adam	13/03/1934	Glasgow		1958	6	0	4	Sheffield Wed.	
Varty WC	William	25/06/1906	Throckley		1935	5	1	11	Gillingham	Carlisle Utd.
Viney EE	Edwin	1904	New Tredegar		1931	1	0	9		
Walker H	Harold				1936	40	12	7	Lincoln City	
Watkin AJ	Alan	16/05/1940	Felling		1959	3	0	11		
Watkin TWS	William	21/09/1932	Grimsby		1952	38	12	0	Grimsby Town	Middlesbrough
Watson A	Albert		Felling		1937	67	24	8	Halifax Town	
Watson TD	Thomas	03/02/1936	Boldon		1957	21	5	0	West Bromwich A.	Grimsby Town
Webster WT	Billy	1909	Sunderland		1935	24	4	11	Port Vale	
Weddle GD	George	24/02/1919	Ashington		1946	48	10	0		
Welsh W	Billy	02/05/1904	Douglas Water	1978	1931	58	22	9	Wrexham	Hartlepool Utd.
Wesley JC	Jack	19/01/1908	Cheltenham		1932	51	31	10		Bradford
Whalley GD	George	30/07/1920	Darlington		1946	6	0	0		
Whitfield JS	John	10/06/1938	Gateshead		1959	1	1	11		
Wilbert GN	George	11/07/1924	Dunston-on-Tyne		1947	266	93	0		
Williamson BW	Brian	06/10/1939	Blyth		1958	55	0	1		Crewe Alexandra
Wilson A	Archie	04/12/1924	South Shields		1946	5	0	1		Lincoln City
Wilson CA	Carl	08/05/1940	Consett		1959	17	4	9	Newcastle United	Doncaster Rovers
Wimshurst KP	Ken	23/03/1938	South Shields		1958	7	0	7	Newcastle United	Wolves
Winters IA	Ian	08/02/1921	Renfrew		1948	152	49	0	York City	Workington
Woodburn J	James	29/01/1917	Rutherglen		1948	133	10	0	Newcastle United	
Woodhouse J	John	05/04/1937	Middlesbrough		1957	2	0	0	Leeds United	
Wyles H	Harold	28/10/1922	Melton Mowbray		1947	235	7	0		
Yeats TB	Tom	30/05/1935	Newcastle		1954	1	0	0	Sunderland	
Young JR	John				1949	4	0	1		
Younger J	Jimmy		Pelton		1934	19	1	11	Bury	

FOOTBALL LEAGUE SEASONAL STATISTICS: 1930 ~ 1960

Basic notes for statistics that follow (pages 105 to 127):

The first column is the (League) match number or cup round, the second the match date, and the third the opposition (upper case - capitals - 'home' games, lower case 'away' matches). The fourth column, shows the match result (Gateshead score first), and the fifth column the goalscorers; 'pen', denotes goal scored from a penalty and 'og' an own goal (with goalscorer where known). Sixth column is the official attendance (where an accurate figure has been traced). The team line-ups follow (where reliably traced) with the normally accepted playing positions, i.e. 1 = goalkeeper, 3 = left back, 8 = inside right, etc. The summaries below the line-ups refer to League appearances and League goals scored by that player.

#	Date	Opponent	Score	Scorers	Att	Barkas HB	Charlton T	Crowther GE	Davies J	Green JH	Kennedy R	Littlewood AJ	Maycock R	McNaughton W	Meek J	Moon G	Neilson GW	Pickard TJ	Reilly WI	Scott I	Sinclair TM	Talbot IH	Taylor A	Turnbull JA
1	Aug 30	DONCASTER ROVERS	2-1	Maycock, Barkas	15545	8		1	5		10		9	7			4		6		2		11	3
2	Sep 1	Halifax Town	0-3		8189	8		1	5		10		9	7			4		6		2		11	3
3	6	Hull City	0-4		8644	8	7		5		10		9				4	1	6		2		11	3
4	8	NEW BRIGHTON	4-0	Charlton, Maycock, Barkas, Taylor	5396	8	7		5		10		9				4	1	6		2		11	3
5	13	LINCOLN CITY	0-1		7505	8	7		5		10		9				4	1	6		2	11		3
6	15	New Brighton	0-0		2488	7			5		10		9	8		2	4	1	6				11	
7	20	Hartlepools United	3-2	McNaughton, Kennedy 2	2100	9	7		5		10			8			4	1	6		2		11	3
8	27	WIGAN BOROUGH	4-2	Charlton 3, Kennedy	7085	9	7		5		10			8			4	1	6		2		11	3
9	Oct 4	Nelson	2-2	Kennedy, McNaughton	2321	7			5		10		9	8			4	1	6		2		11	3
10	11	DARLINGTON	1-1	Barkas	10066	9	7		5		10			8			4	1	6		2		11	3
11	18	Rotherham United	1-1	Kennedy	7013	9	7		5		10			8			4	1	6		2		11	3
12	25	CARLISLE UNITED	1-0	Kennedy	14823	9	7		5		10			8			4	1	6		2		11	3
13	Nov 1	Barrow	0-0		5478	9	7		5		10			8			4	1	6		2		11	3
14	8	SOUTHPORT	2-3	Talbot, Maycock	7439	9	7		5				10	8			4	1	6		2	11		3
15	15	Accrington Stanley	1-2	McNaughton	2811	9	7		5				10	8			4	1	6		2	11		3
16	22	ROCHDALE	0-2		1129		7		5		10		9	8			4	1	6		2		11	3
17	Dec 6	WREXHAM	4-3	Charlton, Kennedy, Taylor, Barkas	5300	9	7		5		10			8			4	1	6		2		11	3
18	20	CHESTERFIELD	3-3	Barkas 2, Kennedy	6405	9	7	1			10	5		8			4		6		2		11	3
19	25	Stockport County	1-3	Barkas	10663	9	7	1			10	5		8			4		6		2		11	3
20	27	Doncaster Rovers	1-1	Taylor	4528	9	7	1			10	5		8			4		6		2		11	3
21	Jan 1	YORK CITY	2-1	Charlton 2	4004		7		5		10		9	8			4	1	6		2		11	3
22	3	HULL CITY	1-0	Maycock	7450		7		5		10		9	8			4	1	6		2		11	3
23	17	Lincoln City	0-0		7091		7	1	5		10		9	8			4		6		2		11	3
24	24	HARTLEPOOLS UNITED	0-0		5649		7	1	5		10		9	8			4		6		2		11	3
25	31	Wigan Borough	3-3	McNaughton, Kennedy, Reilly	982		7	1	5	8	10			9			4		6		2	11		3
26	Feb 4	Crewe Alexandra	2-6	McNaughton 2	1790		7	1	5	8	10			9			4		6		2	11		3
27	7	NELSON	2-0	Kennedy, McNaughton	3161		7	1	5		10			8	9		4			6	2	11		3
28	14	Darlington	2-2	McNaughton, Talbot	3435		7	1	5		10			9	8		4			6	2	11		3
29	21	ROTHERHAM UNITED	2-0	McNaughton, Meek	4383			1	5		10			9	8		4			6	2	11	7	3
30	28	Carlisle United	2-2	Kennedy, McNaughton	9680			1	5		10			8	9	7	4			6	2	11		3
31	Mar 7	BARROW	4-1	McNaughton, Mee, Kennedy, Charlton	2161		7	1	5		10			9	8		4			6	2	11		3
32	14	Southport	0-1		3644		7	1	5		10			9	8		4			6	2	11		3
33	21	ACCRINGTON STANLEY	4-0	McNaughton 2, Meek, Neilson	5034		7	1	5		10			9	8		4			6	2	11		3
34	28	Rochdale	1-0	McNaughton	1555		7	1	5		10			9	8		4			6	2	11		3
35	Apr 3	York City	3-4	Talbot, McNaughton 2	4352		7	1	5		10			9	8		4			6	2	11		3
36	4	CREWE ALEXANDRA	2-2	Sinclair, McNaughton	4735		7	1	5		10			9	8		4			6	2	11		3
37	6	Tranmere Rovers	1-2	Kennedy	7875		7	1	5		10			9	8		4			6	2		11	3
38	11	Wrexham	1-5	McNaughton	4182		7	1	5		10			9	8		4			6	2		11	3
39	15	STOCKPORT COUNTY	2-1	McNaughton 2	2389		7	1	5		10			9	8		4			6	2		11	3
40	18	TRANMERE ROVERS	3-0	McNaughton, Meek 2	1864		7	1	5		10			9	8		4			6	2		11	3
41	25	Chesterfield	1-8	McNaughton	5733		7	1	5		10			9	8		4			6	2		11	3
42	May 2	HALIFAX TOWN	3-1	McNaughton, Meek	3166		7	1	5		10			9	8		4			6	2		11	3
				Apps		19	36	25	39	2	40	3	16	39	15	1	42	17	26	16	41	16	27	42
				Goals		7	8				13		4	24	6		1		1			1	3	3

F.A. Cup

	Date	Opponent	Score	Scorers	Att	Barkas HB	Charlton T	Crowther GE	Davies J	Green JH	Kennedy R	Littlewood AJ	Maycock R	McNaughton W	Meek J	Moon G	Neilson GW	Pickard TJ	Reilly WI	Scott I	Sinclair TM	Talbot IH	Taylor A	Turnbull JA
R1	Nov 29	Tranmere Rovers	4-4	McNaughton 2, Barkas 2		9	7		5		10			8			4	1	6		2		11	3
rep	Dec 3	TRANMERE ROVERS	3-2	Charlton, Barkas 2		9	7		5		10			8			4	1	6		2		11	3
R2	13	FOLKESTONE	3-2	Charlton, McNaughton, Barkas		9	7	1			10	5		8			4		6		2		11	3
R3	Jan 10	SHEFFIELD WEDNESDAY	2-6	Charlton, Kennedy	12490		7		5		10			9	8		4	1	6		2		11	3

FINAL TABLE	Pl.	Home					Against					F.	A.	Pts
		W	D	L	F	A	W	D	L	F	A	(Total)		
1 Chesterfield	42	19	1	1	66	22	7	5	9	36	35	102	57	58
2 Lincoln City	42	16	3	2	60	19	9	4	8	42	40	102	59	57
3 Wrexham	42	16	4	1	61	25	5	8	8	33	37	94	62	54
4 Tranmere Rovers	42	16	3	2	73	26	8	3	10	38	48	111	74	54
5 Southport	42	15	3	3	52	19	7	6	8	36	37	88	56	53
6 Hull City	42	12	7	2	64	20	8	3	10	35	35	99	55	50
7 Stockport County	42	15	5	1	54	19	5	4	12	23	42	77	61	49
8 Carlisle United	42	13	4	4	68	32	7	1	13	30	49	98	81	45
9 GATESHEAD	42	14	4	3	46	22	2	9	10	25	51	71	73	45
10 Wigan Borough	42	14	4	3	48	25	5	1	15	28	61	76	86	43
11 Darlington	42	9	6	6	44	30	7	4	10	27	29	71	59	42
12 York City	42	15	3	3	59	30	3	3	15	26	52	85	82	42
13 Accrington Stanley	42	14	2	5	51	31	1	7	13	33	77	84	108	39
14 Rotherham United	42	9	6	6	50	34	4	6	11	31	49	81	83	38
15 Doncaster Rovers	42	9	8	4	40	18	4	3	14	25	47	65	65	37
16 Barrow	42	13	4	4	45	23	2	3	16	23	66	68	89	37
17 Halifax Town	42	11	6	4	30	16	2	3	16	25	73	55	89	35
18 Crewe Alexandra	42	13	2	6	52	35	1	4	16	14	58	66	93	34
19 New Brighton	42	12	4	5	36	25	1	3	17	13	51	49	76	33
20 Hartlepools United	42	10	2	9	47	37	2	4	15	20	49	67	86	30
21 Rochdale	42	9	1	11	42	50	3	5	13	20	57	62	107	30
22 Nelson	42	6	7	8	28	40	0	0	21	15	73	43	113	19

1931/32   2nd in Division 3 (North)

	Date		Opponent	Score	Scorers	Att	Boland G	Brannigan DM	Charlton T	Crowther GE	Davies J	Frame WG	Kennedy R	McLaughlan F	McNaughton W	Meek J	Neilson GH	Nisbet KH	Paterson A	Scott J	Sinclair TM	Turnbull RA	Viney EE	Welsh W
1	Aug	29	New Brighton	3-1	Welsh 2, Boland	4134	11	6		1	5		10		9	7	4				2	3		8
2		31	Walsall	2-1	McNaughton 2	4237	11	6		1	5		10		9	7	4				2	3		8
3	Sep	5	BARROW	4-0	McNaughton 4	11459	11			1	5		10		9	7	4				2	3		8
4		9	YORK CITY	6-0	McNaughton 4, Welsh, Kennedy	14100	11			1	5		10		9	7	4		6		2	3		8
5		12	Hull City	1-0	Kennedy	9497	11			1	5		10		9	7	4		6		2	3		8
6		16	York City	2-3	McNaughton, Boland	6199	11			1	5		10		9	7	4		6		2	3		8
7		19	LINCOLN CITY	2-3	Meek, Kennedy	14633	11			1	5		10		9	7	4		6		2	3		8
8		26	Chester	1-1	Kennedy	10195	11			1	5		10			7	4		6		2	3	9	8
9	Oct	3	HARTLEPOOLS UNITED	3-1	Charlton, McNaughton, Meek	10223	11		7	1	5				9	8	4		6		2	3		10
10		17	SOUTHPORT	2-0	Charlton, Meek	8904	11		7	1	5		10			8	4		6		2	3		9
11		24	Doncaster Rovers	2-1	Welsh, Charlton	3216	11	4	7	1			10			8	5		6		2	3		9
12		31	ROCHDALE	3-1	Welsh 2, Meek	7227	11	6	7	1			10			8	4		5		2	3		9
13	Nov	7	Crewe Alexandra	5-3	Boland 3, Welsh 2	6853	11	6	7	1			10			8	4		5		2	3		9
14		14	CARLISLE UNITED	4-0	Meek 3, Boland	9910	11	6	7	1			10			8	4		5		2	3		9
15		21	Wrexham	1-2	Kennedy	8487	11	6	7	1			10			8	4		5		2	3		9
16	Dec	5	Stockport County	1-1	Charlton	4081	11	6	7	1			10			8	4		5		2	3		9
17		16	ROTHERHAM UNITED	4-1	Welsh 3, Kennedy	2824	11	6	7			1	10			8	4		5		2	3		9
18		19	Tranmere Rovers	3-4	Charlton, Welsh 2	5565	11		7			1	10			8	4		6	5	2	3		9
19		25	Halifax Town	2-1	Charlton, Welsh	11649	11		7			1	10			8	4		6	5	2	3		9
20		26	HALIFAX TOWN	1-1	Meek	11655	11		7			1	10			8	4		6	5	2	3		9
21	Jan	2	NEW BRIGHTON	4-0	Meek, Charlton, McNaughton, Neilson	8111	11		7			1			10	8	4		6	5	2	3		9
22		9	ACCRINGTON STANLEY	4-0	Kennedy 2, Meek, McNaughton	6480	11		7			1	10		9	8	4		6	5	2	3		
23		16	Barrow	1-3	Neilson	6969	11		7	1			10		9	8	4		6	5	2	3		
24		23	HULL CITY	2-1	Kennedy, McNaughton	4490	11		7	1			10	3	9	8	4		6	5	2			
25		30	Lincoln City	0-1		14178	11		7	1			10	3	9	8	4		6	5	2			
26	Feb	6	CHESTER	1-2	Meek	7688	11		7	1			10	3	9	8	4		6	5	2			
27		13	Hartlepools United	2-1	Boland, Meek	3382	11		7	1			10		9	8	4		6	5	2	3		
28		20	TRANMERE ROVERS	3-3	McNaughton 2, Charlton	5915	11	6	7	1			10		9	8	5		4		2	3		
29		27	Southport	1-1	Kennedy	5719			7	1	5		10		8	11	4	9	6		2	3		
30	Mar	5	DONCASTER ROVERS	2-1	Turnbull, Kennedy	5002		6	7	1			10		8	11	4		5		2	3		9
31		12	Rochdale	3-0	Welsh, Kennedy, Charlton	2526	11		7	1	5		10			8	4		6		2	3		9
32		19	CREWE ALEXANDRA	3-3	Charlton, Boland 2	8386	11		7	1			10			8	4		6	5	2	3		9
33		25	Darlington	2-1	McNaughton, Kennedy	6123	11		7	1			10		9	8	4		6	5	2	3		
34		26	Carlisle United	0-0		5401	11		7	1			10			8	4		6	5	2	3		9
35		28	DARLINGTON	3-2	Meek 2, Kennedy	6311	11		7	1			10		9	11	4		6	5	2	3		8
36	Apr	2	WREXHAM	4-0	Boland, Welsh, Kennedy, Meek	5276	11	6	7	1			10			9	5		4		2	3		8
37		9	Accrington Stanley	2-1	Meek, McNaughton	3786	11	6	7	1			10		9	8	5		4		2	3		
38		16	STOCKPORT COUNTY	2-1	Meek, McNaughton	8655	11	6	7	1			10		9	11	5		4		2	3		8
39		23	Rotherham United	1-2	Kennedy	4091	11	6	7	1			10		9	8	5		4		2	3		
40	May	7	WALSALL	2-0	McNaughton 2	1617	11	6	7	1			10		9	8	5		4		2	3		
					Apps		36	16	32	34	12	6	38	3	24	40	40	1	23	29	40	37	1	28
					Goals		10		10				16		22	17	2					1		16

On October 10, Gateshead lost 2-1 at Wigan Borough, but the result was expunged from the records when Wigan resigned from the League. The Gateshead line-up was the same as for match 9, with Meek the goalscorer.

F.A. Cup

	Date		Opponent	Score	Scorers	Att	Boland G	Brannigan DM	Charlton T	Crowther GE	Davies J	Frame WG	Kennedy R	McLaughlan F	McNaughton W	Meek J	Neilson GH	Nisbet KH	Paterson A	Scott J	Sinclair TM	Turnbull RA	Viney EE	Welsh W
R1	Nov	28	WREXHAM	3-2	Meek 2, Kennedy	9130	11		7	1	5				9	8	4				2	3		10
R2	Dec	12	Burton Town	1-4	Meek	5963	11	6	7	1			10			8	4			5	2	3		9

	FINAL TABLE	Pl.		Home				Against				F.	A.	Pts
			W	D	L	F	A	W	D	L	F	A	(Total)	
1	Lincoln City	40	16	2	2	65	13	10	3	7	41	34	106	47	57
2	GATESHEAD	40	15	3	2	59	20	10	4	6	35	28	94	48	57
3	Chester	40	16	2	2	54	22	5	6	9	24	38	78	60	50
4	Tranmere Rovers	40	15	4	1	76	23	4	7	9	31	35	107	58	49
5	Barrow	40	16	1	3	59	23	8	0	12	27	36	86	59	49
6	Crewe Alexandra	40	15	3	2	64	24	6	3	11	31	42	95	66	48
7	Southport	40	14	5	1	44	15	4	5	11	14	38	58	53	46
8	Hull City	40	14	1	5	52	21	6	4	10	30	32	82	53	45
9	York City	40	14	3	3	49	24	4	4	12	27	57	76	81	43
10	Wrexham	40	14	2	4	42	25	4	5	11	22	44	64	69	43
11	Darlington	40	12	1	7	41	27	5	3	12	25	42	66	69	38
12	Stockport County	40	12	3	5	31	15	1	8	11	24	38	55	53	37
13	Hartlepools United	40	10	4	6	47	37	6	1	13	31	63	78	100	37
14	Accrington Stanley	40	14	4	2	56	20	1	2	17	19	60	75	80	36
15	Doncaster Rovers	40	12	3	5	38	27	4	1	15	21	53	59	80	36
16	Walsall	40	12	3	5	42	30	4	0	16	15	55	57	85	35
17	Halifax Town	40	11	6	3	36	18	2	2	16	25	69	61	87	34
18	Carlisle United	40	9	7	4	40	23	2	4	14	24	56	64	79	33
19	Rotherham United	40	10	3	7	41	23	4	1	15	22	49	63	72	32
20	New Brighton	40	8	5	7	25	23	0	3	17	13	53	38	76	24
21	Rochdale	40	4	2	14	33	63	0	1	19	15	72	48	135	11

106

1932/33   7th in Division 3 (North)

No		Date	Opponent	Result	Scorers	Att	Atkin TL	Boland G	Brannigan DM	Charlton T	Clark RN	Crowther GE	Gowdy WA	Heslop JJ	Kennedy R	Laird JW	Lincoln A	Meek J	Neilson GH	Newton C	O'Donnell W	Paterson A	Ranson JG	Scott J	Sinclair TM	Turnbull RA	Turnbull WJ	Welsh W	Wesley JC
1	Aug	27	DONCASTER ROVERS	4-0	Boland, Charlton, Kennedy, Welsh	6780		11	6	7		1			10			8	5			4				2	3	9	
2		31	Darlington	3-1	Charlton 2, Kennedy	4115		11	6	7					10			8	5		1	4				2	3	9	
3	Sep	3	Hull City	1-1	Kennedy	10204		11	6	7					10			8	5		1	4				2	3	9	
4		7	DARLINGTON	3-0	Welsh 2, Kennedy	5723		11	6	7					10			8	5		1	4				2	3	9	
5		10	BARNSLEY	1-1	Charlton	7328		11		7					10			8	5		1	4		6		2	3	9	
6		17	Hartlepools United	2-2	Charlton, Bowran (og)	5735		11	6	7					10	9		8	5		1				4	2	3		
7		24	HALIFAX TOWN	3-0	Meek, Kennedy, Laird	5467		11	6	7					10	9		8	5		1				4	2	3		
8	Oct	1	Tranmere Rovers	2-4	Kennedy 2	4133		11	6	7					10			9	5		1					2	3		8
9		8	WREXHAM	4-4	Welsh, Kennedy, Meek, Boland	1815		11	6	7					9			8	5		1	4				2	3		10
10		15	Walsall	0-2		5489		11	6	7					9			8	4		1	3		5		2			10
11		22	York City	2-2	Ranson 2	6150		11	6		1				10			7	4				9	5		2	3	8	
12		29	CREWE ALEXANDRA	2-1	Charlton, Kennedy	3116		11	6	7	1				10				4				9	5		2	3	8	
13	Nov	5	Rochdale	0-1		8650		11	6	7					10				4		1		9	5		2	3	8	
14		12	SOUTHPORT	4-1	Charlton 2, Welsh, Brannigan	3997		11	6	7					10				4		1		9	5		2	3	8	
15		19	Mansfield Town	2-1	Boland, Ranson	6823		11	6	7					10				4		1		9	5		2	3	8	
16	Dec	3	Accrington Stanley	3-0	Ranson 2, Charlton	2847		11	6	7					10				4		1		9	5		2	3	8	
17		17	Chester	1-3	Ranson	7030		11	6	7					10				4		1		9	5		2	3	8	
18		24	BARROW	2-3	Ranson 2	6692		11	6	7					10				4		1		9	5		2	3	8	
19		26	Carlisle United	2-1	Boland, Charlton	10177		11	6	7					10			8	4		1		9	5		2	3		
20		27	CARLISLE UNITED	1-0	Kennedy	9283		11	6	7					10			8	4		1		9	5		2	3		
21		31	Doncaster Rovers	1-3		6080	7	11	6						10			8	4		1		9	5		2	3		
22	Jan	3	NEW BRIGHTON	2-0	Meek, Kennedy	3001	8		6						10		4	7			1		9	5		2	3	11	
23		7	HULL CITY	2-3	Kennedy, Ranson	7723	8	11	6	7					10				4		1		9	5		2	3		
24		21	Barnsley	4-2	Atkin 2, Neilson, Wesley	4927	11		6	7	1							8	5	2	4		9				3		10
25		25	ROTHERHAM UNITED	1-1	Meek	1821	11		6	7	1							8	5	2	4		9				3		10
26		28	HARTLEPOOLS UNITED	3-1	Wesley 2, Ranson	4171	11		6	7	1							8	5	2	4		9				3		10
27	Feb	4	Halifax Town	0-1		7477	11		6		1			7				8	5	2	4		9				3		10
28		11	TRANMERE ROVERS	0-2		3849	11		6		1			7					5	2	4		9				3	8	10
29		18	Wrexham	1-5	Atkin	8440	7		6		1				8					2	4		9	5			3	10	11
30	Mar	4	YORK CITY	2-2	Ranson 2	3651	7	11	6		1				10					2	4		9	5			3	8	
31		11	Crewe Alexandra	0-2		4137	7	11	6		1				10					2	4		9	5			3	8	
32		18	ROCHDALE	3-0	Ranson 2, Atkin	2797	7	11	6		1				10					2	4		9	5			3	8	
33		25	Southport	1-4	Ranson	3503	7	11	6		1				10					2	4		9	5			3	8	
34	Apr	1	MANSFIELD TOWN	3-2	Welsh, Meek, Brannigan	2413	7	11	6		1				10					2	4		9	5			3	8	
35		8	Rotherham United	2-1	Kennedy, Atkin	3456	7	11	6		1				10					2	4		9	5			3	8	
36		14	STOCKPORT COUNTY	0-3		7041	7				1		6		10					2	4		9	5			3	8	
37		15	ACCRINGTON STANLEY	1-0	Atkin	1929	7				1		6		10					2	4		9	5			3	8	
38		17	Stockport County	3-4	Ranson, Meek, Atkin	4959	7				1		6		10					2	4		9	5			3	8	
39		22	New Brighton	1-1	Ranson	3559		11			1		6		10			7		2	4		9	5			3		8
40		29	CHESTER	3-0	Ranson 2, Kennedy	1424		11	6		1				10			7		2	4		9	5			3	8	
41	May	3	WALSALL	1-1	Meek	2002		11	6		1				10			7		2	4		9	5			3	8	
42		6	Barrow	2-1	Atkin, Ranson	2578	7	11	6		1				10					2	4		9	5			3	8	
			Apps				19	28	37	23	17	3	4	2	35	2	1	32	30	22	30	23	32	31	10	41	3	29	8
			Goals				8	4	2	10					14	1		7	1				21					6	3

One own goal

F.A. Cup

Rd		Date	Opponent	Result	Scorers	Att	Atkin TL	Boland G	Brannigan DM	Charlton T	Clark RN	Kennedy R	Neilson GH	Ranson JG	Scott J	Turnbull RA	Turnbull WJ	Welsh W
R1	Nov	26	Barrow	1-0	Ranson	5901		11	6	7	1	10	4	9	5	2	3	8
R2	Dec	10	MARGATE	5-2	Ranson 2, Kennedy 3	11499		11	6	7	1	10	4	9	5	2	3	8
R3	Jan	14	MANCHESTER CITY	1-1	Kennedy	9123		11	6	7	1	10	4	9	5	2	3	8
rep		18	Manchester City	0-9		22590	11		6	7	1		4	9	5	2	3	10

FINAL TABLE

		Pl.	W	D	L	F	A	W	D	L	F	A	F	A	Pts
				Home					Against					(Total)	
1	Hull City	42	18	3	0	69	14	8	4	9	31	100	45	59
2	Wrexham	42	18	2	1	75	15	6	7	8	31	106	51	57
3	Stockport County	42	16	2	3	69	30	5	10	6	30	99	58	54
4	Chester	42	15	4	2	57	25	7	4	10	37	94	66	52
5	Walsall	42	16	4	1	53	15	3	6	12	43	75	58	48
6	Doncaster Rovers	42	13	8	0	52	26	4	6	11	25	77	79	48
7	GATESHEAD	42	12	5	4	45	25	7	4	10	33	78	67	47
8	Barnsley	42	14	3	4	60	31	5	5	11	32	92	80	46
9	Barrow	42	12	3	6	41	24	6	4	11	19	86	60	43
10	Crewe Alexandra	42	16	3	2	57	16	4	0	17	23	68	80	84	43
11	Tranmere Rovers	42	11	4	6	49	31	6	4	11	21	35	70	66	42
12	Southport	42	15	3	3	54	20	2	4	15	16	47	70	67	41
13	Accrington Stanley	42	12	4	5	55	29	3	6	12	23	47	78	76	40
14	Hartlepools United	42	15	3	3	56	29	1	4	16	31	87	87	116	39
15	Halifax Town	42	12	4	5	39	23	3	4	14	32	67	71	90	38
16	Mansfield Town	42	13	4	4	57	22	1	3	17	27	78	84	100	35
17	Rotherham United	42	14	3	4	42	21	0	3	18	18	63	60	84	34
18	Rochdale	42	9	4	8	32	33	4	3	14	26	47	58	80	33
19	Carlisle United	42	8	7	6	34	25	5	0	16	17	50	51	75	33
20	York City	42	10	4	7	51	38	3	2	16	21	54	72	92	32
21	New Brighton	42	8	6	7	42	36	3	4	14	21	52	63	88	32
22	Darlington	42	9	6	6	42	32	1	2	18	24	77	66	109	28

1933/34 19th in Division 3 (North)

Match results, goalscorers and attendances (player columns record shirt numbers):

#	Date	Opponent	Score	Scorers	Att.
1	Aug 26	Chesterfield	2-6	Kennedy 2	8771
2	30	DARLINGTON	2-2	Wesley, Temple	5674
3	Sep 2	ROCHDALE	2-1	Temple 2	4226
4	6	Darlington	3-3	Wesley 3	3915
5	9	Tranmere Rovers	1-2	Wesley	6441
6	11	Accrington Stanley	2-5	Atkin, Meek	4457
7	16	BARNSLEY	1-4	Neilson	5986
8	23	Mansfield Town	1-1	Meek	5057
9	30	HARTLEPOOLS UNITED	6-3	Wesley 4, McDermott, Boland	4292
10	Oct 7	Wrexham	3-2	McDermott, Wesley, Atkin	3883
11	14	SOUTHPORT	2-2	McDermott, Birkett (og)	5562
12	21	Stockport County	0-1		5378
13	28	HALIFAX TOWN	4-0	Atkin, Wesley, Meek 2	3239
14	Nov 4	Crewe Alexandra	2-3	Wesley 2 (1 pen)	4422
15	11	NEW BRIGHTON	6-0	Wesley 3, McDermott, Atkin, Meek	3810
16	18	Rotherham United	2-3	Meek, Wesley	3574
17	Dec 2	York City	1-1	Temple	3569
18	16	Doncaster Rovers	2-5	Wesley, Neilson	3551
19	23	BARROW	0-0		3041
20	26	ACCRINGTON STANLEY	2-0	Meek, Atkin	4348
21	30	CHESTERFIELD	2-1	Meek, Wesley	5394
22	Jan 6	Rochdale	0-2		3220
23	17	WALSALL	2-1	McDermott, Meek	1078
24	20	TRANMERE ROVERS	1-2	McDermott	3383
25	27	Barnsley	0-0		7974
26	Feb 3	MANSFIELD TOWN	5-3	Kennedy 4, Meek	2482
27	10	Hartlepools United	3-3	Atkin, Kennedy, Meek	3755
28	17	WREXHAM	0-3		2634
29	24	Southport	1-1	Meek	2028
30	Mar 3	STOCKPORT COUNTY	0-4		2922
31	10	Halifax Town	4-2	Craig (og), Meek 2, Wesley	1874
32	17	CREWE ALEXANDRA	2-1	Neilson, Meek (pen)	2012
33	24	New Brighton	1-3	Wesley	2598
34	30	Carlisle United	0-6		5502
35	31	ROTHERHAM UNITED	4-1	Kennedy 2, Wesley, Atkin	1795
36	Apr 2	CARLISLE UNITED	2-3	Wesley, Kennedy	2624
37	7	Walsall	1-5	Atkin	5737
38	14	YORK CITY	0-2		1482
39	21	Chester	0-4		4564
40	25	CHESTER	1-3	Boland	1043
41	28	DONCASTER ROVERS	2-4	Wesley 2	552
42	May 5	Barrow	1-12	Neilson (pen)	3330

Match no. 2: Some reports give goalscorers as Wesley and Meek

Appearances and goals (totals):

	Askew J	Atkin TL	Atkinson T	Boland G	Brannigan DM	Burke JW	Carr JJ	Clark RN	Dawson T	Inskip JB	Jobson JT	Kennedy R	McDermott I	McLaughlan R	Meek J	Murphy VJ	Neilson GH	Newton C	O'Donnell W	Paterson A	Scott J	Spedding JJ	Temple IL	Turnbull WJ	Welsh W	Wesley JC
Apps	5	35	2	28	3	3	33	13	18	9	8	21	26	3	39	2	33	22	23	34	6	33	18	7	1	37
Goals		8		2								10	6		15		4						4			25

Two own goals

F.A. Cup

	Date	Opponent	Score	Scorers	Att.
R1	Nov 25	DARWEN	5-2	McDermott, Temple, Meek 2, Atkin	7757
R2	Dec 9	NORTH SHIELDS	1-0	Wesley	6642
R3	Jan 13	Workington	1-4	McDermott	11640

Third Division (North) Cup

	Opponent	Score	
R1	Darlingyton	1-1	
rep	DARLINGTON	2-3	(aet)

FINAL TABLE

		Pl.	Home					Against					F.	A.	Pts
			W	D	L	F	A	W	D	L	F	A	(Total)		
1	Barnsley	42	18	3	0	64	18	9	5	7	54	43	118	61	62
2	Chesterfield	42	18	1	2	56	17	9	6	6	30	26	86	43	61
3	Stockport County	42	18	3	0	84	23	6	8	7	31	29	115	52	59
4	Walsall	42	18	2	1	66	18	5	5	11	31	42	97	60	53
5	Doncaster Rovers	42	17	1	3	58	24	5	8	8	25	37	83	61	53
6	Wrexham	42	14	1	6	68	35	9	4	8	34	38	102	73	51
7	Tranmere Rovers	42	16	2	3	57	21	4	5	12	27	42	84	63	47
8	Barrow	42	12	5	4	78	45	7	4	10	38	49	116	94	47
9	Halifax Town	42	15	2	4	57	30	5	2	14	23	61	80	91	44
10	Chester	42	11	6	4	59	26	6	0	15	30	60	89	86	40
11	Hartlepools United	42	14	3	4	54	24	2	4	15	35	69	89	93	39
12	York City	42	11	5	5	44	28	4	3	14	27	46	71	74	38
13	Carlisle United	42	11	6	4	43	23	4	2	15	23	58	66	81	38
14	Crewe Alexandra	42	12	3	6	54	38	3	3	15	27	59	81	97	36
15	New Brighton	42	13	3	5	41	25	1	5	15	21	62	62	87	36
16	Darlington	42	11	4	6	47	35	2	5	14	23	66	70	101	35
17	Mansfield Town	42	9	7	5	49	29	2	5	14	32	59	81	88	34
18	Southport	42	6	11	4	35	29	2	6	13	28	61	63	90	33
19	GATESHEAD	42	10	3	8	46	40	2	6	13	30	70	76	110	33
20	Accrington Stanley	42	10	6	5	44	38	3	1	17	21	63	65	101	33
21	Rotherham United	42	5	7	9	35	35	5	1	15	22	56	53	91	28
22	Rochdale	42	7	5	9	34	30	2	1	18	19	73	53	103	24

1934/35 19th in Division 3 (North)

League — Division 3 (North)

No	Date	Opponent	Score	Scorers	Att
1	Aug 25	CHESTER	2-4	Wsley, McAinsh	6532
2	29	DARLINGTON	3-0	Rivers, Spedding, Wesley	4807
3	Sep 1	Southport	1-1	Meek	3342
4	5	Darlington	1-2	McAinsh	5003
5	8	DONCASTER ROVERS	0-0		5943
6	15	Hartlepools United	2-1	Gray, Rivers	4638
7	22	CREWE ALEXANDRA	5-2	Meek 3(1 pen), Mathison, Wesley	5000
8	29	Stockport County	1-5	Meek	4548
9	Oct 6	BARROW	1-0	Gray	5170
10	13	ACCRINGTON STANLEY	1-1	Carr	5173
11	20	Carlisle United	4-5	Rivers 2, Ferguson 2	4351
12	27	ROCHDALE	2-0	Ferguson, Hale	3197
13	Nov 3	Lincoln City	0-5		4244
14	10	TRANMERE ROVERS	0-2		1303
15	17	Wrexham	1-3	Hale	5353
16	Dec 1	Rotherham United	0-3		4723
17	15	Chesterfield	1-3	Spedding	3054
18	22	MANSFIELD TOWN	2-2	Rivers, Hale	2028
19	25	NEW BRIGHTON	2-1	Rivers, Spedding	2130
20	26	New Brighton	0-3		4047
21	29	Chester	2-2	Ferguson, Younger	5419
22	Jan 5	SOUTHPORT	1-2	Ferguson	2929
23	12	HALIFAX TOWN	3-1	Spedding 2, J Turnbull	2729
24	19	Doncaster Rovers	0-5		6754
25	26	HARTLEPOOLS UNITED	2-1	J Turnbull, Spedding	1899
26	Feb 2	Crewe Alexandra	1-2	J Turnbull	3689
27	9	STOCKPORT COUNTY	3-2	Spedding 2, Robson	3924
28	16	Barrow	2-3	J Turnbull 2	1883
29	23	Accrington Stanley	2-4	Gray 2	2220
30	27	WALSALL	1-0	McDermott	720
31	Mar 2	CARLISLE UNITED	3-2	Hale, Robson, Carr(pen)	2894
32	9	Rochdale	1-6	Rivers	3562
33	16	LINCOLN CITY	0-2		2687
34	23	Tranmere Rovers	2-2	Spedding, O'Donnell	5188
35	30	WREXHAM	1-0	McDermott	2254
36	Apr 6	Halifax Town	0-4		7630
37	13	ROTHERHAM UNITED	1-1	McDermott	2232
38	19	YORK CITY	2-1	McAinsh, J Turnbull	3424
39	20	Walsall	0-5		3923
40	22	York City	0-3		4312
41	27	CHESTERFIELD	1-4	Rivers	1407
42	May 4	Mansfield Town	1-1	Robson	2541

Appearances and Goals

Player	Apps	Goals
Askew J	15	
Burgess C	16	
Burke JW	10	
Carr JJ	19	2
Conroy T	20	
Daglish J	14	
Ferguson JJ	21	5
Goodfellow DO	5	
Gray RA	11	4
Hales W	14	4
Hamilton J	4	
Ince J	22	
Inskip JB	17	
Mathison G	29	1
McAinsh J	27	3
McDermott J	20	3
Meek J	9	5
Mellon JM	18	
Neilson GH	22	
O'Donnell W	8	1
Oxley A	6	
Quigley JA	2	
Rivers W	42	8
Robson E	6	3
Spedding JJ	39	9
Traynor JW	2	
Turnbull JW	13	6
Turnbull JM	5	
Turnbull T		
Wesley JC	7	3
Younger J	19	1

F.A. Cup

Round	Date	Opponent	Score	Scorer
R1	Nov 24	DARLINGTON	1-4	Hamilton

Third Division (North) Cup

Round	Opponent	Score
R1	YORK CITY	2-2
rep	York City	1-3

FINAL TABLE

	Team	Pl	Home W	Home D	Home L	Home F	Home A	Away W	Away D	Away L	Away F	Away A	F	A	Pts
1	Doncaster Rovers	42	16	0	5	53	21	10	5	6	34	23	87	44	57
2	Halifax Town	42	17	2	2	50	24	8	3	10	26	43	76	67	55
3	Chester	42	14	4	3	62	27	6	10	5	29	31	91	58	54
4	Lincoln City	42	14	3	4	55	21	8	4	9	32	37	87	58	51
5	Darlington	42	15	5	1	50	15	6	4	11	30	44	80	59	51
6	Tranmere Rovers	42	15	4	2	53	20	5	7	9	21	35	74	55	51
7	Stockport County	42	15	2	4	57	22	7	1	13	33	50	90	72	47
8	Mansfield Town	42	16	3	2	55	25	3	6	12	20	37	75	62	47
9	Rotherham United	42	14	4	3	56	21	5	3	13	30	52	86	73	45
10	Chesterfield	42	13	4	4	46	21	4	6	11	25	31	71	52	44
11	Wrexham	42	12	5	4	47	25	4	6	11	29	44	76	69	43
12	Hartlepools United	42	12	4	5	52	34	5	3	13	28	44	80	78	41
13	Crewe Alexandra	42	12	6	3	41	25	2	5	14	25	61	66	86	39
14	Walsall	42	11	7	3	51	18	2	3	16	30	54	81	72	36
15	York City	42	12	5	4	50	20	3	1	17	26	62	76	82	36
16	New Brighton	42	9	6	6	32	25	5	2	14	27	51	59	76	36
17	Barrow	42	11	5	5	37	31	2	4	15	21	56	58	87	35
18	Accrington Stanley	42	11	5	5	44	36	1	5	15	19	53	63	89	34
19	GATESHEAD	42	12	4	5	36	28	1	4	16	22	68	58	96	34
20	Rochdale	42	9	5	7	39	35	2	6	13	14	36	53	71	33
21	Southport	42	6	6	9	27	36	4	6	11	28	49	55	85	32
22	Carlisle United	42	7	6	8	34	36	1	1	19	17	66	51	102	23

109

1935/36 14th in Division 3 (North)

No	Date		Opponent	Score	Scorers	Att	Allen IW	Beardshaw EC	Carr JJ	Conroy T	Cook W	Cull JE	Goodfellow DO	Hartley TW	Heslop R	Humble G	Inskip JB	Jones S	Livingstone A	Mathison G	McAinsh J	McDermott I	McKenzie RR	Moore JE	Neilson GH	Oxley A	Quigley JA	Rivers W	Robinson R	Robson E	Robson(James)	Robson (John)	Spedding JJ	Talbot GR	Varty WC	Webster WT
1	Aug 31		Walsall	0-2		10346	9			2					10		5	7						4					6	3			8	1		11
2	Sep 2		Tranmere Rovers	0-2		7428	9			2					10		5	7						4					6	3			8	1		11
3		7	CARLISLE UNITED	1-1	Spedding	8430	9			2			7		10		5							4		5			6	3			8	1		11
4		11	TRANMERE ROVERS	1-1	Spedding	10200	9			2			7		10		5				8	6		4						3			5	1		11
5		14	Hartlepools United	0-2		4487	9			2			7		10		5				8			4					6	3			5	1		11
6		18	BARROW	4-3	Moore, Allen 2, Webster	2830	9			2			7		10		5				8	6								3			4	1		11
7		21	MANSFIELD TOWN	3-1	Webster, Allen 2	3220	9			2			7		10		5				8	4											1		11
8		28	Rotherham United	0-3		6541	9			2			7		10		5				8	4								3				1		11
9	Oct 5		WREXHAM	2-0	Allen 2	3099	9			2	8	7			10		5				6			4						3				1		11
10		12	Oldham Athletic	2-2	Varty, Allen	5993	9			2	8				10		5				6			4						3				1	7	11
11		19	New Brighton	0-1		2173	9			2					10		5				6			4				8	3					1	7	11
12		26	CHESTERFIELD	3-3	Rivers, Cull 2	4452	9			2		7			8		5				6							10	3			4	1		11
13	Nov 2		Stockport County	1-3	Humble	6028				2	8	7			4	9	5											10	3				1		11
14		9	CREWE ALEXANDRA	2-1	Rivers 2	1701	9			2	11	7	1		8		5				6			4				10	3						11
15		16	Accrington Stanley	1-6	Cull	3537	9			2		7	1		8		5				6							10	3				11		
16		23	SOUTHPORT	3-1	Neilson, Allen 2	2360	9			2		7	1		5	11					6				4			10	3			8			
17	Dec 7		LINCOLN CITY	4-0	Allen, Rivers, McAinsh, Spedding	2825	9					11	1		8		5				6	7			2			10	3			4			
18		14	Rochdale	0-5		2966	9					11	1		8		5				6	7			2			10	3			4			
19		21	YORK CITY	0-0		2417	9					11	1				5					7			6	8		10	3			4			
20		25	HALIFAX TOWN	2-2	Allen 2	2718	9			2		11	1				5		3			7			6	8		10				4			
21		26	Halifax Town	1-1	McAinsh	4414	9			2		11	1				5		3			7			6	8		10				4			
22		28	WALSALL	2-2	Cull, Oxley	3069	9			2		11					5		3			7			6	8		10				4			
23	Jan 1		Darlington	2-5	Cull, E Robson	3823	11			2		7					5		3						6	8		10		9		4			
24		4	Carlisle United	0-2		5389	9			2			1		10		5		3			7			6	8						4			11
25		11	Chester	0-4		3581				2			1		8		5		3	6	7		4	10			9								
26	Feb 1		ROTHERHAM UNITED	1-1	Moore	2843				2			1		8	9	5		3	6	7				11	4	10								
27		8	Wrexham	4-2	Oxley, Heslop 2, Livingstone	2468				2			1		8		5		3	6	7				4	9	10								11
28		12	HARTLEPOOLS UNITED	1-0	Quigley	1973				2			1		8		5		3	6	7				4	9									11
29		15	OLDHAM ATHLETIC	0-0		4096				2			1		8		5		3	6	7				4	9	10								11
30		22	NEW BRIGHTON	3-1	McAinsh, Neilson, Mathison	2846				2			1		8	9	5		3	6	7				4	10									11
31		29	Crewe Alexandra	4-2	John Robson, James Robson 2, Quigley	2636		5		2					8				3	6					10	7				9	11				
32	Mar 7		STOCKPORT COUNTY	1-0	Quigley	3639		5		2			1		8				3	6					10	7				9	11				
33		14	Chesterfield	0-2		8595		5		2			1		8				3	6	7				10	11				9					
34		21	ACCRINGTON STANLEY	0-0		3496		5		2			1		8				3	6	7				10	11				9					
35		28	Southport	1-1	Neilson	2160		5		2			1		8				3	6					9	10	7								
36	Apr 4		CHESTER	2-0	Inskip 2	3639		5		2			1		8		4		3	6					9	10	7								
37		11	Lincoln City	0-5		3713		5		2			1		8		4		3	6					9	10	7								
38		13	DARLINGTON	1-1	Inskip	3299		5		2			1	8	10		4		3	6	7				9		7								11
39		14	Mansfield Town	1-3	Webster	3599		5		2			1	8	10		4		3	6					9		7								11
40		18	ROCHDALE	1-0	Mathison	1996		5	2						8		4		3	6	7				9	10									11
41		25	York City	2-2	Webster, Heslop	2264		5	2				1		8		4		3	6	7	9				10									11
42	May 2		Barrow	0-3		2358		5	2						8		4		3		7	9				10									11
	Apps						23	12	3	37	4	19	24	3	35	3	39	3	23	28	18	3	10	7	27	20	13	17	19	1	4	2	16	13	5	24
	Goals						12					5			3	1	3		1	2	3			2	3	2	3	4		1	2	1	3		1	4

Played in two games: Askew (games 22 and 23 at 1),
Dawson (games 31 and 40 at 1)
Played in one game: Harbottle (game 42 at 1),
Hogg (Game 25 at 11)
Cassidy (Game 42 at 6)

F.A. Cup

	Date		Opponent	Score		Att	Allen IW								Heslop R	Humble G	Inskip JB	Jones S			McAinsh J				Neilson GH			Rivers W	Robinson R	Robson E			Spedding JJ	Talbot GR	Varty WC	Webster WT
R1	Nov 30		Chester	0-1		6200	9					7		1	8		5	11			6				2			10	3				4			

Third Division (North) Cup

		Opponent	Score
R2		Carlisle United	2-6

FINAL TABLE

		Pl.	Home W	D	L	F	A	Against W	D	L	F	A	F. A. Pts (Total)		
1	Chesterfield	42	15	3	3	60	14	9	9	3	32	25	92	39	60
2	Chester	42	14	5	2	69	18	8	6	7	31	27	100	45	55
3	Tranmere Rovers	42	17	2	2	75	28	5	9	7	18	30	93	58	55
4	Lincoln City	42	18	1	2	64	14	4	8	9	27	37	91	51	53
5	Stockport County	42	15	2	4	45	18	5	6	10	20	31	65	49	48
6	Crewe Alexandra	42	14	4	3	55	31	5	5	11	25	45	80	76	47
7	Oldham Athletic	42	13	5	3	60	25	5	4	12	26	48	86	73	45
8	Hartlepools United	42	13	6	2	41	18	2	6	13	16	43	57	61	42
9	Accrington Stanley	42	12	5	4	43	24	5	3	13	20	48	63	72	42
10	Walsall	42	15	2	4	58	13	1	7	13	21	46	79	59	41
11	Rotherham United	42	14	3	4	52	13	2	6	13	17	53	69	66	41
12	Darlington	42	16	3	2	60	26	1	3	17	14	53	74	79	40
13	Carlisle United	42	13	5	3	44	19	1	7	13	12	43	56	62	40
14	GATESHEAD	42	11	10	0	37	18	2	4	15	19	58	56	76	40
15	Barrow	42	9	9	3	33	16	4	3	14	25	49	58	65	38
16	York City	42	10	8	3	41	28	3	4	14	21	67	62	95	38
17	Halifax Town	42	12	3	6	34	22	3	4	14	23	39	57	61	37
18	Wrexham	42	12	3	6	39	18	3	4	14	27	57	66	75	37
19	Mansfield Town	42	13	5	3	55	25	1	4	16	25	66	80	91	37
20	Rochdale	42	8	10	3	35	26	2	3	16	23	62	58	88	33
21	Southport	42	9	8	4	31	26	2	1	18	17	64	48	90	31
22	New Brighton	42	8	5	8	29	33	1	1	19	14	69	43	102	24

1936/37 21st in Division 3 (North)

Player columns (left to right): Askew J, Bow J, Cassidy W, Conroy T, Dickinson S, Downie W, Harbottle AN, Hartley TW, Heslop R, Hornsby S, Inskip JB, Livingstone A, Mathison G, McDermott J, McKenzie RR, Miller EC, Moore JH, Neilson GH, Oxley A, Pickard F, Quigley JA, Reay JC, Reed G, Short WI, Smith G, Spedding S, Walker H

#		Date	Opponent	Score	Scorers	Att
1	Aug	29	Rotherham United	0-3		6227
2	Sep	2	STOCKPORT COUNTY	0-0		3978
3		5	PORT VALE	0-1		4538
4		7	Stockport County	2-4	Heslop, Miller	6834
5		12	Oldham Athletic	4-4	Hartley, McDermott 2, Miller	3869
6		19	ACCRINGTON STANLEY	1-1	Reay	3760
7		26	Lincoln City	0-4		5329
8	Oct	3	NEW BRIGHTON	1-1	Pickard	2951
9		10	Hull City	2-3	Pickard, McDermott	8080
10		17	Crewe Alexandra	1-3	Turnbull (og)	3255
11		24	CHESTER	1-1	McDermott	3338
12		31	Rochdale	2-0	McDermott, Reay	3991
13	Nov	7	BARROW	1-1	Oxley	2524
14		14	York City	0-2		5511
15		21	CARLISLE UNITED	1-0	Heslop	2903
16	Dec	5	SOUTHPORT	5-4	Oxley, McKenzie, Reed 2, Heslop	2502
17		19	HALIFAX TOWN	0-2		2135
18		25	DARLINGTON	5-0	McDermott, Walker 2, Miller 2	2287
19		26	ROTHERHAM UNITED	2-1	Miller, McDermott	3825
20		28	Darlington	2-0	Oxley, Walker	1621
21	Jan	1	MANSFIELD TOWN	3-3	McDermott, Walker 2	4753
22		2	Port Vale	2-4	Neilson, Miller	8472
23		9	OLDHAM ATHLETIC	0-3		2698
24		16	Hartlepools United	1-6	Moore	7405
25		23	Accrington Stanley	1-2	Moore	3145
26	Feb	6	New Brighton	1-1	Inskip	2941
27		13	HULL CITY	6-3	McDermott, Miller, Oxley, Heslop 2	2332
28		20	CREWE ALEXANDRA	2-0	Walker 2	2463
29	Mar	6	ROCHDALE	3-1	Carr (og), Neilson, McDermott	1726
30		13	Barrow	0-3		5356
31		20	YORK CITY	3-2	Miller 2, McDermott	2233
32		26	WREXHAM	0-0		2963
33		27	Carlisle United	1-2	Walker	5934
34		29	Wrexham	0-6		4159
35	Apr	3	HARTLEPOOLS UNITED	2-2	Walker, Mathison	2738
36		7	LINCOLN CITY	0-5		1224
37		10	Southport	0-3		3817
38		17	TRANMERE ROVERS	4-0	Walker, McDermott 2, Heslop	1674
39		21	Chester	0-6		1765
40		24	Halifax Town	1-2	Miller	4689
41		26	Tranmere Rovers	1-6	Heslop	2379
42	May	1	Mansfield Town	2-3	Mathison, Heslop	3123

Appearances / Goals (by player column)

	Askew J	Bow J	Cassidy W	Conroy T	Dickinson S	Downie W	Harbottle AN	Hartley TW	Heslop R	Hornsby S	Inskip JB	Livingstone A	Mathison G	McDermott J	McKenzie RR	Miller EC	Moore JH	Neilson GH	Oxley A	Pickard F	Quigley JA	Reay JC	Reed G	Short WI	Smith G	Spedding S	Walker H
Apps	6	1	3	42	1	11	34	2	30	8	34	34	26	28	7	38	17	27	28	4	7	15	23	2	2	2	30
Goals								1	8		1		2	13	1	11	2	2	4	2		2	2				10

Two own goals

F.A. Cup

	Date	Opponent	Score	Scorers	Att
R1	Nov 28	NOTTS COUNTY	2-0	Mathison (pen), Reid	11456
R2	Dec 12	Millwall	0-7		18550

F.A. Cup line-ups (shirt numbers): R1 — Askew 1, Conroy 2, Heslop 8, Inskip 5, Livingstone 3, Mathison 6, Neilson 4, Oxley 10, Reay 11, Reed 9, Walker 7. R2 — same.

Third Division (North) Cup

		Opponent	Score
R1		DARLINGTON	3-3
rep		Darlington	0-3

FINAL TABLE

		Pl.	Home W	D	L	F	A	Against W	D	L	F	A	F (Total)	A	Pts
1	Stockport County	42	17	3	1	59	18	6	11	4	25	21	84	39	60
2	Lincoln City	42	18	1	2	65	20	7	6	8	38	37	103	57	57
3	Chester	42	15	5	1	68	21	7	4	10	19	36	87	57	53
4	Oldham Athletic	42	13	7	1	49	25	7	4	10	28	34	77	59	51
5	Hull City	42	13	6	2	39	22	4	6	11	29	47	68	69	46
6	Hartlepools United	42	16	1	4	53	21	3	6	12	22	48	75	69	45
7	Halifax Town	42	12	4	5	40	20	6	5	10	28	43	68	63	45
8	Wrexham	42	12	3	6	41	21	4	9	8	30	36	71	57	44
9	Mansfield Town	42	13	1	7	64	35	5	7	9	27	41	91	76	44
10	Carlisle United	42	13	6	2	42	19	5	2	14	23	49	65	68	44
11	Port Vale	42	12	6	3	39	23	5	4	12	19	41	58	64	44
12	York City	42	13	3	5	54	27	3	6	12	25	43	79	70	43
13	Accrington Stanley	42	14	2	5	51	26	2	7	12	25	43	76	69	41
14	Southport	42	10	8	3	39	28	2	5	14	34	59	73	87	37
15	New Brighton	42	10	8	3	36	16	3	3	15	19	54	55	70	37
16	Barrow	42	11	5	5	42	25	2	5	14	28	61	70	86	36
17	Rotherham United	42	11	7	3	52	28	3	0	18	26	63	78	91	35
18	Rochdale	42	12	3	6	44	27	1	6	14	25	59	69	86	35
19	Tranmere Rovers	42	10	8	3	52	30	2	1	18	19	58	71	88	33
20	Crewe Alexandra	42	6	8	7	31	31	4	4	13	24	52	55	83	32
21	GATESHEAD	42	9	8	4	40	31	2	2	17	23	67	63	98	32
22	Darlington	42	6	8	7	42	46	2	6	13	24	50	66	95	30

1937/38 5th in Division 3 (North)

#	Date	Opponent	Score	Scorers	Att	Cassidy W	Conroy T	Davidson DL	Dudgeon A	Felton ET	Gallantree WL	Harvey GMH	Heslop R	Inskip JB	Keane J	Lawrence W	Livingstone A	McDermott J	McInroy A	Miller EC	Milne W	Neilson GH	Oxley A	Ross J	Smith JT	Storey WCG	Thompson JE	Walker H	Watson A
1	Aug 28	CREWE ALEXANDRA	2-0	Gallantree, Smith	8600		2		5		7		4				3		1	11		6	10		9				8
2	30	Port Vale	2-2	Smith, Gallantree	6699		2		5		7		4				3		1	11		6	10		9				8
3	Sep 4	Barrow	3-1	Inskip, Smith, Watson	5965		2		5		7		4				3		1	11		6	10		9				8
4	8	PORT VALE	2-1	Inskip, Smith	9641		2		5		7		4				3		1	11		6	10		9				8
5	11	WREXHAM	2-2	Oxley, Watson	11210		2		5		7		4				3		1	11		6	10		9				8
6	15	Darlington	2-1	Oxley, Smith	5474		2		5				4				3		1	11		6	10		9			7	8
7	18	Hartlepools United	3-1	Smith, Watson, Oxley	7503		2		5				4				3		1	11		6	10		9			7	8
8	25	LINCOLN CITY	1-1	Watson	20792		2		5				4				3		1	11		6	10		9			7	8
9	Oct 2	Hull City	1-3	Inskip	11082		2		5				4				3		1	11		6	10		9			7	8
10	9	NEW BRIGHTON	3-1	Watson, Oxley, Smith	10713		2		5				4				3		1	11		6	10		9			7	8
11	16	TRANMERE ROVERS	2-1	Miller, Smith	12303		2		5				4				3		1	11		6	10		9			7	8
12	23	Halifax Town	0-2		4075		2		5				4				3		1	11		6	10		9			7	8
13	30	CARLISLE UNITED	2-1	Walker, Oxley	10514		2		5				4				3		1	11		6	10		9			7	8
14	Nov 6	Accrington Stanley	5-1	Smith 3, Inskip, Watson	4647		2		5				4				3		1	11		6	10		9			7	8
15	13	CHESTER	3-1	Watson, Oxley, Miller	13170		2	6	5				4				3		1	11			4		9				8
16	20	Rotherham United	1-1	Smith	8251		2	6	5				4				3		1	11			4		9				8
17	Dec 4	Doncaster Rovers	0-1		10359		2	6	5					10	4		3		1	11					7	9				8
18	25	YORK CITY	2-2	Davidson, Smith	10439		2	6	5				4				3		1	11					9				8
19	27	York City	1-5	Inskip	9069		2	6	5					11	4				1	11	3		9	10					8
20	Jan 1	Crewe Alexandra	3-1	Inskip, Watson, Neilson	4463		2	6	5					11	4	1		7			3		9	10					8
21	8	ROCHDALE	3-1	Smith, McDermott	9504		2	6	5					11	4			7			3		9	10					8
22	15	BARROW	6-0	Smith 2, Inskip, Watson 2, Dudgeon	5894		2	6	5					11	4			7			3			10					8
23	22	Wrexham	0-0		4765		2	6	5					11	4			7			3			10					8
24	29	HARTLEPOOLS UNITED	2-1	McDermott, Miller	7308		2	6	5						4			7	1	11	3		10		9				8
25	Feb 5	Lincoln City	2-3	Davidson, Smith	10944		2	6	5						4			7	1	11	3		10		9				8
26	12	HULL CITY	3-2	Smith, Watson, Inskip	10307		2	6	5						4	3	7	1	11		6	10		9				8
27	19	New Brighton	1-4	Walker	4262		2	6	5						4		3		1	11			10		9			7	8
28	26	Tranmere Rovers	2-4	Watson, Oxley	11662	6	2								4	5	3		1	11			10		7	9			8
29	Mar 5	HALIFAX TOWN	4-1	Felton, Smith, Thompson 2	12276	6	2			5	7				8	4		1	3				10			11	9		
30	12	Carlisle United	0-1		9139	6	2			5	7				10	4				1		3			11		9		8
31	19	ACCRINGTON STANLEY	1-0	Watson	7788	6	2	5								4			1		3			7	11	10	9		8
32	26	Chester	1-2	Smith	3154		2	6	5				7						1	11	3				9	10			8
33	Apr 2	ROTHERHAM UNITED	0-0		8796	6	2		5										1	11	3		10			9			
34	9	Rochdale	2-2	Thompson 2	5240	6	2		5				4		7				1	11	3		10			9			
35	15	Oldham Athletic	1-3	Miller	18615	6	2		5				4		7				1	11	3		10			9			
36	16	DONCASTER ROVERS	2-3	Oxley, Watson	9791	6	2		5						7				1	11	3	4	10		9				8
37	18	OLDHAM ATHLETIC	0-0		6509	6	2		5	7							3		1			4	10		9	11			8
38	23	Southport	0-0		4253	6	2		5	7							3		1			4	10			11	9		
39	25	Bradford City	1-1	Heslop	2585	10	2		5				8	4			3			6	11				7				
40	30	BRADFORD CITY	3-0	Watson, Smith 2	2679	6	2		5				10	4			3		1	11					7		9		8
41	May 2	SOUTHPORT	5-0	Cassidy, Miller 2, Watson 2	1614	6	2		5				10				3		1	11			4		7		9		8
42	7	DARLINGTON	5-2	Smith, Thompson 2, Cassidy, Watson	3002	6	2		5				10				3		1	11			4		7		9		8
		Apps				14	42	14	40	4	13	1	11	33	3	2	16	8	40	31	26	25	35	3	38	3	11	10	39
		Goals				2		2	1	1	2		1	7				2		6		2	8		24		6	2	18

F.A. Cup

	Date	Opponent	Score		Att	Cassidy W	Conroy T	Davidson DL	Dudgeon A	Felton ET	Gallantree WL	Harvey GMH	Heslop R	Inskip JB	Keane J	Lawrence W	Livingstone A	McDermott J	McInroy A	Miller EC	Milne W	Neilson GH	Oxley A	Ross J	Smith JT	Storey WCG	Thompson JE	Walker H	Watson A
R1	Nov 27	Walsall	0-4		7825		2	6					10	7			5					1	11	3	4		9			8

Third Division (North) Cup

	Opponent	Score
R1	Rotherham United	1-0
R3	Bradford City	1-1
rep	BRADFORD CITY	1-4

Bye in R2

	FINAL TABLE	Pl.		Home					Against					F.	A.	Pts
			W	D	L	F	A	W	D	L	F	A		(Total)		
1	Tranmere Rovers	42	15	4	2	57	21	8	6	7	24	20	81	41	56
2	Doncaster Rovers	42	15	4	2	48	16	6	8	7	26	33	74	49	54
3	Hull City	42	11	8	2	51	19	9	6	6	29	24	80	43	53
4	Oldham Athletic	42	16	4	1	48	18	3	9	9	19	28	67	46	51
5	GATESHEAD	42	15	5	1	53	20	5	6	10	31	39	84	59	51
6	Rotherham United	42	13	6	2	45	21	7	4	10	23	35	68	56	50
7	Lincoln City	42	14	3	4	48	17	5	5	11	18	33	66	50	46
8	Crewe Alexandra	42	14	3	4	47	17	4	6	11	24	36	71	53	45
9	Chester	42	13	4	4	54	31	3	8	10	23	41	77	72	44
10	Wrexham	42	14	4	3	37	15	2	7	12	21	48	58	63	43
11	York City	42	11	4	6	40	25	5	6	10	30	43	70	68	42
12	Carlisle United	42	11	5	5	35	19	4	4	13	22	48	57	67	39
13	New Brighton	42	12	5	4	43	18	3	3	15	15	43	60	61	38
14	Bradford City	42	12	6	3	46	21	2	4	15	20	48	66	69	38
15	Port Vale	42	11	8	2	45	27	1	6	14	20	46	65	73	38
16	Southport	42	8	8	5	30	26	4	6	11	23	56	53	82	38
17	Rochdale	42	7	10	4	38	27	6	1	14	29	51	67	78	37
18	Halifax Town	42	9	7	5	24	19	3	5	13	20	47	44	66	36
19	Darlington	42	10	4	7	37	31	1	6	14	17	48	54	79	32
20	Hartlepools United	42	10	8	3	36	20	0	4	17	17	60	53	80	32
21	Barrow	42	9	6	6	28	20	2	4	15	13	51	41	71	32
22	Accrington Stanley	42	9		2 10	31	32	2	5	14	14	43	45	75	29

112

1938/39   10th in Division 3 (North)

	Date		Opponent	Score	Scorers	Att	Barrass RK	Cassidy W	Conroy T	Dudgeon A	Embleton E	Gallacher HR	Harvey GMH	Heslop R	Inskip JB	Keane I	Lawrence W	Livingstone A	McArdle P	McDermott J	McInroy A	McLaughlin JW	Miller EC	Morley JF	Neilson GH	Oxley A	Render I	Sinton IT	Smith IT	Thompson JE	Watson A
1	Aug	27	Crewe Alexandra	2-3	Watson, Heslop	5916		6	2	5				4				3			1				9	10				7	8
2		31	BARROW	2-1	Watson 2	8457		6	2	5		9						3	11		1				4	10		7			8
3	Sep	3	SOUTHPORT	0-0		10742		6	2	5		9						3	11		1				4	10		7			8
4		8	Carlisle United	2-2	Watson, Embleton	11813		6	2	5	10	9					1	3					11			4				7	8
5		10	Doncaster Rovers	3-2	Embleton 2, Gallacher	11334		6	2	5	10	9					1	3					11			8				7	4
6		17	ROTHERHAM UNITED	7-1	Gallacher 5, Oxley, Embleton	12470		6	2	5	10	9		4			1	3					11			8				7	
7		24	Rochdale	2-5	Miller, Embleton	6393		6	2	5	10	9					1	3					11			8				7	4
8	Oct	1	YORK CITY	2-3	Gallacher 2	8723			2	5	10	9		4				3			1		11		6					7	8
9		8	Wrexham	0-2		4433			2		10	9		4	5			3	11		1				6				7		8
10		15	Chester	2-2	Embleton, Oxley	9033			2	5	10	9		4	6			3			1		11			8		7			
11		22	BRADFORD CITY	0-0		7291			2	5	10	9	7	4	6			3			1		11			8					
12		29	Hull City	0-1		9985			2	5	10		7	4	6			3			1		11							9	8
13	Nov	5	LINCOLN CITY	4-0	Smith 3, Miller	4623			2	5	10		7	4	6			3			1		11						9		8
14		12	Stockport County	2-3	Smith, Watson	9425			2	5	10		7	4	6		1	3			1		11						9		8
15		19	ACCRINGTON STANLEY	4-1	Smith 3, Oxley	3947			2	5	7			4	6			3			1		11			10			9		8
16	Dec	3	OLDHAM ATHLETIC	2-0	Barrass, Miller	3735	9	6	2	5				8	4			3			1		11						7	10	
17		10	Barnsley	0-2		11423	9	6	2	5			7		4			3	11		1		10							8	
18		17	NEW BRIGHTON	0-3		2469	9	6	2	5				4		7		3			1		11						10		8
19		24	CREWE ALEXANDRA	0-5		2905		6	2	5	10	9		4	7			3			1		11			8					
20		26	DARLINGTON	0-2		2787	7	6	2	5				4							1		11		3	8			9	10	
21		27	Darlington	2-5	Smith, Thompson	5510		6	2					4						8	1		11		3	10	5		7	9	
22		31	Southport	0-2		6395		6	2	5	10	9										1	11		3				7	8	4
23	Jan	14	DONCASTER ROVERS	2-0	Gallacher, McDermott	2460		6	2	5		9		4					10	7	1		11		3						8
24		21	Rotherham United	2-2	Embleton 2, Gallacher	4133		6	2	5	10	9		4			1		11	7					3						8
25		28	ROCHDALE	2-2	Embleton, McDermott	2846		6	2	5	10	9		4			1		11	7					3						8
26	Feb	4	York City	1-1	Gallacher	5754		6	2	5		9		4			1		11	7					3	10					8
27		11	WREXHAM	5-1	Inskip, Oxley, Gallacher, McArdle 2	2303		6	2	5		9		4					11	7	1				3	10					8
28		18	CHESTER	3-0	Gallacher, Oxley, McDermott	4492		6	2	5		9		4					11	7	1				3	10					8
29		25	Bradford City	1-1	Oxley	6728		6	2	5		9		4					11	7	1			8	3	10					8
30	Mar	4	HULL CITY	2-2	Gallacher, McArdle	4933			2			9	6	4			3	11		7	1					10	5				8
31		11	Lincoln City	0-1		5796			2	5		9		4					11	7	1				3	10		6			8
32		18	STOCKPORT COUNTY	4-1	McArdle, Gallacher, Oxley 2	3746		6	2	5		9		4					11	7	1				3	10					8
33		25	Accrington Stanley	1-1	Oxley	2810		6	2	5		9		4					11	7	1				3	10					8
34	Apr	1	BARNSLEY	1-1	McArdle	8701		6	2	5		9		4					11	7	1				3	10					8
35		7	Hartlepools United	1-3	Cassidy	3992		6	2	5	7			4						7	1				3	10			9		8
36		8	Oldham Athletic	3-1	Miller, Watson, Gallacher	5444		6	2	5		9		4						10		1	11		3				7		8
37		10	HARTLEPOOLS UNITED	2-0	Smith, Miller	4593		6	2	5		9		4						8		1	11		3	10			7		
38		15	HALIFAX TOWN	2-0	Miller, Allsopp (og)	3149		6	2	5		9		4						7	1		11		3	10					8
39		22	New Brighton	1-0	McDermott	2725		6	2	5		9	4						10	7	1		11		3	8					
40		24	Halifax Town	3-3	Gallacher 2, Oxley	1574		6	2	5		9	4						10	7	1		11		3	8					
41		29	Barrow	1-1	Dudgeon	4669			2	5		9	4					3	10		1		11		6	8		7			
42	May	6	CARLISLE UNITED	1-1	Gallacher	3483		6	2	5		9	4						10	7	1		11		3	8					

	Barrass RK	Cassidy W	Conroy T	Dudgeon A	Embleton E	Gallacher HR	Harvey GMH	Heslop R	Inskip JB	Keane I	Lawrence W	Livingstone A	McArdle P	McDermott J	McInroy A	McLaughlin JW	Miller EC	Morley JF	Neilson GH	Oxley A	Render I	Sinton IT	Smith IT	Thompson JE	Watson A
Apps	4	31	42	39	17	31	5	19	26	2	8	21	20	19	31	3	28	1	27	29	2	3	13	13	28
Goals	1	1			9	18		1	1				5	4			6			10			9	1	6

One own goal

F.A. Cup

		Date		Opponent	Score	Scorers	Att			Conroy T	Dudgeon A	Embleton E				Inskip JB						McInroy A		Miller EC			Oxley A			Smith IT	Thompson JE	Watson A
R1	Nov	26	Gainsborough Trinity	1-2	Miller	5000			2	5	10			6				3			1		11			8			9	7	4

Third Division (North) Cup

		Opponent	Score
R1		CARLISLE UNITED	4-2
R2		HARTLEPOOLS UNITED	0-0
rep		Hartlepools United	1-5

	FINAL TABLE	Pl.	Home W	D	L	F	A	Against W	D	L	F	A	F. (Total)	A.	Pts
1	Barnsley	42	18	2	1	60	12	12	5	4	34	22	94	34	67
2	Doncaster Rovers	42	12	5	4	47	21	9	9	3	40	26	87	47	56
3	Bradford City	42	16	2	3	59	21	6	6	9	30	35	89	56	52
4	Southport	42	14	5	2	47	16	6	5	10	28	38	75	54	50
5	Oldham Athletic	42	16	1	4	51	21	6	4	11	25	38	76	59	49
6	Chester	42	12	5	4	54	31	8	4	9	34	39	88	70	49
7	Hull City	42	13	5	3	57	25	5	5	11	26	49	83	74	46
8	Crewe Alexandra	42	12	5	4	54	23	7	1	13	26	47	82	70	44
9	Stockport County	42	13	6	2	57	24	4	3	14	34	53	91	77	43
10	GATESHEAD	42	11	6	4	45	24	3	8	10	29	43	74	67	42
11	Rotherham United	42	12	4	5	45	21	5	4	12	19	43	64	64	42
12	Halifax Town	42	9	10	2	33	22	4	6	11	19	32	52	54	42
13	Barrow	42	11	5	5	46	22	5	4	12	20	43	66	65	41
14	Wrexham	42	15	2	4	46	28	2	5	14	20	51	66	79	41
15	Rochdale	42	10	5	6	58	29	5	4	12	34	53	92	82	39
16	New Brighton	42	11	2	8	46	32	4	7	10	22	41	68	73	39
17	Lincoln City	42	9	6	6	40	33	3	3	15	26	59	66	92	33
18	Darlington	42	12	2	7	43	30	1	5	15	19	62	62	92	33
19	Carlisle United	42	10	5	6	44	33	3	2	16	22	78	66	111	33
20	York City	42	8	5	8	37	34	4	3	14	27	58	64	92	32
21	Hartlepools United	42	10	4	7	36	33	2	3	16	19	61	55	94	31
22	Accrington Stanley	42	6	5	10	30	39	1	1	19	19	64	49	103	20

1946/47 14th in Division 3 (North)

#	Date		Opponent	Score	Scorers	Att.
1	Aug	31	CREWE ALEXANDRA	2-1	Clark, Howdon	5146
2	Sep	4	HARTLEPOOLS UNITED	0-1		3740
3		7	Lincoln City	0-4		9099
4		14	SOUTHPORT	2-2	Gallon, Rutherford	4322
5		16	Hull City	2-1	McCormack 2	17770
6		21	Rotherham United	0-4		13956
7		28	CHESTER	3-4	McCormack 3	4842
8	Oct	5	York City	1-3	McCormack	8502
9		12	TRANMERE ROVERS	3-1	Oliver, Johnson, McCorm...	5132
10		19	CARLISLE UNITED	1-3	Temple	7037
11		26	Halifax Town	1-2	McCormack	3372
12	Nov	2	NEW BRIGHTON	3-0	Oxley, Ramsey, J Callend...	4264
13		9	Rochdale	3-2	Small 2, McCormack	8031
14		16	DONCASTER ROVERS	1-3	McCormack	7646
15		23	Wrexham	0-2		6480
16	Dec	7	Oldham Athletic	1-1	Small	9368
17		21	Barrow	0-1		4478
18		25	ACCRINGTON STANLEY	2-1	McCormack, Small	3540
19		26	Accrington Stanley	3-0	McCormack 2, Briggs (o...	5099
20		28	Crewe Alexandra	1-1	McCormack	6057
21	Jan	1	HULL CITY	1-0	Cassidy	5277
22		2	BRADFORD CITY	1-2	Small (p)	6208
23		4	LINCOLN CITY	3-0	Gallon, McCormack 2	5263
24		15	STOCKPORT COUNTY	1-2	Johnson	2271
25		18	Southport	1-2	Johnson	4729
26		25	ROTHERHAM UNITED	2-0	J Callender, Johnson	5673
27	Feb	1	Chester	1-0	Beattie	5454
28		15	Tranmere Rovers	0-1		7282
29		22	Carlisle United	1-3	McCormack	7196
30	Mar	8	New Brighton	3-2	Johnson, Beattie 2	4252
31		22	Doncaster Rovers	0-3		15481
32		29	WREXHAM	3-3	McCormack, Johnson, Beattie	1874
33	Apr	4	Darlington	0-2		8139
34		5	Stockport County	0-2		7693
35		7	DARLINGTON	1-0	J Callender	4998
36		12	OLDHAM ATHLETIC	1-0	T Callender	3692
37		19	Bradford City	2-2	Bradford (og), McCorma...	9340
38		26	BARROW	0-5		2365
39	May	3	HALIFAX TOWN	6-1	Forster 2, Small, Skeen, Johnson 2	1292
40		17	ROCHDALE	2-2	Johnson, Forster	4314
41		24	YORK CITY	1-2	Skeen	3756
42		26	Hartlepools United	3-1	Small 3	7000

Played in one game: TB Hetherington (game 9, at 1), JD Lough (game 37 at 11)

Player columns: Atkinson FJ, Beattie T, Bell JH, Callender JW, Callender TS, Cassidy W, Clark H, Dawson E, Forster LJ, Gallon JW, Howdon S, Hutchinson D, Johnson T, McCormack JC, McDougall L, Oliver G, Passmore E, Purvis B, Oxley A, Ramsay GA, Robinson E, Rutherford R, Skeen G, Small ML, Temple W, Thompson KH, Thompson W, Weddle GD, Whalley GD, Wilson A

Apps: 3, 17, 35, 36, 42, 16, 21, 36, 12, 20, 2, 3, 31, 29, 28, 13, 1, 1, 2, 9, 8, 6, 32, 21, 10, 9, 2, 5, 5, 5

Goals: 4, –, 3, 1, 1, 1, –, –, 3, 2, 1, –, –, 9, 19, –, 1, –, –, 1, 1, –, 1, 2, 9, 1, –, –, –, –

Two own goals

F.A. Cup

R	Date		Opponent	Score	Scorers	Att.
R1	Nov	30	BRADFORD CITY	3-1	Small 2, McCormack	8653
R2	Dec	14	LANCASTER CITY	4-0	Gallon, T Callender, McC...	7640
R3	Jan	11	Manchester City	0-3		38575

FINAL TABLE

		Pl.	W	D	L	F	A	W	D	L	F	A	F.	A.	Pts
				Home					Against					(Total)	
1	Doncaster Rovers	42	15	5	1	67	16	18	1	2	56	24	123	40	72
2	Rotherham United	42	20	1	0	81	19	9	5	7	33	34	114	53	64
3	Chester	42	17	2	2	53	13	8	4	9	42	38	95	51	56
4	Stockport County	42	17	0	4	50	19	7	2	12	28	34	78	53	50
5	Bradford City	42	12	5	4	40	20	8	5	8	22	27	62	47	50
6	Rochdale	42	9	5	7	39	25	10	5	6	41	39	80	64	48
7	Wrexham	42	13	5	3	43	21	4	7	10	22	30	65	51	46
8	Crewe Alexandra	42	12	4	5	39	26	5	5	11	31	48	70	74	43
9	Barrow	42	10	2	9	28	24	7	5	9	26	38	54	62	41
10	Tranmere Rovers	42	11	5	5	43	30	6	2	13	23	44	66	77	41
11	Hull City	42	9	5	7	23	19	7	3	11	24	34	49	53	40
12	Lincoln City	42	12	3	6	52	32	5	2	14	34	55	86	87	39
13	Hartlepools United	42	10	5	6	36	26	5	4	12	28	47	64	73	39
14	GATESHEAD	42	10	3	8	39	33	6	3	12	23	39	62	72	38
15	York City	42	8	4	11	36	42	8	5	8	32	39	67	81	37
16	Carlisle United	42	10	5	6	45	38	4	4	13	25	55	70	93	37
17	Darlington	42	12	4	5	48	26	3	2	16	20	54	68	80	36
18	New Brighton	42	11	3	7	37	30	3	5	13	20	47	57	77	36
19	Oldham Athletic	42	6	5	10	29	31	6	3	12	26	49	55	80	32
20	Accrington Stanley	42	8	3	10	37	38	6	1	14	19	54	56	92	32
21	Southport	42	6	5	10	35	41	1	6	14	18	44	53	85	25
22	Halifax Town	42	6	3	12	28	36	2	3	16	15	56	43	92	22

1947/48 4th in Division 3 (North)

#		Date	Opponent	Score	Scorers	Att	Atkinson FJ	Beattie T	Bell JH	Callender JW	Callender TS	Cassidy W	Dawson E	Forster LJ	Gray R	Harrison R	Hawkins GH	Hood GW	Ingham RJ	Johnson T	Marley G	McDougall L	Passmore E	Robinson E	Rutherford R	Skeen G	Small ML	Smirk AH	Thompson W	Weddle GD	Wilbert GN	Wyles H
1	Aug	23	Rotherham United	0-0		12205			3	4	5					11	8								2			6	9		10	
2		27	DARLINGTON	1-2	Harrison	5721				4	5		1	7		11	8								3			6	9		10	
3		30	CARLISLE UNITED	1-3	T Callender (pen)	8831				4	5		1			11	9		7	8					3		2	6	10			
4	Sep	1	Darlington	1-1	Johnson	7151			3		5	4	1				10		7	8								6	9		11	
5		6	Crewe Alexandra	1-0	Small	7829			3		5	4	1				10		7	8			2					6	9		11	
6		9	Tranmere Rovers	0-3		9124	2				5	4		1				3	7	8				9				6	10		11	
7		13	CHESTER	2-1	Hawkins, Weddle	5987			3		5	4	1				10		7	8			2					6	9		11	
8		20	Mansfield Town	2-1	Ingham, Johnson	9879			2		5	4	1				10		7	8			3	9				6			11	
9		27	YORK CITY	0-0		6723					5	4	1				10		7	8			3	9	2			6			11	
10	Oct	4	Oldham Athletic	1-0	Ingham	16992	3	9			5	4	1				10		7			8	2					6			11	
11		11	Accrington Stanley	0-1		7265			3		5	4	1				9		7				10	2				6	8		11	
12		18	HULL CITY	0-1		7684			3	4	5		1				9		7	8	10		2					6			11	
13		25	Stockport County	1-1	Robinson	10237				4	5		1					3	7			10	2	9	11			6	8			
14	Nov	1	BRADFORD CITY	2-2	J Callender, Hawkins	5623				4	5		1				9	3	7			10	2					6	8			11
15		8	Barrow	2-1	Small, Wilbert	8307				4	5		1			10	9	3	7				2					6	8			11
16		15	WREXHAM	2-2	T Callender (p), Johnson	5414				4	5		1			7	9	3			10		2					6	8			11
17		22	Halifax Town	0-0		5277				8	5	4	1			7		3			10		2					6	9			11
18	Dec	6	New Brighton	2-1	Johnson, Ingham	4025				4	5	6	1			7	3	9	8				2								10	11
19		13	Southport	1-2	Hawkins	5065				4	5	6	1			7	3	9	8				2								10	11
20		20	ROTHERHAM UNITED	1-1	Weddle	5200			3	4	5				1		9		10	8			2				6				7	11
21		25	HARTLEPOOLS UNITED	7-0	T Callender,Weddle,Cassidy,Hawkins 2,Johnson 2	6329			3	4	5	6			1		9		10	8			2								7	11
22		27	Hartlepools United	2-3	Hawkins, T Callender(pen)	6608			3	4	5	6			1		10		7	8			2	9								11
23	Jan	1	TRANMERE ROVERS	3-0	J Callender, Johnson, Hawkins	3885				8	5	4	1				9	3	7	10			2				6					11
24		3	Carlisle United	1-1	Small	14771				8	5	4	1				9	3					2				6	10			7	11
25		10	ROCHDALE	5-0	Hawkins 3, Wilbert, Weddle	3857				8	5	4	1				9	3					2				6	10			7	11
26		17	CREWE ALEXANDRA	2-0	Hawkins, Wilbert	7291				8	5	4	1				9	3					2				6	10			7	11
27		24	SOUTHPORT	3-2	Small 2, J Callender	7048			3	8	5	4	1				9	2									6	10			7	11
28		31	Chester	3-2	J Callender 2, Weddle	6721				8	5	4	1				9	3					2				6	10			7	11
29	Feb	7	MANSFIELD TOWN	2-1	J Callender, Small	9718				8	5	4	1				7	3		10			2				6	9				11
30		14	York City	1-3	Johnson	7611				8	5	4	1				3	7	10				2				6	9				11
31		21	OLDHAM ATHLETIC	3-5	Small 2, Hawkins	4572				4	5		1				9	3	7				2				6	8			10	11
32		28	ACCRINGTON STANLEY	4-2	Wilbert 2, Skeen, Small	7262				4	5		1				3		8				9				6	10	7		11	2
33	Mar	6	Hull City	3-2	Passmore, Johnson 2	17737				4	5		1						10				9		3	6	8	7		11	2
34		13	STOCKPORT COUNTY	1-1	Smirk	6967				4	5		1						10		3	9				6	8	7		11	2
35		20	Bradford City	2-2	Small, Weddle	9152				4	5		1				3					9				6	8	7		10	11	2
36		26	Lincoln City	0-3		17657				4	5		1				3					9				6	8	7		10	11	2
37		27	BARROW	0-2		7619				8	5	4		1			3									6	10	7	9		11	2
38		29	LINCOLN CITY	3-2	Wilbert, Smirk, T Callender(pen)	9673				8	5	4	1				3									6	9	7		10	11	2
39	Apr	3	Wrexham	3-0	Wilbert, Smirk, Weddle	10197				8	5	4		1			3									6	9	7		10	11	2
40		10	HALIFAX TOWN	3-0	Small 2, T Callender(pen)	4826				8	5	4		1			3									6	9	7		10	11	2
41		17	Rochdale	1-2	J Callender	7031				8	5	4		1			3									6	9	7		10	11	2
42		24	NEW BRIGHTON	3-1	Weddle, Smirk, J Callender	2923				8	5	4		1			3									6	9	7		10	11	2
			Apps				2	1	11	34	42	27	31	2	11	6	27	26	21	21	5	29	11	5	1	38	31	11	1	28	29	11
			Goals							8	6	1				1	12		3	10			1	1		1	12	4		8	7	

F.A. Cup

		Date	Opponent	Score	Scorers	Att				Callender JW	Callender TS		Dawson E				Hawkins GH	Hood GW	Ingham RJ			McDougall L				Skeen G	Small ML					Wyles H
R1	Nov	29	BRADFORD CITY	1-3	Small	9223				4	5		1				7	10	3			8		2			6	9				11

FINAL TABLE

		Pl.	Home					Against					F.	A.	Pts
			W	D	L	F	A	W	D	L	F	A	(Total)		
1	Lincoln City	42	14	3	4	47	18	12	5	4	34	22	81	40	60
2	Rotherham United	42	15	4	2	56	18	10	5	6	39	31	95	49	59
3	Wrexham	42	14	3	4	49	23	7	5	9	25	31	74	54	50
4	GATESHEAD	42	11	5	5	48	28	8	6	7	27	29	75	57	49
5	Hull City	42	12	5	4	38	21	6	6	9	21	27	59	48	47
6	Accrington Stanley	42	13	1	7	36	24	7	5	9	26	35	62	59	46
7	Barrow	42	9	4	8	24	19	7	9	5	25	21	49	40	45
8	Mansfield Town	42	11	4	6	37	24	6	7	8	20	27	57	51	45
9	Carlisle United	42	10	4	7	50	35	8	3	10	38	42	88	77	43
10	Crewe Alexandra	42	12	4	5	41	24	6	3	12	20	39	61	63	43
11	Oldham Athletic	42	6	10	5	25	25	8	3	10	38	39	63	64	41
12	Rochdale	42	12	4	5	32	23	3	7	11	16	49	48	72	41
13	York City	42	8	7	6	36	25	5	7	9	27	35	65	60	40
14	Bradford City	42	10	4	7	38	27	5	6	10	27	39	65	66	40
15	Southport	42	10	4	7	34	27	4	7	10	26	36	60	63	39
16	Darlington	42	7	8	6	30	31	6	5	10	24	39	54	70	39
17	Stockport County	42	9	6	6	42	28	4	6	11	21	39	63	67	38
18	Tranmere Rovers	42	10	1	10	30	28	6	3	12	24	44	54	72	36
19	Hartlepools United	42	10	6	5	34	23	4	2	15	17	50	51	73	36
20	Chester	42	11	6	4	44	25	2	3	16	20	42	64	67	35
21	Halifax Town	42	4	10	7	25	27	3	3	15	18	49	43	76	27
22	New Brighton	42	5	6	10	20	28	3	3	15	18	53	38	81	25

1948/49 5th in Division 3 (North)

No	Date	Opponent	Score	Scorers	Att	Atkinson FJ	Bell JH	Cairns RL	Callender IW	Callender TS	Cassidy W	Dawson E	Gray R	Hetherington H	Hood GW	Ingham RJ	Kendall JB	Marley G	McDougall L	Passmore E	Robinson E	Skeen G	Small ML	Weddle GD	Wilbert GN	Winters IA	Woodburn J	Wyles H
1	Aug 21	NEW BRIGHTON	3-0	Ingham, Passmore 2	6100	6			5	4			1		3	7				9					8	10	11	2
2	24	Rochdale	0-3		9955	6			5	4			1		3	7				9					8	10	11	2
3	28	Chester	1-1	Weddell	8734	6			4	5			1		3	7				9				10	8		11	2
4	30	ROCHDALE	2-1	Weddell, Small	7410	4	3		8	5			1			7				9			6	10			11	2
5	Sep 4	SOUTHPORT	2-2	Passmore, Wilbert	6359	4			8	5			1		3	7				9			6	10			11	2
6	8	Darlington	3-1	Passmore 2, Small	10609	4		2	8	5			1			7				9			6	10			11	3
7	11	Crewe Alexandra	1-2	Passmore	8577	6		2	4	5			1			7			8	9				10			11	3
8	13	DARLINGTON	1-3	Small	7293	6		2	4	5			1			7			8	9				10			11	3
9	18	YORK CITY	1-1	Passmore	6502	4	3		8	5			1			7				9			6	10			11	2
10	25	Stockport County	1-3	J Callender	12325	4			8	5			1			7	10			9	3		6				11	2
11	Oct 2	CARLISLE UNITED	3-0	J Callender 2, Small	11674	8			4	5			1			7	10			9	3		6				11	2
12	9	DONCASTER ROVERS	0-3		8552	8			4	5			1			7	10			9	3		6				11	2
13	16	Bradford City	1-1	Hinsley (og)	11335	4		2	8	5			1			7				9	6			10			11	3
14	23	HALIFAX TOWN	1-2	Small	6026	4		2	8	5			1			7	10			9			6				11	3
15	30	Wrexham	4-1	Wilbert 3, Small	8989	8		2	4	5			1			7	10			11			6		9			3
16	Nov 6	BARROW	3-0	Ingham, Robinson, Wilbert	5631	8		2	4	5			1			7	10			11	6				9			3
17	13	Mansfield Town	1-1	Ingham	8983	8	3		4	5			1			7	10			11					9	6		2
18	20	TRANMERE ROVERS	3-3	Atkinson 2, J Callender	5439	8		2	4	5			1			7	10			11					9	6		3
19	Dec 4	ACCRINGTON STANLEY	1-1	Ingham	5916	8		2	4	5			1			7	10			11					9	6		3
20	18	Rotherham United	0-1		12716	8		2	4	5			1			7	10			11					9	6		3
21	25	HARTLEPOOLS UNITED	2-1	Ingham, Robinson	7146	8		2	4	5			1			7	10			11					9	6		3
22	27	Hartlepools United	3-1	T Callender (p), Wilbert 2	9035	8		2	4	5			1			7	10			11					9	6		3
23	Jan 1	CHESTER	2-1	Wilbert, Atkinson	8720	8		2	4	5			1			7	10			11					9	6		3
24	15	Southport	3-0	Wilbert, Atkinson, Hetherington	4604	8		2	4	5			1	7		10				11					9	6		3
25	22	CREWE ALEXANDRA	4-1	Wilbert, Atkinson, Ingham 2	10139	8		2	4	5			1	7		10				11					9	6		3
26	Feb 5	York City	1-0	Robinson	9704	8		2	4	5			1			7	10			11	6				9			3
27	19	STOCKPORT COUNTY	0-1		8619	8		2	4	5			1			7	10			11					9	6		3
28	26	Carlisle United	1-2	Simpson (og)	10375			2	4	5			1			7	10			11					9	6	8	3
29	Mar 5	Doncaster Rovers	1-2	Ingham	6273			2	4	5						7	10			11	6	1			9		8	3
30	12	BRADFORD CITY	6-2	Wilbert 2, Winters, T Callender, Kendall, Ingham	4476			2	4	5						7	10			11	6	1			9	8		3
31	19	Halifax Town	2-2	Ingham 2	7692			2	4	5						7	10			11	6	1			9	8		3
32	26	WREXHAM	2-0	Wilbert 2	4620			2	4	5						7	10			11	6	1			9	8		3
33	Apr 2	Barrow	0-3		3662			2	4	5						7	10			11	6	1			9	8		3
34	9	MANSFIELD TOWN	0-0		3958			2	4	5						7	10			11	6	1			9	8		3
35	12	Oldham Athletic	0-0		13317					5	6					9	10	7	2	4	11	1				8		3
36	15	Hull City	0-2		43795			2	8	5	6	7				9		4		11	10	1						3
37	16	Tranmere Rovers	1-1	Robinson	6411			2	4	5		7				9				11	6	1				10	8	3
38	18	HULL CITY	0-2		17538			2	8	5	6	7				9		4		11	10	1						3
39	23	OLDHAM ATHLETIC	2-2	Ingham, Winters	5308			2	8	5	6	7				9		4		11		1				10		3
40	30	Accrington Stanley	2-1	Winters, Kendall	3564			2	4	5	6	7					10			11		1			9	8		3
41	May 4	New Brighton	2-2	Atkinson, Passmore	5032	8		2	4	5	6	7								9		1				11	10	3
42	7	ROTHERHAM UNITED	3-2	Winters 2, Passmore	6586	8		2	4	5	6	7								9		1				11	10	3
Apps						27	3	31	39	42	11	16	26	2	4	35	22	2	3	16	24	14	23	13	34	15	18	42
Goals						6			4	2				1		12	2			9	4		6	2	14	5		

Two own goals

F.A. Cup

R	Date	Opponent	Score	Scorers	Att	Atkinson FJ	Cairns RL	Callender IW	Callender TS	Gray R	Hetherington H	Ingham RJ	Kendall JB	Passmore E	Robinson E	Small ML	Wilbert GN	Winters IA	Woodburn J	Wyles H
R1	Nov 27	NETHERFIELD	3-0	J Callender (p), Small, Atkinson	7028	8	2	4	5	1		7	10	11		6	9			3
R2	Dec 11	SCARBOROUGH	3-0	T Callender (p), Ingham, Robinson	9114		2	4	5	1	8	7	10	11	6		9	3		
R3	Jan 8	ALDERSHOT	3-1	Kendall 2, Wilbert	11266	8	2	4	5	1		7	10	11			9	6		3
R4	29	WEST BROMWICH ALB.	1-3 (aet)	J Callender	17000	8	2	4	5	1		7	10	11			9	6		3

116

1949/50 2nd in Division 3 (North)

#		Date	Opponent	Score	Scorers	Att.	Bell JH	Buchan WRM	Cairns RL	Callender JW	Callender TS	Campbell J	Cassidy W	Charlton JA	Fowler HN	Gray R	Ingham RJ	Kendall JB	Malpass FL	Marley G	Passmore E	Robinson E	Skeen G	Small ML	Wilbert GN	Winters IA	Woodburn J	Wyles H	Young JR
1	Aug	20	Rochdale	3-1	Wilbert, Ingham 2	6837			2	4	5					1	7				9				10	11	8	6	3
2		22	HALIFAX TOWN	7-1	Passmore 4, Wilbert, Ingham, Small	9740			2	4	5						7				9				10	11	8	6	3
3		27	BRADFORD CITY	4-2	Callender T(pen),Callender J,Winters,Passmore	13384			2	4	5			1			7				9				10	11	8	6	3
4			Halifax Town	2-5	Callender T(pen), Passmore	5923			2	6	5						7				9				10	11	8	4	3
5	Sep	3	Chester	3-0	Passmore 3	7695			2	4	5						7				9				10	11	8	6	3
6		5	Hartlepools United	5-3	Passmore 5	12078			2		5	4					7				9				10	11	8	6	3
7		10	SOUTHPORT	3-2	Cassidy,Callender T(pen), Passmore	14254			2		5	4			1	7					9				10	11	8	6	3
8		17	Stockport County	1-2	Small	11948			2	4	5				1	7					9				10	11	8	6	3
9		24	DONCASTER ROVERS	1-1	Wilbert	14973			2	4	5				1	7					9				10	11	8	6	3
10	Oct	1	Lincoln City	0-2		13405			2	4	5					7					9	3			10	11	8	6	
11		8	ROTHERHAM UNITED	2-2	Wilbert 2	10943			2	4	5					7		1			9				10	11	8	6	3
12		15	Carlisle United	2-4	Callender T(pen), Passmore	16578			2	8	5	4				7		1		6	9				10	11		3	
13		22	MANSFIELD TOWN	0-1		11157			2	4	5				1	7				6	9				10	11	8		3
14		29	Accrington Stanley	1-0	Robinson	5636			2	4	5				1	7						11			10	9	8	6	3
15	Nov	5	WREXHAM	0-1		7231			2	4	5				1	7						11			10	9	8	6	3
16		12	Oldham Athletic	0-1		10224	3			4	5				1	7						8			9	10	6	2	
17		19	YORK CITY	1-1	J Callender	5617				4	5	11			1	7						3	8		9	10	6	2	
18	Dec	3	CREWE ALEXANDRA	1-1	Ingham	9003		8		4	5	11			3	1	7				10				9		6	2	
19		17	ROCHDALE	1-3	Kendall	3997				4	5	11			3	1	7	9		10					8		6	2	
20		24	Bradford City	1-2	Wilbert	16003		10		4	5				3	1	8	9				7			11		6	2	
21		26	Darlington	3-2	Callender J 2, Robinson	10021		10		4	5				3	1	7	8				11			9		6	2	
22		27	DARLINGTON	3-3	Wilbert,Ingham,Callender T(pen)	9381		10		4	5				3	1	7	8				11			9		6	2	
23		31	CHESTER	4-0	Kendall 2, Ingham,Callender T	6542				4	5				3	1	7	8				11			9		6	2	
24	Jan	2	HARTLEPOOLS UNITED	2-0	Kendall, Wilbert	9813				4	5				3	1	7	8				10			9	11	6	2	
25		14	Southport	3-0	Woodburn, Marley, Wilbert	7765				4	5				3	1	7	8		10					9	11	6	2	
26		21	STOCKPORT COUNTY	1-0	Ingham	7723				4	5				3	1	7	8		10		11			9		6	2	
27		28	Tranmere Rovers	0-1		7414		11		4	5				3	1	7	8		10					9		6	2	
28	Feb	4	Doncaster Rovers	1-1	Callender T	22207				4	5	11			3	1	7	8		10					9		6	2	
29		11	Barrow	1-1	Campbell	4952				4	5	11			3	1	7	8		10					9		6	2	
30		18	LINCOLN CITY	2-1	Callender T(pen), Campbell	10751				4	5	11			3	1	7	8		10					9		6	2	
31		25	York City	5-1	Kendall 2, Wilbert, Marley, Ingham	5465				4		11	5		3	1	7	8		10					9		6	2	
32	Mar	4	TRANMERE ROVERS	5-1	Wilbert 3, Kendal, Campbell	7422				4	5	11	6		3	1	7	8		10					9		6	2	
33		11	Mansfield Town	0-1		8530				4	5	11			3	1	7	8		10					9		6	2	
34		18	ACCRINGTON STANLEY	5-0	Kendall 3, Wilbert, Campbell	6851		10		4	5	11			3	1	7	8							9		6	2	
35		25	Wrexham	1-0	Wilbert	5291		10		4	5	11			3	1	7	8							9		6	2	
36	Apr	1	OLDHAM ATHLETIC	2-0	Buchan 2	7898		10		4	5	11			3	1	7	8							9		6	2	
37		7	New Brighton	1-0	Kendall	6095		10		4	5	11			3	1	7	8							9		6	2	
38		8	Rotherham United	2-1	Ingham, Wilbert	8405		10		4	5	11			3	1	7	8							9		6	2	
39		10	NEW BRIGHTON	2-1	Ingham. Campbell	9172		10		4	5	11			3	1	7	8							9		6	2	
40		15	CARLISLE UNITED	2-1	Kendall. Wilbert	12067		10		4	5	11			3	1	7	8							9		6	2	
41		22	Crewe Alexandra	1-3	Wilbert	6380		10		4	5	11			3	1	7	8							9		6	2	
42		29	BARROW	3-1	Kendall, Buchan,Callender J	5303		10		4	5	11			3	1	7	8							9		6	2	
					Apps		1	14	15	40	41	18	5	1	25	34	42	24	3	15	13	12	2	15	40	17	40	41	4
					Goals			3		5	8	5	1				10	13		2	16	2		2	18	1	1		

F.A. Cup

		Date	Opponent	Score	Scorers	Att.	Buchan WRM	Callender JW	Callender TS	Campbell J	Fowler HN	Gray R	Ingham RJ	Kendall JB	Marley G	Winters IA	Wilbert GN	Woodburn J	Wyles H
R1	Nov	26	YORK CITY	3-1	Marley 2, Campbell	6144		4	5	11		1	7	8	10	3	9	6	2
R2	Dec	10	Newport County	1-1	Winters	15184	10	4	5	11	3	1	7	8			9	6	2
rep		15	NEWPORT COUNTY	1-2 (aet)	J Callender	13634	10	4	5	11	3	1	7	8			9	6	2

	FINAL TABLE	Pl.	Home W	D	L	F	A	Away W	D	L	F	A	F.	A.	Pts
1	Doncaster Rovers	42	9	9	3	30	15	10	8	3	36	23	66	38	55
2	GATESHEAD	42	13	5	3	51	23	10	2	9	36	31	87	54	53
3	Rochdale	42	15	3	3	42	13	6	6	9	26	28	68	41	51
4	Lincoln City	42	14	5	2	35	9	7	4	10	25	30	60	39	51
5	Tranmere Rovers	42	15	3	3	35	21	4	8	9	16	27	51	48	49
6	Rotherham United	42	10	6	5	46	28	9	4	8	34	31	80	59	48
7	Crewe Alexandra	42	10	6	5	38	27	7	8	6	30	28	68	55	48
8	Mansfield Town	42	12	4	5	37	20	6	8	7	29	34	66	54	48
9	Carlisle United	42	12	6	3	39	20	4	9	8	29	31	68	51	47
10	Stockport County	42	14	2	5	33	21	5	5	11	22	31	55	52	45
11	Oldham Athletic	42	10	4	7	32	31	6	7	8	26	32	58	63	43
12	Chester	42	12	3	6	47	33	5	3	13	23	46	70	79	40
13	Accrington Stanley	42	12	5	4	41	21	4	2	15	16	41	57	62	39
14	New Brighton	42	10	5	6	27	25	4	5	12	18	38	45	63	38
15	Barrow	42	9	6	6	27	20	5	3	13	20	33	47	53	37
16	Southport	42	7	10	4	29	26	5	3	13	22	45	51	71	37
17	Darlington	42	9	8	4	35	27	2	5	14	21	42	56	69	35
18	Hartlepools United	42	10	3	8	37	35	4	2	15	15	44	52	79	33
19	Bradford City	42	11	1	9	38	32	1	7	13	23	44	61	76	32
20	Wrexham	42	8	7	6	24	17	2	5	14	15	37	39	54	32
21	Halifax Town	42	9	5	7	35	31	3	3	15	23	54	58	85	32
22	York City	42	6	7	8	29	33	3	6	12	23	37	52	70	31

1950/51   8th in Division 3 (North)

#	Mon	Date	Opponent	Res	Scorers	Att	Gray	Wyles	Fowler	Callender J	Callender T	Woodburn	Ingham	Kendall	Wilbert	Buchan	Campbell	Winters	Cairns	Cassidy	Small	Robinson	Palmer	Johnson	Brown
1	Aug	19	ACCRINGTON STANLEY	7-0	Kendall 4, Wilbert 2, Buchan	9623	1	2	3	4	5	6	7	8	9	10	11								
2		24	Carlisle United	0-3		12016	1	2	3	4	5	6	7	8	9	10	11								
3		26	Crewe Alexandra	1-0	Winters	8359	1	2	3	4	5	6	8		9	10	11	7							
4		28	CARLISLE UNITED	4-3	Winters, Wilbert 3	14896	1	2	3	4	5	6	8		9	10	11	7							
5	Sep	2	NEW BRIGHTON	4-0	Winters, Buchan 2, Campbell	14037	1	2	3	4	5	6	7		9	10	11	8							
6		4	HALIFAX TOWN	5-0	Winters 2, Wilbert, Buchan, Campbell	13035	1	2	3	4	5	6	7		9	10	11	8							
7		9	Bradford City	2-2	Callender T.(pen), Wilbert	15607	1	2	3	4	5	6	7		9	10	11	8							
8		11	Halifax Town	0-1		6468	1	2	3	4	5	6	7	8	9	10	11								
9		16	ROCHDALE	4-1	Callender T.(pen), Winters, Wilbert 2	13607	1	2	3	4	5	6	7		9	10	11	8							
10		18	STOCKPORT COUNTY	2-0	Callender J. 2	11196	1	2	3	4	5	6	7		9	10	11	8							
11		23	Chester	2-2	Winters, Buchan	10363	1	2	3	4	5	6	7		9	10	11	8							
12		30	SHREWSBURY TOWN	3-0	Ingham, Winters 2	9570	1	2	3	4	5	6	7		9	10	11	8							
13	Oct	7	SCUNTHORPE UNITED	1-0	Ingham	11903	1	2	3	4	5	6	7		9	10	11	8							
14		14	Wrexham	0-0		11228	1	2	3	4	5	6	7		9	10	11	8							
15		21	ROTHERHAM UNITED	0-3		14039	1	2	3	4	5	6	7		9	10	11	8							
16		28	Mansfield Town	1-2	Ingham	13349	1	2	3	4	5	6	7		9	10	11	8							
17	Nov	4	YORK CITY	3-0	Callender T.(pen), Ingham, Winters	7614	1	2	3	4	5	6	7		9	10	11	8							
18		11	Barrow	1-1	Woodburn	6061	1	2	3	4	5	6	7		9	10	11	8							
19		18	OLDHAM ATHLETIC	3-2	Callender T.(pen), Wilbert, Campbell	8570	1	2	3	4	5	6	7		9	10	11	8							
20		25	Shrewsbury Town	0-1		9709	1	2	3	4	5	6	7		9	10	11	8							
21	Dec	2	TRANMERE ROVERS	2-0	Woodburn, Wilbert	8956	1	3			5	4	7		9	10	11	8	2	6					
22		23	CREWE ALEXANDRA	4-0	Winters, Wilbert 2, Buchan	6638	1	3			5	4	7		9	10	11	8	2	6					
23		25	HARTLEPOOLS UNITED	0-1		8595	1	2	3		5	4	7		9	10	11	8		6					
24		26	Hartlepools United	0-3		9269	1	2	3	6	5		7		9	10	11	8				4			
25	Jan	1	Darlington	2-4	Wilbert 2	5821	1	3	4		5			7	9	10	11	8	2						6
26		13	BRADFORD CITY	2-0	Woodburn, Buchan	6437	1	2	3	6	5	4	7		9	10	11	8							
27		20	Rochdale	0-2		5612	1	2		6	5	4	7		9	10	11	8				3			
28		27	Southport	0-1		3599	1	2		6	5	4	7		9	10	11	8				3			
29		31	Stockport County	2-5	Wyles, Winters	6045	1	2		6	5	4	7		9	10		8	2			11			
30	Feb	3	CHESTER	2-1	Woodburn, Wilbert	4804	1	2		8	5	4	11		9	10		7		6		3			
31		10	DARLINGTON	5-2	Callender T.2, Palmer, Woodburn 2	5694	1	2	3	4	5	8	7		9	10				6			11		
32		24	Scunthorpe United	1-2	Buchan	9688	1	2	3	4	5	8	7		9	10	11			6					
33	Mar	3	WREXHAM	0-0		5642	1	2		4	5	6	7		9	8	11					3		10	
34		10	Rotherham United	2-1	Kendall, Campbell	14655	1	2		4	5	6		7	9	8	11					3		10	
35		17	MANSFIELD TOWN	1-3	Wilbert	4342	1	2		4	5	6		7	9	8	11					3		10	
36		23	Lincoln City	1-2	Callender T.(pen)	11245	1	2		4	5	6	7	8	9			11				3		10	
37		24	York City	1-1	Ingham	5848	1	2		4	5	6	7	8	9			11				3		10	
38		26	LINCOLN CITY	1-2	Johnson	5672	1	2		4	5	6	7	8	9			11				3		10	
39		31	BARROW	1-0	Ingham	2916	1	2		4	5	6	7	8	9			11				3		10	
40	Apr	4	New Brighton	1-0	Buchan	2668	1	2		4	5	6	7		9	10		8				3		11	
41		7	Oldham Athletic	3-2	Callender J., Winters, Wilbert	11707	1	2		4	5	6	7		9	10		8				3		11	
42		14	BRADFORD PARK AVE.	5-0	Callender T.(2pen.), Woodburn, Ingham, Johnson	4717	1	2		4	5	6	7		9	10		8				3		11	
43		18	Bradford Park Avenue	0-2		7003	1	2		4	5	6	7		9	10		8				3		11	
44		21	Tranmere Rovers	2-2	Ingham, Winters	8929	1	2		4	5	6	7		9	10		8				3		11	
45		30	SOUTHPORT	1-3	Winters	3006	1	2		4	5	6	7		9	10		8				3		11	
46	May	5	Accrington Stanley	2-2	Ingham 2	2782	1	2	3	4	5	6	7					8		9		10	11		
						Apps	46	46	27	42	46	44	44	9	45	42	36	34	4	6	2	17	2	13	1
						Goals		1		3	9	7	10	5	18	9	4	15					1	2	

F.A. Cup

Rd	Mon	Date	Opponent	Res		Att	Gray	Wyles	Fowler	Callender J	Callender T	Woodburn	Ingham	Kendall	Wilbert	Buchan	Campbell	Winters	Cairns	Cassidy	Small	Robinson	Palmer	Johnson	Brown
R3	Jan	6	Sheffield United	0-1		25881	1	2	3	6	5	4	7		9	10	11	8							

		Pl.	Home					Against					F.	A.	Pts
			W	D	L	F	A	W	D	L	F	A	(Total)		
1	Rotherham United	46	16	3	4	55	16	15	6	2	48	25	103	41	71
2	Mansfield Town	46	17	6	0	54	19	9	6	8	24	29	78	48	64
3	Carlisle United	46	18	4	1	44	17	7	8	8	35	33	79	50	62
4	Tranmere Rovers	46	15	5	3	51	26	9	6	8	32	36	83	62	59
5	Lincoln City	46	18	1	4	62	23	7	7	9	27	35	89	58	58
6	Bradford Park Ave.	46	15	3	5	46	23	8	5	10	44	49	90	72	54
7	Bradford City	46	13	4	6	55	30	8	6	9	35	33	90	63	52
8	GATESHEAD	46	17	1	5	60	21	4	7	12	24	41	84	62	50
9	Crewe Alexandra	46	11	5	7	38	26	8	5	10	23	34	61	60	48
10	Stockport County	46	15	3	5	45	26	5	5	13	18	37	63	63	48
11	Rochdale	46	11	6	6	38	18	6	5	12	31	44	69	62	45
12	Scunthorpe United	46	10	12	1	32	9	3	6	14	26	48	58	57	44
13	Chester	46	11	6	6	42	30	6	3	14	20	34	62	64	43
14	Wrexham	46	12	6	5	37	28	3	6	14	18	43	55	71	42
15	Oldham Athletic	46	10	5	8	47	36	6	3	14	26	37	73	73	40
16	Hartlepools United	46	14	5	4	55	26	2	2	19	9	40	64	66	39
17	York City	46	7	12	4	37	24	5	3	15	29	53	66	77	39
18	Darlington	46	10	8	5	35	29	3	5	15	24	48	59	77	39
19	Barrow	46	12	3	8	38	27	4	3	16	13	49	51	76	38
20	Shrewsbury Town	46	11	6	6	28	30	4	4	15	15	44	43	74	37
21	Southport	46	9	4	10	29	25	4	6	13	27	47	56	72	36
22	Halifax Town	46	11	6	6	36	24	0	6	17	14	45	50	69	34
23	Accrington Stanley	46	10	4	9	28	29	1	6	16	14	72	42	101	32
24	New Brighton	46	7	6	10	22	32	4	2	17	18	58	40	90	30

1951/52 5th in Division 3 (North)

#		Date	Opponent	Score	Scorers	Att	Gray	Wyles	Robinson	Callender J	Callender T	Woodburn	Ingham	Winters	Wilbert	Buchan	Johnson	Kendall	Campbell	Thompson	Fowler	Brown	Cairns	Rutherford	Cassidy	Small	Myers	Davis
1	Aug	18	Accrington Stanley	2-1	Ingham, Winters	9189	1	2	3	4	5	6	7	8	9	10	11											
2		21	Oldham Athletic	0-2		13931	1	2	3	4	5	6	7		9	11		10	8									
3		25	CREWE ALEXANDRA	1-0	Winters	7072	1	2	3	4	5	6		8	9	10		7	11									
4		27	HALIFAX TOWN	3-0	Callender T., Wilbert 2	5674	1	2	3	4	5	6	7	10	9	8			11									
5	Sep	1	Southport	2-0	Ingham 2	6617	1	2	3	4	5	6	7	10	9	8			11									
6		3	Hartlepools United	0-1		12225	1	2	3	4	5	6	7	10	9	8			11									
7		8	TRANMERE ROVERS	4-1	Callender J, Woodburn, Wilbert, Campbell	7630	1	2	3	4	5	6	7	10	9	8			11									
8		10	HARTLEPOOLS UNITED	2-0	Buchan, Winters	9367	1	2	3	4	5	6	7	9	8	10			11									
9		15	Scunthorpe United	1-1	Johnson	8539	1	2	3	4	5	6		10	9	8	7		11									
10		22	LINCOLN CITY	3-1	Buchan, Winters 2	13287	1	2	3	4	5	6	7	10	9	8			11									
11		29	Chester	3-0	Wilbert 2, Winters	8072	1	2	3	4	5	6	7	10	9	8			11									
12	Oct	6	Stockport County	0-0		14807	1	2	3	4	5	6	7	10	9	8			11									
13		13	WORKINGTON	4-1	Callender J, Ingham, Winters 2	11630	1	2	3	4	5	6	7	10	9	8			11									
14		20	Barrow	1-2	Woodburn	8428	1	2	3	4	5	6	7	10	9	8			11									
15		27	GRIMSBY TOWN	1-1	Winters	11398	1	2	3	4	5	6	7	10		8			11		9							
16	Nov	3	Wrexham	1-2	Winters	8794	1	2	3	4	5	6	7	10	11	8					9							
17		10	CHESTERFIELD	1-1	Wilbert	8030	1	2		4	5	6	7	10	9	8			11				3					
18		17	Bradford Park Avenue	0-2		13611	1	2		4	5		7	10	9	8			11			6	3					
19	Dec	1	Mansfield Town	3-2	Ingham 2, Campbell	10171	1	2		4	5	6	7	10		8			11	9	3							
20		8	ROCHDALE	1-0	Winters	6055	1	2		4	5	6	7	10		8			11	9	3							
21		22	Crewe Alexandra	2-4	Callender T.(pen), Winters	6434	1	2		4	5	6	7	10		8			11	9	3							
22		25	CARLISLE UNITED	1-1	Winters	8848	1	2		4	5	6	7	10	11	8				9	3							
23		26	Carlisle United	0-0		13021	1	2		4	5	6	7	10	9			8	11		3							
24		29	SOUTHPORT	3-0	Callender J., Buchan, Johnson	6461	1	2		4	5	6	7	10		8	11		9		3							
25	Jan	5	Tranmere Rovers	1-5	Buchan	7782	1	2		4	5	6	7	10	8	11			9		3							
26		19	SCUNTHORPE UNITED	2-1	Wilbert, Rutherford	5586	1	3		4	5		7	10	9			8						6	2	11		
27		23	DARLINGTON	2-2	Thompson, Campbell	2677	1	3		4	5	6		10		8			11	7	9				2			
28		26	Lincoln City	0-1		12907	1	3		4		6	7	10	9	8			11						2	5		
29	Feb	9	CHESTER	1-0	Campbell	5416	1	3		4	5		7	10	9	8			11				6		2			
30		13	Darlington	2-3	Wilbert, Campbell	2211	1	3		4	5		7	8	9			10	11				6		2			
31		16	STOCKPORT COUNTY	0-2		6591	1	3		4	5		7		9			10	11	8			6		2			
32		23	BRADFORD CITY	2-2	Campbell 2	4770	1	2		4	5		7		9			10	11		3		6					
33	Mar	1	Workington	2-1	Ingham, Wyles	5306	1	10		4	5		7		9	8			11		3		6		2			
34		8	BARROW	2-0	Wilbert, Campbell	3426	1	3		4	5		7	10	9	8			11				6		2			
35		15	Grimsby Town	0-2		16306	1	3		4	5		7	10	9	8			11				6		2			
36		22	WREXHAM	1-1	Winters	3324	1	3		4	5		7	10	9	8			11				6		2			
37		26	ACCRINGTON STANLEY	1-0	Campbell	622	1	3		4	5		7	10		8	9		11				6		2			
38		29	Chesterfield	0-1		4361	1	3		4	5		7	10		8	11			9			6		2			
39	Apr	2	OLDHAM ATHLETIC	1-0	Winters	2548	1	3		4	5		7	10	8		11			9			6		2	8		
40		5	BRADFORD PARK AVE.	0-1		2803		3		4	5		7	10			11			9			6		2	8	1	
41		11	York City	0-1		12166	1	3	11	4	5		7	10	9	8							6		2			
42		12	Halifax Town	1-0	Wilbert	7553	1	3		4	5		7	10	9	8			11				6		2			
43		14	YORK CITY	1-1	Johnson	3916	1	3		4	5		7	8	9		10		11				6		2			
44		19	MANSFIELD TOWN	4-1	Wilbert, Winters 2, Campbell	3501	1	3		8	5		7	10	9				11				6		2			4
45		26	Rochdale	3-0	Callender J., Wilbert 2	3174	1	3		8	5		7	10	9				11				6		2			4
46	May	3	Bradford City	1-1	Winters	5275	1	3		8	5		7	10	9				11				6		2			4
				Apps			45	42	21	46	45	29	42	43	39	33	23	2	25	13	12	3	19	1	17	2	1	3
				Goals				1		4	2		6	18	13	4	3		10	1			1					

F.A. Cup

		Date	Opponent	Score	Scorers	Gray	Wyles	Robinson	Callender J	Callender T	Woodburn	Ingham	Winters	Wilbert	Buchan	Johnson	Kendall	Campbell	Thompson	Fowler	Brown	Cairns	Rutherford	Cassidy	Small	Myers	Davis
R1	Nov	24	Stockport County	2-2	Callender T.(pen), Buchan	1	2		4	5	6	7	10		8			11		9		3					
rep		28	STOCKPORT COUNTY *	1-1	Campbell	1	2		4	5	6	7	10		8			11		9		3					
rep2	Dec	3	Stockport County	2-1	Thompson 2	1	2		4	5	6	7	10		8				9	3							
R2		15	GUILDFORD CITY	2-0	Ingham, Winters	1	2		4	5	6	7	10		8			11		9		3					
R3	Jan	12	Ipswich Town	2-2	Ingham, Wilbert	1	2		4	5	6	7	10	9	8	11						3					
rep		16	IPSWICH TOWN *	3-3	Callender J, Buchan, Johnson	1	2		4	5	6	7	10	9	8	11						3					
rep2		21	Ipswich Town *	2-1	Buchan, Johnson	1	3		4	5	6	7	10	9	8	11						2					
R4	Feb	6	West Bromwich Albion	0-2	Ingham 2	1	3		4	5	6	7	10	9	8							2		11			

* After Extra Time. R1 2nd replay at Hillsborough R3 2nd replay at Bramall Lane R4 at Newcastle United

FINAL TABLE	Pl.	Home W	D	L	F	A	Against W	D	L	F	A	F (Total)	A	Pts
1 Lincoln City	46	19	2	2	80	23	11	7	5	41	29	121	52	69
2 Grimsby Town	46	19	2	2	59	14	10	6	7	37	31	96	45	66
3 Stockport County	46	12	9	2	47	17	11	4	8	27	23	74	40	59
4 Oldham Athletic	46	19	2	2	65	22	5	7	11	25	39	90	61	57
5 GATESHEAD	46	14	7	2	41	17	7	4	12	25	32	66	49	53
6 Mansfield Town	46	10	7	6	50	23	5	5	13	23	37	73	60	52
7 Carlisle United	46	10	7	6	31	24	9	6	8	31	33	62	57	51
8 Bradford Park Ave.	46	13	6	4	51	28	6	6	11	23	36	74	64	50
9 Hartlepools United	46	17	3	3	47	19	4	5	14	24	46	71	65	50
10 York City	46	16	4	3	53	19	2	9	12	20	33	73	52	49
11 Tranmere Rovers	46	17	2	4	59	29	4	4	15	17	42	76	71	48
12 Barrow	46	13	5	5	33	19	4	7	12	24	42	57	61	46
13 Chesterfield	46	15	7	1	47	16	2	4	17	18	50	65	66	45
14 Scunthorpe United	46	10	11	2	39	23	4	5	14	26	51	65	74	44
15 Bradford City	46	12	5	6	40	32	4	5	14	21	36	61	68	42
16 Crewe Alexandra	46	12	6	5	42	28	5	2	16	21	54	63	82	42
17 Southport	46	12	6	5	36	22	3	5	15	17	49	53	71	41
18 Wrexham	46	14	5	4	41	22	1	4	18	22	51	63	73	39
19 Chester	46	13	4	6	46	30	2	5	16	26	55	72	85	39
20 Halifax Town	46	11	4	8	31	23	3	3	17	30	74	61	97	35
21 Rochdale	46	10	5	8	32	34	1	8	14	15	45	47	79	35
22 Accrington Stanley	46	6	8	9	30	34	4	4	15	31	58	61	92	32
23 Darlington	46	10	5	8	39	34	1	4	18	25	69	64	103	31
24 Workington	46	8	4	11	33	34	3	3	17	17	57	50	91	29

1952/53 9th in Division 3 (North)

#	Date		Opponent	Score	Scorers	Att.	Turnbull	Wyles	March	Callender J	Callender T	Cassidy	Ingham	Smith	Wilbert	Winters	Campbell	Cairns	Brown	Robinson	Gray	Price	Johnson	Watkin	Rutherford
1	Aug	23	CARLISLE UNITED	2-0	Wilbert, Campbell	11390	1	2	3	4	5	6	7	8	9	10	11								
2		25	Mansfield Town	0-2		12685	1	2	3	4	5	6	7	8	9	10	11								
3		30	Southport	2-3	Callender T(Pen), Winters	4808	1		3	4	5		7	8	9	10		2	6	11					
4	Sep	1	MANSFIELD TOWN	1-2	Wilbert	5388			3	4	5			8	9	10		2	6	11	1		7		
5		6	CREWE ALEXANDRA	6-1	Callender T,Price 2,Winters 2,Wilbert	5089			3	4	5			8	9	10		2	6	11	1		7		
6		8	HARTLEPOOLS UNITED	1-1	Wilbert	3147			3	4	5			8	9	10		2	6	11	1		7		
7		13	Port Vale	1-1	Winters	17803			3	4	5			8	9	10		2	6		1		7		
8		15	Hartlepools United	0-0		8370			3		4	5			9	10	11	2	6		1		7	8	
9		20	CHESTER	4-1	Wilbert 2,Winters,Price	6186			3	4	5		7	8	9	10		2	6		1	11			
10		22	TRANMERE ROVERS	0-1		4363			3	4	5		7	8	9	10		2	6		1	11			
11		27	Scunthorpe United	0-0		6940			3	4	5		7	8	9	10		2	6		1	11			
12		30	Rochdale	3-2	Wilbert,Winters,Price	4848			3	4	5		7	8	9	10		2	6		1	11			
13	Oct	4	STOCKPORT COUNTY	2-0	Ingham, Price	7062			3	4	5		7	8	9	10		2	6		1	11			
14		11	OLDHAM ATHLETIC	1-0	Winters	10935			3	4	5		7	8	9	10		2	6		1	11			
15		18	Bradford Park Avenue	0-3		13022			3	4	5		7	8	9	10	11	2	6		1				
16		25	WREXHAM	1-0	Callender T	6577			3	4	5		7	8	9	10		2	6		1	11			
17	Nov	1	Barrow	2-2	Ingham, Wilbert	5655			3	4	5		7	8	9	10		2	6		1	11			
18		8	GRIMSBY TOWN	2-0	Wilbert, Johnson	11451			3	4	5		7	8	9	10		2	6		1		11		
19		15	York City	2-1	Smith 2	9013			3	4	5		7	8	9	10		2	6		1		11		
20		29	Chesterfield	1-1	Price	4163			3	4	5		7	8	9	10		2	6		1	11			
21	Dec	13	Accrington Stanley	1-1	Winters	4278			3	4	5		7	8	9	10		2	6		1	11			
22		20	Carlisle United	2-2	Wilbert, Winters	4465			3	4	5		7	8	9	10		2	6		1	11			
23		25	Bradford City	1-3	Smith	12312			3	4	5		7	8	9	10		2	6		1	11			
24		27	BRADFORD CITY	2-2	Callender J, Wilbert	4574			3	4	5		7	8	9	10		2	6		1				11
25	Jan	1	ROCHDALE	3-1	Callender T(pen),Smith,Price	3729			3	4	5		7	8	9	10		2	6		1	11			
26		3	SOUTHPORT	1-2	Ingham	5268			3	4	5		7	8	9	10		2	6		1	11			
27		12	Halifax Town	3-1	Callender J, Wilbert,Campbell	4000		2	3	4	5		7		9	8	11		6		1			10	
28		17	Crewe Alexandra	3-4	Callender T(pen), Ingham,Campbell	7034		2	3	4	5		7		9	8	11		6		1			10	
29		24	PORT VALE	1-1	Campbell	7785			3	4	5		7	8		9	11	2	6		1			10	
30	Feb	4	HALIFAX TOWN	3-1	Callender T,Wilbert,Watkin	4020			3	4	5		7	8	9	8	11	2	6		1			10	
31		7	Chester	0-2		5075			3	4	5		7	8	9	10	11	2	6		1				
32		18	SCUNTHORPE UNITED	1-1	Callender T	4126			3	4	5		7	8	9	10	11	2	6		1				
33		21	Stockport County	1-3	Brown	9616			3	4	5		7	8	9	10	11	2	6		1				
34	Mar	3	Oldham Athletic	1-1	Ingham	8379	9	3	4	5		7				8	11	2	6		1			10	
35		7	BRADFORD PARK AVE.	3-2	Ingham,Wyles,Winters	7303	9	3	4	5		7		8		10	11	2	6		1				
36		14	Wrexham	0-1		10105	9	3	4	5		7		8		10	11	2	6		1				
37		21	BARROW	3-1	Wyles 3	5164	9	3	4	5		7		8			11	2	6		1			10	
38		28	Grimsby Town	0-0		10445	9	3	4	5		7			8		11	2	6		1			10	
39	Apr	3	Darlington	0-1		7144	9	3	4	5		7		8		10	11	2	6		1				
40		4	YORK CITY	1-1	Ingham	5745	9	3	4	5		7		8			11	2	6		1			10	
41		6	DARLINGTON	5-1	Wyles,Campbell 3,Davison(og)	4248	9	3	4	6		7		8			11	2			1			10	5
42		11	Tranmere Rovers	0-2		6502	2	3	4	5		7		8	9	6	11				1			10	
43		15	WORKINGTON	1-1	Callender T	771	2	3	4	6		7			9	8	11	2	6	5	1			10	
44		18	CHESTERFIELD	2-4	Price, Wilbert	3253			3	4	5			9	8		2	6		1	7	10	11	
45		25	Workington	2-0	Smith, Wilbert	8256	2	3	4	5			8	9	10	11		6		1	7			
46		29	ACCRINGTON STANLEY	5-0	Smith 2,Wilbert,Watkin,Holliday(og)	1599	2	3	4	5		7	8	9	10			6		1			11	

| | | | | | | Apps | 3 | 30 | 33 | 46 | 46 | 2 | 39 | 38 | 37 | 43 | 23 | 37 | 42 | 4 | 43 | 20 | 10 | 9 | 1 |
| | | | | | | Goals | | 5 | | 1 | 8 | | 7 | 7 | 15 | 10 | 7 | | 1 | | | 8 | 1 | 2 | |

Two own goals

F.A. Cup

R	Date		Opponent	Score	Scorers	Att.	March	Callender J	Callender T	Ingham	Smith	Wilbert	Winters	Campbell	Cairns	Brown	Gray	Price	Johnson
R1	Nov	22	CREWE ALEXANDRA	2-0	Smith, Price	10371	3	4	5	7	8	9	10		2	6	1	11	
R2	Dec	6	Bradford Park Avenue	2-1	Ingham 2	13149	3	4	5	7	8	9	10		2	6	1	11	
R3	Jan	10	LIVERPOOL	1-0	Winters	15193	3	4	5	7	8	9	10		2	6	1	11	
R4		31	Hull City	2-1	Ingham, Phillips(og)	37063	3	4	5	7	8	9	10	11	2	6	1		
R5	Feb	14	Plymouth Argyle	1-0	Winters	29736	3	4	5	7	8	9	10	11	2	6	1		
R6		28	BOLTON WANDERERS	0-1		17692	3	4	5	7	8	9		11	2	6	1		10

FINAL TABLE

		Pl.	Home W	D	L	F	A	Away W	D	L	F	A	F (Total)	A	Pts
1	Oldham Athletic	46	15	4	4	48	21	7	11	5	29	24	77	45	59
2	Port Vale	46	13	9	1	41	10	7	9	7	26	25	67	35	58
3	Wrexham	46	18	3	2	59	24	6	5	12	27	42	86	66	56
4	York City	46	14	5	4	35	16	6	8	9	25	29	60	45	53
5	Grimsby Town	46	15	5	3	47	19	6	5	12	28	40	75	59	52
6	Southport	46	16	4	3	42	18	4	7	12	21	42	63	60	51
7	Bradford Park Ave.	46	10	8	5	37	23	9	4	10	38	38	75	61	50
8	GATESHEAD	46	13	6	4	51	24	4	9	10	25	36	76	60	49
9	Carlisle United	46	13	7	3	57	24	5	6	12	25	44	82	68	49
10	Crewe Alexandra	46	13	5	5	46	28	7	3	13	24	40	70	68	48
11	Stockport County	46	13	8	2	61	28	4	5	14	21	43	82	69	47
12	Tranmere Rovers	46	16	4	3	45	16	5	1	17	20	47	65	63	47
13	Chesterfield	46	13	6	4	40	23	5	5	13	25	40	65	63	47
14	Halifax Town	46	13	5	5	47	31	3	10	10	21	37	68	68	47
15	Scunthorpe United	46	10	6	7	38	21	6	8	9	24	35	62	56	46
16	Bradford City	46	14	7	2	54	29	0	11	12	21	51	75	80	46
17	Hartlepools United	46	14	6	3	39	16	2	8	13	18	45	57	61	46
18	Mansfield Town	46	11	9	3	34	25	5	5	13	21	37	55	62	46
19	Barrow	46	15	6	2	48	20	1	6	16	18	51	66	71	44
20	Chester	46	10	7	6	39	27	1	8	14	25	58	64	85	37
21	Darlington	46	13	4	6	33	27	1	2	20	25	69	58	96	34
22	Rochdale	46	12	5	6	41	27	2	0	21	21	56	62	83	33
23	Workington	46	9	5	9	40	33	2	5	16	15	58	55	91	32
24	Accrington Stanley	46	7	9	7	25	29	1	2	20	14	60	39	89	27

1953/54 4th in Division 3 (North)

#		Date	Opponent	Score	Scorers	Att	Gray	Cairns	Hewson	Callender J	Callender T	Brown	Campbell	Ingham	Wilbert	Johnson	Watkin	Price	Smith	March	Haley	Wyles	Davis	Robson	Anderson	Moran	Conway
1	Aug	19	Halifax Town	0-0		9696	1	2	3	4	5	6	7	8	9	10	11										
2		22	Southport	4-2	Brown,Wilbert 2,Johnson	5572	1	2	3	4	5	6		8	9	10	11	7									
3		24	SCUNTHORPE UNITED	0-0		8727	1	2	3	4	5	6		8	9	10	11	7									
4		29	CHESTER	2-1	Ingham, Johnson	8013	1	2	3	4	5	6		7	9	10	11		8								
5	Sep	3	Scunthorpe United	1-1	Smith	11302	1		3	4	5	6		7	9	10	11		8	2							
6		5	Crewe Alexandra	1-3	Johnson	6862	1		3	4	5	6		7	9	10	11		8	2							
7		7	YORK CITY	3-0	Smith,Ingham,Watkin	6781	1	2	3	4	6	5			9				8		7						
8		12	PORT VALE	1-0	Ingham, Johnson	11382	1	2	3	4	6	5			9		10	11	7	8							
9		14	York City	1-1	Wilbert	7777	1	2	3	4	6	5		9	11	10			7	8							
10		19	Bradford Park Avenue	1-3	Ingham, Johnson	12581	1	2	3	4	6	5		9	11	10			7	8							
11		21	WORKINGTON	4-1	Price,Johnson,Ingham,Callender T	3949	1		3	4	10	5		9		8	11	7		2	6						
12		26	BARNSLEY	0-0		10417	1	2	3	4	10	5		9		8	11	7			6						
13		28	Workington	0-2		6280	1	2	3	4	10	5		9		8	11	7			6						
14	Oct	3	Darlington	2-0	Wilbert, Watkin	8443	1	2	3	4	10	5		8	9		11	7			6						
15		10	Grimsby Town	0-2		9116	1	2	3	4	10	5		8	9		11	7			6						
16		17	STOCKPORT COUNTY	4-2	Callender T.2(1 pen), Smith 2	8541	1		3	4	10	5		7	9		11		8		6	2					
17		24	Rochdale	1-0	Callender J	6308	1		3	4	10	5		7	9		11		8		6	2					
18		31	WREXHAM	3-1	Callender J, (2), Smith	8538	1		3	8	6	5		7	11		9		10		4	2					
19	Nov	7	Mansfield Town	1-1	Callender J	7355	1		3	8	6	5		7	11		9		10		4	2					
20		14	BARROW	1-0	Wilbert	7369	1		3	8	6	5	9	7	11				10		4	2					
21		28	CHESTERFIELD	3-3	Callender J, Haley, Campbell	6005	1		3	4	10	5	11	7			9		8		6	2					
22	Dec	5	Tranmere Rovers	4-1	Ingham,Watkin 2,Wilbert	5913	1		3	8	6	5		7	11		9		10		4	2					
23		12	HALIFAX TOWN	4-0	Ingham 2,Smith,Callender J	4758	1		3	8	5	6		7	11		9		10		4	2					
24		19	SOUTHPORT	1-0	Watkin	4787	1		3	8	5	6		7	11		9		10		4	2					
25		25	CARLISLE UNITED	2-2	Watkin, Smith	7210	1		3	8	5	6		7	11		9		10		4	2					
26		26	Carlisle United	0-1		8534	1		3	8	5	6		7	11		9		10		4	2					
27	Jan	2	Chester	0-5		4197	1		3	8	5	6			11		9		10			2	4				
28		9	ACCRINGTON STANLEY	4-0	Watkin, Smith,Callender T,Callender J	2514	1		3	8	5	6			11	7	9		10			4	2				
29		16	CREWE ALEXANDRA	2-0	Calledner T, Ingham	4033	1				5	6		7	11	10	9		8	3	4	2					
30		23	Port Vale	0-0		20370	1				5	6		7	11	10	9		8	3	4	2					
31		30	Accrington Stanley	2-2	Smith, Watkin	5113	1			4	5	6		7	11	10	9		8	3		2					
32	Feb	20	DARLINGTON	1-2	Smith	5450	1			8	5	6		7	11		9		10	3	4	2					
33		27	GRIMSBY TOWN	7-1	Watkin 4,Haley,Johnson,Campbell	4922	1		2	4	5	6	11			7	10	9			3	8					
34	Mar	6	Stockport County	1-0	Wilbert	6334	1		2	4	5	6	11	7	9						10	3	8				
35		13	ROCHDALE	2-1	Ingham, Robson	4847	1		2	4	5	6	11	7							8	3		9	10		
36		20	Wrexham	1-5	Ingham	7545	1		2	4	5			11	7						8	3	6	9	10		
37		27	MANSFIELD TOWN	1-3	Callender T.(pen)	4678	1		2		5	6	11	7							3			9	10	4	8
38		31	Barnsley	2-0	Johnson, Price	12960	1			4	5			7	9	10		11	8	3		2				6	
39	Apr	3	Barrow	0-0		3712	1			4	5	10	11	7	9				8	3		2				6	
40		7	BRADFORD PARK AVE.	0-1		2228	1			4	5			11	7	9	10		8	3		2				6	
41		10	BRADFORD CITY	1-0	Wilbert	3537	1		2	4	5	6		8	9	11		7		3					10		
42		16	Hartlepools United	0-1		8701	1		2	4	5	6	11	8	9			7		3						10	
43		17	Chesterfield	1-1	Callender T (pen)	7570	1			4	5	6	11	8	9			7	10	3		2					
44		19	HARTLEPOOLS UNITED	1-3	Wilbert	3962	1		2	4	5	6	11	8	9			7	10			3					
45		24	TRANMERE ROVERS	2-1	Price 2	3033	1	2	3	4	5	6			7	9	10	11	8								
46		28	Bradford City	2-2	Smith, Price	4616	1	2	3	4	5	6			7	9	10	11	8								
			Apps				46	15	37	43	46	43	13	44	36	23	30	19	34	18	23	22	1	3	4	5	1
			Goals							7	7	1	2	11	9	6	12	5	11		2			1			

F.A. Cup

#		Date	Opponent	Score	Scorers	Att	Gray	Cairns	Hewson	Callender J	Callender T	Brown	Campbell	Ingham	Wilbert	Johnson	Watkin	Price	Smith	March	Haley	Wyles	Davis	Robson	Anderson	Moran	Conway
R1	Nov	21	TRANMERE ROVERS	1-2	Smith	9701	1		3	4		5		7		10	9		8		6	2					

	FINAL TABLE	Pl	Home					Against					F.	A.	Pts
			W	D	L	F	A	W	D	L	F	A			(Total)
1	Port Vale	46	16	7	0	48	5	10	10	3	26	16	74	21	69
2	Barnsley	46	16	3	4	54	24	8	7	8	23	33	77	57	58
3	Scunthorpe United	46	14	7	2	49	24	7	8	8	32	32	77	56	57
4	GATESHEAD	46	15	4	4	49	22	6	9	8	25	33	74	55	55
5	Bradford City	46	15	6	2	40	14	7	3	13	20	41	60	55	53
6	Chesterfield	46	13	6	4	41	19	6	8	9	35	45	76	64	52
7	Mansfield Town	46	15	5	3	59	22	5	6	12	29	45	88	67	51
8	Wrexham	46	16	4	3	59	19	5	5	13	22	49	81	68	51
9	Bradford Park Ave.	46	13	6	4	57	31	5	8	10	20	37	77	68	50
10	Stockport County	46	14	6	3	57	20	4	5	14	20	47	77	67	47
11	Southport	46	12	5	6	41	26	5	7	11	22	34	63	60	46
12	Barrow	46	12	7	4	46	26	4	5	14	26	45	72	71	44
13	Carlisle United	46	10	8	5	53	27	4	7	12	30	44	83	71	43
14	Tranmere Rovers	46	11	4	8	40	34	7	3	13	19	36	59	70	43
15	Accrington Stanley	46	12	7	4	41	22	4	3	16	25	52	66	74	42
16	Crewe Alexandra	46	9	8	6	30	25	5	5	13	19	41	49	67	41
17	Grimsby Town	46	14	5	4	31	15	2	4	17	20	62	51	77	41
18	Hartlepools United	46	10	8	5	40	21	3	6	14	19	44	59	65	40
19	Rochdale	46	12	5	6	40	20	3	5	15	19	57	59	77	40
20	Workington	46	10	9	4	36	22	3	5	15	23	58	59	80	40
21	Darlington	46	11	3	9	31	27	1	11	11	19	44	50	71	38
22	York City	46	8	7	8	39	32	4	6	13	25	54	64	86	37
23	Halifax Town	46	9	6	8	26	21	3	4	16	18	52	44	73	34
24	Chester	46	10	7	6	39	22	1	3	19	9	45	48	67	32

1954/55   7th in 3rd Division (North)

#	Date	Opponent	Score	Scorers	Att.	Gray	Hewson	March	Callender J	Callender T	Brown	Ingham	Smith	Wilbert	Johnson	Oliver	Conway	Campbell	Moran	Davis	Anderson	Cairns	Haley	Herron	Johnston	Robson	Thompson	Yeats
1	Aug 21	CHESTERFIELD	1-3	Smith	6374	1	2	3	4	5	6	7	8		9	10	11											
2	24	Southport	2-1	Campbell, Oliver	6638	1	2	3	4	5	6	7			9		11	8	10									
3	28	Crewe Alexandra	1-1	Ingham	6243	1	2	3	4	5	6	7			9		11	8	10									
4	30	SOUTHPORT	1-0	Campbell	4781	1	2	3	4	5	6	7					11	8	10							9		
5	Sep 4	CARLISLE UNITED	0-0		7361	1	2	3	4	5	6	7	8	9			11	10										
6	6	HARTLEPOOLS UNITED	3-0	Smith,Campbell,Oliver	4577	1	2	3	4	5	6	7	8	9			11	10										
7	11	Chester	2-1	Ingham, Oliver	5801	1	2	3	4	5		7	8	9			11	10	6									
8	13	Hartlepools United	0-0		8628	1	2	3	4	5	6	7	8	9			11	10										
9	18	GRIMSBY TOWN	1-0	Campbell	6698	1	2	3	4	5	6	7	8	9			11	10										
10	21	Tranmere Rovers	2-1	Ingham, Johnson	4336	1	2	3	4	5	6	7	8		10	11		9										
11	25	Bradford Park Avenue	2-2	Ingham, Campbell	8779	1	2	3	4	5	6	7	8		10	11		9										
12	27	TRANMERE ROVERS	3-1	Smith 2, Campbell	4403	1	2	3	4	5	6	7	8		10	11		9										
13	Oct 2	ROCHDALE	0-1		8010	1	2	3	4	5	6	7	8			11		9		10								
14	9	YORK CITY	1-1	Ingham	6926	1	2	3			5	6	7	8		10	11		9		4							
15	16	Halifax Town	0-4		7025	1	2	3			5	6	7	8	9		10	4	8									
16	23	OLDHAM ATHLETIC	2-2	Brown, Anderson	7089	1	2	3			5	6	7	8			11	9	4	10								
17	30	Bradford City	1-1	Smith	10494	1	2	3			5	6	9	8		10	11		4	7								
18	Nov 6	BARNSLEY	0-4		5290	1	2	3			5	6	7	8			11	9	10									
19	13	Scunthorpe United	2-0	Campbell, Oliver	9159	1	2	3	4	5	6	7	8			11	9		10									
20	27	Accrington Stanley	2-6	Calleder T, Smith	6503	1			3	4	5	6	7	8		11	9		10	2								
21	Dec 4	MANSFIELD TOWN	4-0	Smith, Oliver 3	3774	1	2	3	4			5	7	8		11	9		10	6								
22	18	Chesterfield	3-1	Ingham, Campbell, Oliver	6272	1	2	3	4	5	6	7	8		11	9		10										
23	25	BARROW	3-1	Ingham, Smith, Campbell	7385	1	2	3	4	5	6	7	8		11	9		10										
24	27	Barrow	1-0	Callender T	7655	1	2	3	4	5	6	7	8		11	9		10										
25	Jan 1	CREWE ALEXANDRA	1-0	Ingham	10828	1	2	3	4	5	6	7	8		11	9		10										
26	29	Stockport County	1-2	Campbell	8768	1	2	3	4	5	6	7	8		11	9		10										
27	Feb 5	Grimsby Town	1-1	Oliver	6982	1	2	3	4	5	6	7	8		11	9		10										
28	19	Rochdale	0-4		4823	1	2	3	4	5	6	7	8		11	9		10										
29	26	York City	1-2	Smith	13246	1	2	3	4	5	6	9	8		11	10				7								
30	Mar 5	HALIFAX TOWN	4-0	Smith, Ingham 2, Oliver	4322	1	2	3	4	5	6	9	8		11	10				7								
31	9	BRADFORD PARK AVE.	3-2	Callender T, Oliver, Johnston	1813	1	2	3	4	5	6	9	8		11					7	10							
32	12	Oldham Athletic	2-1	Ingham, Oliver	7267	1	2	3	4	5	6	9	8		11					7	10							
33	19	BRADFORD CITY	2-1	Smith, Oliver 3	4427	1	2	3	4	5	6	9	8		11					7	10							
34	23	STOCKPORT COUNTY	4-4	Smith, Anderson,Campbell,Oliver	924	1	2	3	4	5	6		8		11	9		7		10								
35	26	Barnsley	0-3		6253	1	2	3	4	5	6		8		11	9		7		10								
36	30	CHESTER	0-0		887	1	2	3	4	5	6		8		11	9				10				7				
37	Apr 2	SCUNTHORPE UNITED	0-1		4217	1	2	3	4	5			8		11	9				6	7	10						
38	8	DARLINGTON	1-1	Smith	4311	1	2	3			5		9	8	11	10	6		7		4							
39	9	Wrexham	0-2		5742	1	2	3			5	7	8		11	10	6		4					9				
40	11	Darlington	1-5	Ingham	7043	1	2	3			5	6	7	8		10			11	4				9				
41	16	ACCRINGTON STANLEY	1-1	Robson	3132	1		3			5	7	8		10	6	11	2	4				9					
42	20	Workington	0-4		3797	1		3			5	7	8		11	6		2	4	10	9							
43	23	Mansfield Town	1-0	Ingham	4334	1		3	4	10		7	8		11		5	2	6							9		
44	25	WREXHAM	0-1		1304	1		3	4	10		7	8		11		5	2	6							9		
45	30	WORKINGTON	3-2	Ingham, Thompson,Campbell	2573	1		3	4		6	7	8		10		5	2							9			
46	May 3	Carlisle United	2-1	Smith, Campbell	2719	1		3	4		6	7	8		10		5	2							9			
Apps						46	40	46	37	43	38	42	42	9	6	41	3	41	5	10	16	7	9	7	8	5	4	1
Goals										3	1	14	14		1	14		13			2				1	1	1	

F.A. Cup

R	Date	Opponent	Score	Scorers	Att.	Gray	Hewson	March	Callender J	Callender T	Brown	Ingham	Smith	Oliver	Campbell	Anderson
R1	Nov 20	CHESTER	6-0	Ingham,Smith,Anderson 2,Oliver,Campbell	8643	1	2	3	4	5	6	7	8	11	9	10
R2	Dec 11	BARNSLEY	3-3	Ingham 2, Campbell	11394	1	2	3	4	5	6	7	8	11	9	10
rep	16	Barnsley	1-0	Smith	11351	1	2	3	4	5	6	7	8	11	9	10
R3	Jan 8	TOTTENHAM HOTSPUR	0-2		18840	1	2	3	4	5	6	7	8	11	9	10

FINAL TABLE

		Pl.	Home W	D	L	F	A	Away W	D	L	F	A	F (Total)	A	Pts
1	Barnsley	46	18	3	2	51	17	12	2	9	35	29	86	46	65
2	Accrington Stanley	46	18	2	3	65	32	7	9	7	31	35	96	67	61
3	Scunthorpe United	46	14	6	3	45	18	9	6	8	36	35	81	53	58
4	York City	46	13	5	5	43	27	11	5	7	49	36	92	63	58
5	Hartlepools United	46	16	3	4	39	20	9	2	12	25	29	64	49	55
6	Chesterfield	46	17	1	5	54	33	7	5	11	27	37	81	70	54
7	GATESHEAD	46	11	7	5	38	26	9	5	9	27	43	65	69	52
8	Workington	46	11	7	5	39	23	7	7	9	29	32	68	55	50
9	Stockport County	46	13	4	6	50	27	5	8	10	34	43	84	70	48
10	Oldham Athletic	46	14	5	4	47	22	5	5	13	27	46	74	68	48
11	Southport	46	10	9	4	28	18	6	7	10	19	26	47	44	48
12	Rochdale	46	13	7	3	39	20	4	7	12	30	46	69	66	48
13	Mansfield Town	46	14	4	5	40	28	4	5	14	25	43	65	71	45
14	Halifax Town	46	9	9	5	41	27	6	4	13	22	40	63	67	43
15	Darlington	46	10	7	6	41	28	4	7	12	21	45	62	73	42
16	Bradford Park Ave.	46	11	7	5	29	21	4	4	15	27	49	56	70	41
17	Barrow	46	12	4	7	39	34	5	2	16	31	55	70	89	40
18	Wrexham	46	9	6	8	40	35	4	6	13	25	42	65	77	38
19	Tranmere Rovers	46	9	6	8	37	30	4	5	14	18	40	55	70	37
20	Carlisle United	46	12	1	10	53	39	3	5	15	25	50	78	89	36
21	Bradford City	46	9	5	9	30	26	4	5	14	17	29	47	55	36
22	Crewe Alexandra	46	8	10	5	45	35	2	4	17	23	56	68	91	34
23	Grimsby Town	46	10	4	9	28	32	3	4	16	19	46	47	78	34
24	Chester	46	10	3	10	23	25	2	6	15	21	52	44	77	33

122

1955/56 13th in 3rd Division (North)

#		Date	Opponent	Score	Scorers	Att	Gray	Hewson	March	Callender J	Davis	Brown	Ingham	Smith	Callender T	Campbell	Oliver	Robson	Moran	Herron	Lydon	Thompson	Anderson	Cairns	Haley	Hunter	Dawson
1	Aug	20	Accrington Stanley	2-2	Callender T 2	10795	1	2	3	4	5	6	7	8	9	10	11										
2		22	TRANMERE ROVERS	3-3	Callender J,Smith, Callender T	3576	1	2	3	4	5	6	7	8	9	10	11										
3		27	BARROW	3-2	Ingham,Callender T, Campbell	3823	1	2	3	4	5	6	7	8	9	10	11										
4		30	Tranmere Rovers	1-1	Robson	6070	1	2	3	4	5	6	7	8			10	11	9								
5	Sep	3	Chester	0-3		7900	1	2	3	4	5	6	7	8	10		9	11									
6		6	Southport	0-2		3806	1	2	3	4	5	6	7	8			10	11	9								
7		10	CARLISLE UNITED	2-3	Ingham, Campbell	6400	1	2	3	4	5	6	7	8	10	9	11										
8		12	SOUTHPORT	2-0	Brown, Smith	2332	1	2	3	4	5	6	7	8	10			11	9								
9		17	Grimsby Town	1-3	Callender T	11266	1	2	3	4	5	6	7	8	10			11	9								
10		21	Crewe Alexandra	0-1		3738	1	2	3	4	5	6	7	8	10	9	11										
11		24	BRADFORD PARK AVE.	3-0	Robson 2,Hindle(og)	2905	1	2	3	4	5	6	7	8	10	11			9								
12		26	CHESTERFIELD	3-3	Callender T 2, Smith	2014	1	2	3		5	6	7	8	10	11			9	4							
13	Oct	1	Rochdale	1-1	Robson	5358	1	2		4	5	6	7	8	3	11	10	9									
14		8	Stockport County	2-1	Ingham, Oliver	9204	1	2		4	5	6	7	8	3	11	10	9									
15		15	DERBY COUNTY	2-4	Campbell 2	6335	1	2		4	5	6	7	8	3	11	10	9									
16		22	Wrexham	1-1	Oliver	5995	1	2	3	4	5		7	8	6	10	11	9									
17		29	HALIFAX TOWN	1-1	Smith	2569	1	2	3	4	5		9	8	6	10	11			7							
18	Nov	5	Bradford City	1-3	Lydon	10484	1	2		4	5	3	7	8	6		11	9			10						
19		12	SCUNTHORPE UNITED	1-0	Callender T	3765	1	2		4	5	3	7	8	6		11	9			10						
20		26	WORKINGTON	4-3	Smith,Thompson 2,Lydon	2882	1	2		4	5	3	7	8	6		11				10	9					
21	Dec	3	York City	0-1		9714	1	2	3	4	5			8	6	11					10	9	7				
22		17	ACCRINGTON STANLEY	4-0	Ingham,Thompson,Lydon,Oliver	3179	1		3	4	5		7	8	6		11				10	9		2			
23		24	Barrow	0-4		6196	1		3	4	5		7	8	6		11				10	9		2			
24		26	DARLINGTON	0-1		3229	1		3	4	5		7	8	6		11				10	9		2			
25		27	Darlington	0-0		6683	1		3	4	5		7	8	6		11				10	9		2			
26		31	CHESTER	1-1	Lydon	3007	1	3			5			8	6		11	9		7	10			2	4		
27	Jan	2	Chesterfield	0-3		6721	1	3			5		7	8	6	9	11				10			2	4		
28		7	Oldham Athletic	2-1	Ingham, Oliver	2549	1		3	4	5		7	8	6	9	11				10			2			
29		14	Carlisle United	1-2	Callender T	3337	1		2	4	5	3	7	8	6	9	11				10						
30		21	GRIMSBY TOWN	2-0	Callender T, Ingham	4247	1		2	4	5	3	7	8	6	9	11				10						
31		28	MANSFIELD TOWN	3-0	Smith 2, Lydon	3701	1		2	4	5	3	7	8	6	9	11				10						
32	Feb	4	Bradford Park Avenue	1-3	Lydon	4357	1		2	4	5	3	7	8	6	9	11				10						
33		11	ROCHDALE	4-1	Robson 2, Lydon 2	1932	1	2		4	5	3	7	8	6			11	9		10						
34		18	STOCKPORT COUNTY	2-1	Robson, Lydon	1601	1	2		4	5	3	7	8	6			11	9		10						
35		25	Derby County	1-4	Ingham	19203	1	2		4	5	3	7	8	6			11	9		10						
36	Mar	3	WREXHAM	2-1	Smith, Lydon	2337	1	2		4	5	3	7	8	6			11	9		10						
37		10	Halifax Town	3-3	Callender T, Smith,Lydon	7429	1		2	4	5	3	7	8	6		9	11			10						
38		17	OLDHAM ATHLETIC	1-3	Oliver	2128	1		2	4	5	3	7	8	6		9	11			10						
39		24	Scunthorpe United	1-1	Oliver	4702	1		2	4	5	3	9	8	6			11			10	7					
40		30	HARTLEPOOLS UNITED	2-1	Ingham, Lydon	5757			2	4	5	3	9	8	6			11		7	10					1	
41		31	BRADFORD CITY	4-1	Smith,Ingham 2,Callender T	3431			2	4	5	3	9	8	6			11		7	10					1	
42	Apr	2	Hartlepools United	1-3	Ingham	8450			2	4	5	3	9	8	6		7	11			10					1	
43		7	Workington	1-6	Smith	4291			2	4	5	3	9	8	6			11		7	10					1	
44		14	YORK CITY	3-2	Ingham,Lydon,Oliver (pen)	2301	1	2	3	4	5		7	8	9			11			10					6	
45		21	Mansfield Town	1-3	Ingham	7348	1	2	3	4	5		7	8	9			11			10					6	
46		28	CREWE ALEXANDRA	4-1	Ingham,Smith 2, Oliver	2148	1			4	5	3	7	8	9			11			10					6	2

	Gray	Hewson	March	Callender J	Davis	Brown	Ingham	Smith	Callender T	Campbell	Oliver	Robson	Moran	Herron	Lydon	Thompson	Anderson	Cairns	Haley	Hunter	Dawson
Apps	42	29	33	43	46	34	44	46	44	25	43	17	1	5	29	7	1	7	5	4	1
Goals			1		1	14	13	12	4	8	7				13	3					

One own goal

F.A. Cup

		Date	Opponent	Score		Att	Gray	Hewson	March	Callender J	Davis	Brown	Ingham	Smith	Callender T	Campbell	Oliver	Robson	Moran	Herron	Lydon
R1	Nov	19	Hartlepools United	0-3		10890	1	3		4	5	2	7	8	6			11	9		10

	FINAL TABLE	Pl.	W	D	L	F	A	W	D	L	F	A	F.	A.	Pts
				Home					Against				(Total)		
1	Grimsby Town	46	20	1	2	54	10	11	5	7	22	19	76	29	68
2	Derby County	46	18	4	1	67	23	10	3	10	43	32	110	55	63
3	Accrington Stanley	46	17	4	2	61	19	8	5	10	31	38	92	57	59
4	Hartlepools United	46	18	2	3	47	15	8	3	12	34	45	81	60	57
5	Southport	46	12	9	2	39	18	11	2	10	27	35	66	53	57
6	Chesterfield	46	18	1	4	61	21	7	3	13	33	45	94	66	54
7	Stockport County	46	16	4	3	65	22	5	5	13	25	39	90	61	51
8	Bradford City	46	16	5	2	57	25	2	8	13	21	39	78	64	49
9	Scunthorpe United	46	12	4	7	40	26	8	4	11	35	37	75	63	48
10	Workington	46	13	4	6	47	20	6	5	12	28	43	75	63	47
11	York City	46	12	4	7	44	24	7	5	11	41	48	85	72	47
12	Rochdale	46	13	5	5	46	39	4	8	11	20	45	66	84	47
13	GATESHEAD	46	15	4	4	56	32	2	7	14	21	52	77	84	45
14	Wrexham	46	11	5	7	37	28	5	5	13	29	45	66	73	42
15	Darlington	46	11	6	6	41	28	5	3	15	19	45	60	73	41
16	Tranmere Rovers	46	11	4	8	33	25	5	5	13	26	59	59	84	41
17	Chester	46	10	8	5	35	33	3	6	14	17	49	52	82	40
18	Mansfield Town	46	13	6	4	59	21	1	5	17	25	60	81	39	39
19	Halifax Town	46	10	6	7	40	27	4	5	14	26	49	66	76	39
20	Oldham Athletic	46	7	12	4	48	36	3	6	14	28	50	76	86	38
21	Carlisle United	46	11	3	9	45	36	4	5	14	26	59	71	95	38
22	Barrow	46	11	6	6	44	25	1	3	19	17	58	61	83	33
23	Bradford Park Ave.	46	13	4	6	47	38	0	3	20	14	84	61	122	33
24	Crewe Alexandra	46	9	4	10	32	35	0	6	17	18	70	50	105	28

123

1956/57 17th in Division 3 (North)

League matches

#	Month	Date	Opponent	Score	Scorers	Att
1	Aug	18	Derby County	3-5	Ingham, Oliver, Robson	19059
2		20	BRADFORD CITY	1-2	Oliver	3414
3		25	WREXHAM	4-2	Brown (pen), Ingham, Coatsworth, Oliver	3444
4		29	Bradford City	1-3	Lydon	12127
5	Sep	1	HARTLEPOOLS UNITED	4-3	Smith 2, Lydon, Oliver (pen)	7246
6		3	Crewe Alexandra	3-0	Callender J, Smith, Oliver	4784
7		8	Bradford Park Avenue	1-0	Ingham	9431
8		10	CREWE ALEXANDRA	1-1	Ingham	3607
9		15	DARLINGTON	1-2	Oliver	5447
10		17	WORKINGTON	1-2	Oliver	6707
11		22	Barrow	2-1	Smith, Lydon	6166
12		26	Workington	1-2	Smith	8629
13		29	HULL CITY	2-0	Coatsworth, Oliver (pen)	5535
14	Oct	6	Stockport County	1-1	Coatsworth	9337
15		13	CARLISLE UNITED	4-2	Ingham 3, Lydon	6034
16		20	Chesterfield	0-6		7800
17		27	TRANMERE ROVERS	3-1	Ingham, Lydon, Oliver	4189
18	Nov	3	York City	0-1		7325
19		10	OLDHAM ATHLETIC	2-3	Smith, Coatsworth	3145
20		24	SOUTHPORT	3-1	Smith, Lydon 2	2831
21	Dec	1	Accrington Stanley	0-2		7677
22		8	Mansfield Town	4-2	Ingham, Smith, Oliver 2	7560
23		15	DERBY COUNTY	1-1	Smith	3937
24		22	Wrexham	1-4	Brown	7326
25		25	HALIFAX TOWN	2-1	Brown, Oliver	2653
26		29	Hartlepools United	1-4	Slater	9254
27	Jan	5	ROCHDALE	1-2	Smith, Oliver	1430
28		12	BRADFORD PARK AVE.	1-3	Robson	2593
29		19	Darlington	0-7		4938
30		26	Rochdale	0-0		4561
31	Feb	2	BARROW	2-2	Ingham, Slater	2948
32		9	Hull City	1-1	Lydon	11689
33		16	STOCKPORT COUNTY	1-5	Ingham	3170
34		23	Carlisle United	2-3	Dawson, Ingham	5000
35	Mar	2	CHESTERFIELD	1-3	Herron	3245
36		9	Tranmere Rovers	0-0		5013
37		16	YORK CITY	0-2		4934
38		23	Oldham Athletic	2-1	Ingham, Gibson	7856
39		30	MANSFIELD TOWN	1-1	Lydon	3471
40	Apr	6	Southport	3-2	Ingham, Gibson 2	4226
41		13	ACCRINGTON STANLEY	1-1	Callender J	3225
42		15	Halifax Town	1-0	Callendar J	3717
43		19	Scunthorpe United	2-1	Gibson 2	4044
44		20	Chester	1-4	Gibson	5545
45		22	SCUNTHORPE UNITED	0-0		3324
46		27	CHESTER	4-1	Callender J, Gibson 2, Kirtley	2599

Appearances / shirt numbers

#	Gray	Dawson	Oldham	March	Davis	Brown	Ingham	Smith	Robson	Lydon	Oliver	Callender J	Callender T	Haley	Cairns	Milburn	Stokoe	Coatsworth	Herron	Beeston	Slater	Moran	Hewson	Baldridge	Kirtley	Gibson	Trewick
1	1	2	3	4	5	6	7	8	9	10	11																
2	1			2		3	7	8	9	10	11	4	5	6													
3	1				5	3	7	8		10	11				2	4	6	9									
4	1		3		5	6	7	8	9	10	11	4			2												
5	1		3		5	6	9	8		10	11				2	4			7								
6	1		3		5	6	7	8		10	11	4	2					9									
7	1	2	3		5	6	7	8		10	11	4						9									
8		2	3		5	6	7			10	11	8					4	9	1								
9	1	2	3		5	6	7	8		10	11						4	9									
10	1	2	3		5	6	7	8		10	11	4						9									
11	1	2	3		5	6	7	8		10	11	4						9									
12	1	2	3		5	6	7	8		10	11	4						9									
13	1	2	3		5		7	8		10	11	4					6	9									
14	1	2	3		5		7	8		10	11	4					6	9									
15	1	2	3		5		7	8		10	11	4					6	9									
16	1	2	3	10	5		7	8			11	4					6	9									
17	1	2	3		5		7	8		10	11	4					6	9									
18	1	2	3		5		7	8		10	11	4					6	9									
19	1		3		5	6	7	8		10	11	4	2					9									
20	1	2	3		5		9	7	8	11	10	4					6										
21	1	2	3		5		9	7	8	11	10	4					6										
22	1	2	3		5		9	7	8	11	10	4										6					
23	1	2	3		5		9	8		11	10	4									6	7					
24	1	2	3		5		9	8		11	10	4									6	7					
25	1	2	3		5		9	8		11	10	4									6	7					
26	1	2	3		5		9	8		11	10	4									6	7					
27	1	2	3		5		9	8		11	10	4							7		6						
28	1	2			5		9		8		11	4							7						6	3	
29	1	2					5		8	9	11	4							7						6	3	
30	1	2	3	6			5	7	8	9	10	11	4														
31	1	2	3	6	5		7	8		10	11	4									9						
32	1	6	3		5		7	8	9	10	11	4										2					
33	1	6	3		5		7	8	9		11	4										2			10		
34	1	6	3		5		7		9	10	11	4										2		8			
35	1	9	3		5	6					11	4							7			2		8	10		
36	1	2	3	4	5	6		8			11							9	7						10		
37	1	2	3		5	6					11	4						9	7					8	10		
38	1	6	3		5		7	8			11	4											2		10	9	
39	1	6	3		5		7	8			11	4											2		10	9	
40	1		3			6	7	8			11	4											2		10	9	5
41	1		3			6	7	8			11	4											2		10	9	5
42	1		3			6		8			11	4										7	2		10	9	5
43	1		3			6		8			11	4										7	2		10	9	5
44	1		3			6		8			11	4										7	2		10	9	5
45	1		3			6		8	3		7	11	4										2		10	9	5
46	1	6	3				7	8			11	4											2		10	9	5
Apps	45	35	40	4	27	42	35	38	9	37	41	42	2	1	4	2	13	16	10	1	6	8	15	6	10	10	7
Goals		1				3	14	10	2	9	13	4						4	1		2				1	8	

F.A. Cup

Round	Month	Date	Opponent	Score	Att	Gray	Dawson	Oldham	Davis	Brown	Ingham	Smith	Lydon	Oliver	Callender J	Coatsworth
R1	Nov	17	Hull City	0-4	12260	1	2	3	5	6	7	8	10	11	4	9

FINAL TABLE

		Pl.	Home W	D	L	F	A	Away W	D	L	F	A	F (Total)	A	Pts
1	Derby County	46	18	3	2	69	18	8	8	7	42	35	111	53	63
2	Hartlepools United	46	18	4	1	56	21	7	5	11	34	42	90	63	59
3	Accrington Stanley	46	15	4	4	54	22	10	4	9	41	42	95	64	58
4	Workington	46	16	4	3	60	25	8	6	9	33	38	93	63	58
5	Stockport County	46	16	3	4	51	26	7	5	11	40	49	91	75	54
6	Chesterfield	46	17	5	1	60	22	5	4	14	36	57	96	79	53
7	York City	46	14	4	5	43	21	7	6	10	32	40	75	61	52
8	Hull City	46	14	6	3	45	24	7	4	12	39	45	84	69	52
9	Bradford City	46	14	3	6	47	31	8	5	10	31	37	78	68	52
10	Barrow	46	16	2	5	51	22	5	7	11	25	40	76	62	51
11	Halifax Town	46	16	2	5	40	24	5	5	13	25	46	65	70	49
12	Wrexham	46	12	7	4	63	33	7	3	13	34	41	97	74	48
13	Rochdale	46	14	6	3	38	19	4	6	13	27	46	65	65	48
14	Scunthorpe United	46	9	5	9	44	36	6	10	7	27	33	71	69	45
15	Carlisle United	46	9	9	5	44	36	7	4	12	32	49	76	85	45
16	Mansfield Town	46	13	3	7	58	38	4	7	12	33	52	91	90	44
17	GATESHEAD	46	9	6	8	42	40	7	4	11	30	50	72	90	42
18	Darlington	46	11	5	7	47	36	6	3	14	35	59	82	95	42
19	Oldham Athletic	46	9	7	7	35	31	3	8	12	31	43	66	74	39
20	Bradford Park Ave.	46	11	2	10	41	40	5	1	17	25	53	66	93	35
21	Chester	46	8	7	8	40	35	2	6	15	15	49	55	84	33
22	Southport	46	7	8	8	31	34	3	4	16	21	60	52	94	32
23	Tranmere Rovers	46	5	9	9	33	38	2	4	17	18	53	51	91	27
24	Crewe Alexandra	46	5	7	11	31	46	1	2	20	12	64	43	110	21

124

1957/58   14th in 3rd Division (North)

League

No		Date	Opponent	Score	Scorers	Att.
1	Aug	24	CREWE ALEXANDRA	3-1	Gibson, Watson 2	5022
2		26	Bradford Park Avenue	2-2	Smith 2	10568
3		31	Wrexham	2-1	Smith, Gibson	12553
4	Sep	2	BRADFORD PARK AVE.	2-4	Kirtley, Watson	7631
5		7	SCUNTHORPE UNITED	1-2	Gibson	5666
6		9	Halifax Town	1-4	Callender	3753
7		14	Darlington	2-2	Kirtley, Gibson	4939
8		16	HALIFAX TOWN	0-0		3169
9		21	HARTLEPOOLS UNITED	0-0		5976
10		23	Stockport County	1-5	Watson	7650
11	Oct	5	Workington	1-1	Ingham	7045
12		12	Chesterfield	3-5	Gibson 2, Sutherland(og)	9196
13		14	STOCKPORT COUNTY	3-0	Kirtley, Hogg 2	4024
14		19	SOUTHPORT	2-1	Gibson 2	4955
15		26	York City	2-2	Ingham , Kirtley	6898
16	Nov	2	BARROW	0-2		4890
17		9	Oldham Athletic	0-0		7303
18		23	Accrington Stanley	0-3		6895
19		30	CHESTER	3-2	Ingham 3	3844
20	Dec	7	Barrow	2-1	Gibson, Baldridge	4604
21		14	TRANMERE ROVERS	2-3	Gibson, Baldridge	3146
22		21	Crewe Alexandra	2-2	Smith, Baldridge	4158
23		25	Hull City	1-1	Watson	8950
24		26	HULL CITY	3-1	Ingham, Smith, Gibson	5148
25		28	WREXHAM	1-1	Smith	4501
26	Jan	1	BRADFORD CITY	0-0		5881
27		4	BURY	1-2	Hogg	3815
28		11	Scunthorpe United	1-2	Hogg	7750
29		18	DARLINGTON	4-0	Ingham, Smith, Hogg 2	3865
30	Feb	1	Hartlepools United	2-2	Hogg, Oliver	6183
31		15	WORKINGTON	3-0	Smith 2, Hogg	4353
32		18	Carlisle United	1-5	Gibson	8913
33		22	ACCRINGTON STANLEY	1-3	Baldridge	5035
34	Mar	1	Southport	0-1		2643
35		11	Bradford City	1-0	Ashe	7136
36		22	CHESTERFIELD	3-0	Smith, Hogg, Kirtley(pen)	4033
37		24	YORK CITY	0-0		3971
38		29	Bury	1-4	Smith	6078
39	Apr	4	Rochdale	0-0		5106
40		5	CARLISLE UNITED	3-2	Hogg 2, Kirtley	4278
41		7	ROCHDALE	3-2	Hogg 2, Kirtley	5110
42		12	Chester	1-1	Kirtley	4752
43		14	MANSFIELD TOWN	2-1	Smith, Hogg	3258
44		19	OLDHAM ATHLETIC	1-0	Smith	6629
45		26	Tranmere Rovers	1-2	Oliver	8901
46		28	Mansfield Town	0-3		7478

Appearances / Goals (shirt-number grid)

Player	Apps	Goals
Gray	41	
Hewson	10	
Oldham	13	
Callender	23	1
Trewick	46	
Dawson	22	
Ingham	42	7
Smith	32	13
Gibson	31	10
Kirtley	37	10
Watson	21	5
Taylor	3	
Brown	13	
Lydon	27	
Inglis	2	
Hogarth	8	
Woodhouse	2	
Oliver	21	2
Granville	2	
Hogg	26	14
Robson	6	
Moffitt	15	
Baldridge	12	4
Ashe	28	1
Herron	2	
Carolin	12	
Batty	9	

One own goal

F.A. Cup

Round	Date	Opponent	Score	Scorers	Att.
R1	Nov 16	Chester	3-4	Callender, Kirtley, Baldridge	7539

Final Table

		Pl.	Home						Against						F.	A.	Pts
			W	D	L	F	A		W	D	L	F	A			(Total)	
1	Scunthorpe United	46	16	5	2	46	19		13	3	7	42	31		88	50	66
2	Accrington Stanley	46	16	4	3	53	28		9	5	9	30	33		83	61	59
3	Bradford City	46	13	7	3	42	19		8	8	7	31	30		73	49	57
4	Bury	46	17	4	2	61	18		6	6	11	33	44		94	62	56
5	Hull City	46	15	6	2	49	20		4	9	10	29	47		78	67	53
6	Mansfield Town	46	16	3	4	68	42		6	5	12	32	50		100	92	52
7	Halifax Town	46	15	5	3	52	20		5	6	12	31	49		83	69	51
8	Chesterfield	46	13	3	7	39	28		6	7	10	32	41		71	69	48
9	Stockport County	46	15	4	4	54	28		3	7	13	20	39		74	67	47
10	Rochdale	46	14	4	5	50	25		5	4	14	29	42		79	67	46
11	Tranmere Rovers	46	12	6	5	51	32		6	4	13	31	44		82	76	46
12	Wrexham	46	13	8	2	39	18		4	4	15	22	45		61	63	46
13	York City	46	11	8	4	40	26		6	4	13	28	50		68	76	46
14	GATESHEAD	46	12	5	6	41	27		3	10	10	27	49		68	76	45
15	Oldham Athletic	46	11	7	5	44	32		3	10	10	28	52		72	84	45
16	Carlisle United	46	13	3	7	56	35		6	3	14	24	43		80	78	44
17	Hartlepools United	46	11	6	6	45	26		5	6	12	28	50		73	76	44
18	Barrow	46	9	7	7	36	32		4	8	11	30	42		66	74	41
19	Workington	46	11	6	6	46	33		3	7	13	26	48		72	81	41
20	Darlington	46	15	3	5	53	25		2	4	17	25	64		78	89	41
21	Chester	46	7	10	6	36	26		6	3	14	35	55		73	81	39
22	Bradford Park Ave.	46	8	6	9	41	41		5	5	13	27	54		68	95	37
23	Southport	46	8	3	12	29	40		3	3	17	23	48		52	88	28
24	Crewe Alexandra	46	6	5	12	29	41		2	2	19	18	52		47	93	23

#	Date		Opponent	Score	Scorers	Att	Gray	Ashe	Batty	Hogarth	Trewick	Moffitt	Robinson	Smith K (1)	Hogg	Kirtley	Lydon	Stalker	Appleton	Herron	Gibson	Carolin	Baldridge	O'Connor	Robson	Patterson	Turner	Dawson	Alexander	Johnstone	Kemp	Smith K (2)	Williamson	Aitken	Grant
1	Aug	23	Barrow	3-0	Robinson, Smith K(1), Lydon	5933	1	2	3	4	5	6	7	8	9	10	11																		
2		25	SHREWSBURY TOWN	1-2	Lydon	7204	1	2	3	4	5	6	7	8	9	10	11																		
3		30	OLDHAM ATHLETIC	2-1	Hogg, Kirtley	6686		2	3	4	5		7	8	9	10	11	1	6																
4	Sep	1	Shrewsbury Town	1-1	Robinson	9552		2	3		5		7	8	11	10		1		4	6	9													
5		6	BRADFORD PARK AVE.	1-4	Gibson	6399		2	3		5		7	8	11	10		1		4	6	9													
6		8	COVENTRY CITY	1-1	Gibson	5208		2	3		5		7	8	11	10		1		4	6	9													
7		13	Aldershot	1-8	Gibson	4849	1	2	3		5		7	8	11	10				4	6	9													
8		15	Coventry City	1-4	Robinson	16299	1	2			5	3	7		11	9	6			8		10	4												
9		20	MILLWALL	1-2	Gibson	4978	1	2			5	3	7	8	11	9	6			4		10													
10		27	Walsall	1-0	Baldridge	10529	1	2				3	7		9	6				10	5		4	8	11										
11	Oct	4	DARLINGTON	1-3	Robinson	4088	1	2				3	7		9	6				8	10		4	11	5										
12		8	Gillingham	0-3		4335		2	3		5		7		9	8				6		10	11			1	4								
13		11	Crystal Palace	1-3	Hogg	13643		2	3		5		7		11	8				6		9	10			1	4								
14		18	CHESTER	0-1		3963		2	3		5		7		9	8				6						1	4		10	11					
15		25	Watford	1-5	Baldridge	14156		2			5	3	11			8				6			9			1	4		10		7				
16		27	EXETER CITY	1-2	Alexander	3582		2	3		5		7			8				6			9			1	4		10	11					
17	Nov	1	HARTLEPOOLS UNITED	3-0	Baldridge, Smith K(1), Johnstone	3927		2	3		5		7							6			9			1	4		10	11	8				
18		8	Southport	2-2	Kemp, Smith K(2)	3704		2	3		5					6							8			1	4		10	11	7	9			
19		22	Crewe Alexandra	0-0		5840		2	3		5		11		7	6							8			1	4		10			9			
20		29	NORTHAMPTON T	4-1	Robinson, Baldridge 2, Smith K(1)	2870		2	3		5		7	10		11				4			9			1			6			8			
21	Dec	5	Workington	2-4	Smith K(2), Baldridge	3584		2	3		5		7	10		11				4			9			1			6			8			
22		13	YORK CITY	1-0	Baldridge	2825	3				5		7		11	4				2			9	10		1			6			8			
23		20	BARROW	4-0	Smith K(2), Hogg 2	2734	2				5	3		11	10	4							9			1			6			7	8		
24		26	Port Vale	0-8		16899	2				5	3		11	10	4							9			1			6			7	8		
25	Jan	1	PORT VALE	0-4		4674	3			4	5			11	10	6							9			1			2			7	8		
26		3	Oldham Athletic	0-3		4215	3						7	8	11	6				4			10			1			2			9			
27		17	Bradford Park Avenue	1-4	Moffatt	5918			3		5	6			11	4							8			1			2	10	9	7	9		
28		31	ALDERSHOT	1-0	McMahon(og)	2903			3		5	6		8	11	4							9			1			2	10	7				
29	Feb	7	Millwall	2-0	Kirtley(pen), Baldridge	12050			3		5	6		8	9	4	11						7			1			2			10			
30		14	WALSALL	2-1	Smith K(1) 2	2814			3		5	6		8	9	4	11						7			1			2			10			
31		21	Darlington	2-3	Baldridge 2	3575			3		5	6		8	9	4	11						7			1			2			10			
32		28	CRYSTAL PALACE	1-3	McNichol(og)	3614			3		5	6		8	9	4	11						7			1			2			10			
33	Mar	7	Chester	1-0	Smith K(2)	4881			3		5	6		8	11	7										1			2	10		9	1	4	
34		14	WATFORD	1-0	Kirtley(pen)	3509			3		5	6		8	11	7										1			2	10		9	1	4	
35		21	Hartlepools United	0-0		4156			3		5	6		8	11											1			2	10		9	1	4	
36		27	CARLISLE UNITED	4-1	Smith K(1), Smith K(2), Baldridge 2	7623			3		5	6		8	11	7							9						2			10	1	4	
37		28	SOUTHPORT	1-1	Baldridge	4040					5	3		8		7	11						9						2	6		10	1	4	
38		30	Carlisle United	2-4	Baldridge 2	5029			3		5	6		8	11								9						2			10	1	4	7
39	Apr	4	Torquay United	1-0	Smith K(2)	4398			3		5	6		8	11	10							9						2				1	4	7
40		6	Exeter City	1-1	Smith K(1)	7739			3		5	6		9	7		11	8											2			10	1	4	
41		11	CREWE ALEXANDRA	0-0		3371			3		5	3		8	11			4					9						2			10	1	6	7
42		13	TORQUAY UNITED	1-0	Smith K(2)	2914			3		5	3		8	11		6						9						2			10	1	4	7
43		18	Northampton Town	0-1		5799			3		5	6			7	10							9						2		11	8	1	4	
44		20	GILLINGHAM	2-0	Smith K(2) 2	3094			3		5	6			11	10							9						2			8	1	4	7
45		25	WORKINGTON	0-3		2242					2	6			11	4							9						3			10	1	5	7
46		27	York City	0-1		9033					5	3			11	8	6						9						2			10	1	4	7

Played in one game: Firman (game 45 at 8), Wimshurst (game 46 at 7).

	Gray	Ashe	Batty	Hogarth	Trewick	Moffitt	Robinson	Smith K (1)	Hogg	Kirtley	Lydon	Stalker	Appleton	Herron	Gibson	Carolin	Baldridge	O'Connor	Robson	Patterson	Turner	Dawson	Alexander	Johnstone	Kemp	Smith K (2)	Williamson	Aitken	Grant
Apps	7	26	31	4	44	29	22	26	38	39	13	4		26	6	8	33			3	2	1	21	6	24	17	5	7	28
Goals						1	5	7	4	3	2				4		15						1	1	1	9			

Two own goals.

F.A. Cup

	Date		Opponent	Score	Scorers			Batty		Trewick														Alexander	Johnstone	Kemp	Smith K (2)	Williamson	
R1	Nov	15	BRADFORD PARK AVE.	1-4	Johnstone			2	3	5				6				8			1	4		10	11	7	9	

FINAL TABLE	Pl.	Home					Against					F.	A.	Pts
		W	D	L	F	A	W	D	L	F	A	(Total)		
1 Port Vale	46	14	6	3	62	30	12	6	5	48	28	110	58	64
2 Coventry City	46	18	4	1	50	11	6	8	9	34	36	84	47	60
3 York City	46	12	10	1	37	17	9	8	6	36	35	73	52	60
4 Shrewsbury Town	46	15	5	3	59	24	9	5	9	42	39	101	63	58
5 Exeter City	46	16	4	3	55	24	7	7	9	32	37	87	61	57
6 Walsall	46	13	5	5	56	25	8	5	10	39	39	95	64	52
7 Crystal Palace	46	12	8	3	54	27	8	4	11	36	44	90	71	52
8 Northampton Town	46	14	5	4	48	25	7	4	12	37	53	85	78	51
9 Millwall	46	13	6	4	46	23	7	4	12	30	46	76	69	50
10 Carlisle United	46	11	6	6	37	30	8	6	9	25	35	62	65	50
11 Gillingham	46	14	6	3	53	27	6	3	14	29	50	82	77	49
12 Torquay United	46	11	5	7	45	32	5	7	11	33	45	78	77	44
13 Chester	46	10	5	8	39	33	6	7	10	33	51	72	84	44
14 Bradford Park Ave.	46	15	1	7	51	29	3	6	14	24	48	75	77	43
15 Watford	46	10	6	7	46	36	6	4	13	35	43	81	79	42
16 Darlington	46	7	8	8	37	36	6	8	9	29	32	66	68	42
17 Workington	46	9	10	4	40	32	3	7	13	23	46	63	78	41
18 Crewe Alexandra	46	11	5	7	52	32	4	5	14	18	50	70	82	40
19 Hartlepools United	46	11	4	8	50	41	4	6	13	24	47	74	88	40
20 GATESHEAD	46	11	3	9	33	30	5	5	13	23	55	56	85	40
21 Oldham Athletic	46	15	0	8	39	29	1	4	18	20	55	59	84	36
22 Aldershot	46	8	4	11	37	45	6	3	14	26	52	63	97	35
23 Barrow	46	6	6	11	34	45	3	4	16	17	59	51	104	28
24 Southport	46	7	8	8	26	25	0	4	19	15	61	41	86	26

1959/60 22nd in 4th Division (Voted out of Football League)

#	Date		Opponent	Score	Scorers	Att.	Williamson	Lackenby	Moffitt	Hobson	Trewick G	Aitken	Kirtley	Lumley	Smith	Murray	Hogg	Armstrong	Patterson	Hedley	Baldridge	Stephenson	Redhead	Dawson	Trewick A	Watkin	Steele	Carolin	Whitfield	Wilson	Wimshurst	Doran
1	Aug	22	Gillingham	4-5	Smith, Murray 2, Hogg	7352	1	2	3	4	5	6	7	8	9	10	11															
2		24	BARROW	3-1	Smith 3	5654	1	2	3	4	5	6	7	8	9			11	10													
3		29	SOUTHPORT	1-0	Rankin (og)	6187			3	4	5	6	7	8	9			11	10	1	2											
4		31	Barrow	2-2	Smith, Armstrong	6042			3	4	5	6		8	9			11	10	1	2	7	7									
5	Sep	5	Millwall	0-4		14120			3	4	5	6	7	8	9			11		1	2	10										
6		7	NOTTS COUNTY	0-0		6618		5	3	4		6		8	9			11	10	1	2	7										
7		12	TORQUAY UNITED	0-2		6169		5	3	4		6	7	8	9			11		1	2		10									
8		17	Notts County	0-4		8793	1		3	4	5	6		8	9	10	11				2	7										
9		19	Northampton Town	0-2		9426	1	5	3	4		6		8	9	10	11				2	7										
10		21	Aldershot	2-3	Smith, Armstrong	5793	1	5	3	4		6		8	9			11	10		2	7										
11		26	DONCASTER ROVERS	5-0	Lumley, Armstrong 3, Hogg	4318	1	5	3	4		6		8	9			11	10		7	2										
12		28	ALDERSHOT	4-1	Stephenson, Armstrong 2, Hogg	5794	1	5	3	4		6			9	8		11	10		7	2										
13	Oct	3	Workington	1-1	Smith	5494	1	5	3	4		6		8	9			11	10		7	2										
14		5	ROCHDALE	1-2	Lumley	5804	1	5	3	4		6		8				11	10		7	2		9								
15		10	Hartlepools United	0-3		3832	1	5	3	4		6		8	9			11	10		7	2										
16		13	Rochdale	0-2		4770	1	4	3					5	8	10						9		7	6	2	11					
17		17	CREWE ALEXANDRA	4-2	Stephenson, Kirtley, Smith 2	3471	1	9		4				5	8	10					3	7	6	2	11							
18		24	Chester	2-4	Kirtley(pen), Lackenby	4790	1	9		4				5	8	10					3	7	6	2	11							
19		31	CRYSTAL PALACE	0-2		3901	1	4						5	8	9	10	11			3	7	6	2								
20	Nov	7	Bradford Park Avenue	2-4	Stephenson, Lumley	5702	1	4	3					5	8			10				7	6	2	9	11						
21		21	Exeter City	1-2	Armstrong	6992	1	3			5			8				10				7	6	2	9	11	4					
22		28	WATFORD	1-3	Lackenby(pen)	2615	1	6	3					5	10			8				7		2	9	11	4					
23	Dec	12	CARLISLE UNITED	1-0	Stephenson	2442	1	5	3	4		6		8	9	10						7		2	11							
24		19	GILLINGHAM	2-2	Hobson, Murray	1884	1	5	3	4		6		8	9	10						7		2	11							
25		26	Walsall	2-2	Lumley, Whitfield	13191	1	5	3	4		6		8	9							7		2	11				10			
26	Jan	2	Southport	0-1		3389	1	5	3	4		6		8	9							11		2	10		7					
27		9	STOCKPORT COUNTY	2-1	Steele 2	1868	1	5	3	4		6		8	9							11		2	10		7					
28		16	MILLWALL	1-0	Wilson	2468	1	5	3	4		6		8				9				11		2	10		7					
29		23	Torquay United	0-1		4278	1	5	3	4		6		8				10				7		2	11		9					
30		30	Oldham Athletic	1-1	Steele	3421	1	5	3	4		6		8	10							7		2	11		9					
31	Feb	6	NORTHAMPTON T	1-3	Wilson	3164	1	5	3	4		6		8				10						2	11		9			7		
32		13	Doncaster Rovers		2710		1	5	3	4		6		10	9									2			7		8		
33		27	HARTLEPOOLS UNITED	1-1	Baldridge	2652	1	5	3	4		6		10							9	11		2			7		8		
34	Mar	5	Crewe Alexandra	1-4	Wilson	6251	1	5	3	4		10		8										6	2		11		9	7	
35		12	CHESTER	0-1		1735	1	5	3	4		10										8		6	2		11		9	7	
36		19	Crystal Palace	2-2	Lumley, Wilson	13568	1	5	3			6		8		10							7	4	2		11		9		
37		26	BRADFORD PARK AVE.	1-2	Steele	1488	1	5	3			6		8		10							7	4	2		11		9		
38		28	WORKINGTON	2-1	Moffit, Stephenson	1852	1		3	5	6			6									11	4	2	9		10		7	
39	Apr	2	Stockport County	0-0		4072	1	3			5	6		8									7	4	2	9		11		10	
40		9	EXETER CITY	1-0	Murray	2227	1	3			5	6		8		10							7	4	2	9		11			
41		15	Darlington	1-2	Trewick A	4331	1	3			5	6		8							10	7	4	2	9		11				
42		16	Watford	0-5		13495	1	6		3	5			8							10	7	4	2	9		11				
43		18	DARLINGTON	1-3	Armstrong	2144	1	3			5	6						10				7	4	2	9		11				8
44		23	OLDHAM ATHLETIC	2-0	Stephenson, Steele	1492	1	5			6			8	10							7	4	2			11		9		3
45		25	WALSALL	3-0	Lumley, Murray 2	2539	1	5			6			8	10	3						7	4	2			11		9		
46		30	Carlisle United	0-4		2303	1	5			6			8	10	3						7	4	2			11		9		
					Apps		41	43	32	31	13	44	9	40	17	18	16	22	5	11	8	35	20	36	10	3	25	2	1	17	6	1
					Goals			2	1	1			2	6	9	6	3	9			1	6			1		5		1	4		

One own goal

F.A. Cup

	Date		Opponent	Score	Scorers	Att.	Williamson	Lackenby	Moffitt	Hobson	Trewick G	Aitken	Kirtley	Lumley	Smith	Murray	Hogg	Armstrong	Patterson	Hedley	Baldridge	Stephenson	Redhead	Dawson	Trewick A	Watkin	Steele	Carolin	Whitfield	Wilson	Wimshurst	Doran
R1	Nov	14	HALIFAX TOWN	3-4	Trewick A 2, Armstrong	4570	1	4			5			8				10			3	7	6	2	9		11					

FINAL TABLE

		Pl.	Home						Against						F. A. Pts		
			W	D	L	F	A	W	D	L	F	A		(Total)		
1	Walsall	46	14	5	4	57	33	14	4	5	45	27	102	60	65		
2	Notts County	46	19	1	3	66	27	7	9	41	42	107	69	60			
3	Torquay United	46	17	3	3	56	27	9	5	28	31	84	58	60			
4	Watford	46	17	2	4	62	28	7	7	30	39	92	67	57			
5	Millwall	46	12	8	3	54	28	6	9	30	33	84	61	53			
6	Northampton Town	46	13	6	4	50	22	9	3	35	41	85	63	53			
7	Gillingham	46	17	4	2	47	21	4	6	27	48	74	69	52			
8	Crystal Palace	46	12	6	5	61	27	7	6	10	23	37	84	64	50		
9	Exeter City	46	13	7	3	50	30	6	4	13	30	40	80	70	49		
10	Stockport County	46	15	6	2	35	10	4	5	14	23	44	58	54	49		
11	Bradford Park Ave.	46	12	10	1	48	25	5	5	13	22	43	70	68	49		
12	Rochdale	46	15	4	4	46	19	3	6	14	19	41	65	60	46		
13	Aldershot	46	14	5	4	50	22	4	4	15	27	52	77	74	45		
14	Crewe Alexandra	46	14	3	6	51	31	4	6	13	28	57	79	88	45		
15	Darlington	46	11	6	6	40	30	6	4	13	23	43	63	73	43		
16	Workington	46	10	8	5	41	20	4	6	13	27	40	68	60	43		
17	Doncaster Rovers	46	13	3	7	40	23	3	7	13	29	53	69	78	42		
18	Barrow	46	11	8	4	52	29	4	3	16	25	58	77	87	41		
19	Carlisle United	46	9	6	8	28	28	6	5	12	23	38	51	66	41		
20	Chester	46	10	8	5	37	28	4	4	15	22	51	59	77	40		
21	Southport	46	9	7	7	30	32	1	7	15	18	60	48	92	34		
22	GATESHEAD	46	12	3	8	37	27	0	6	17	21	59	58	86	33		
23	Oldham Athletic	46	5	7	11	20	30	3	5	15	21	53	41	83	28		
24	Hartlepools United	46	9	2	12	40	41	1	5	17	19	68	59	109	27		

127